A Century of

WISDEN

A Century of

WISDEN

An Extract from Every Edition
1900–1999

Edited by Christopher Lane

WISDEN

www.wisden.com

A CENTURY OF WISDEN

ISBN 0 947766 62 6

Published in 2000 by
JOHN WISDEN & CO LTD
25 Down Road, Merrow, Guildford, Surrey GU1 2PY
Tel: 01483 570358 Fax: 01483 533153
E-mail: wisden@ndirect.co.uk
Website: www.wisden.com

Printed and bound in Great Britain by Clays Ltd, St Ives plc
Distributed by The Penguin Group
Distributed in Australia by Hardie Grant Books, Melbourne

Cover images from Hulton Getty and Patrick Eagar
Group photo constructed by Nigel Davies

Contents

The 1900s

The 1910s

The 1920s

The 1930s

The 1940s

The 1950s

The 1960s

The 1970s

The 1980s

The 1990s

Preface

"From the frequency with which the Almanack is quoted and the cordial way in which it is always received, I am bound to believe that it fulfils its mission in supplying a readable record of the year's cricket."

Sydney Pardon, *Wisden*'s editor from 1891 to 1925, prefaced the 1900 Almanack with this modest appraisal. First published in 1864, thirteen years before the start of Test cricket, *Wisden* was now in its 37th edition, already a remarkable achievement. But even the esteemed Mr Pardon might not have gone so far as to predict that a new edition of *Wisden Cricketers' Almanack* would appear every year of the new century, or that it would go into the next as an annual bestseller. That it does so in prime health, universally admired and respected as "the bible of cricket", illustrates how faithfully it continues to fulfil Sydney Pardon's stated mission with its reputation for accuracy, independence and integrity.

Many readers will find my first discovery of *Wisden* familiar. It was 1976, and I was given the 113th edition as a twelfth birthday present. Every day for months I thumbed through it, fascinated by its style and keen to soak up as much as I could of its immense mass of information. A resolve subsequently grew to build a collection, not because I knew how good an investment it might be (the 2000 edition records that a full set was sold in 1999 for £29,500) but because the image of a bookcase lined with yellow-jacketed *Wisden*s was irresistibly alluring. Twelve years later, in 1988, I acquired my thirteenth Almanack, by now a Wisden employee, a position which, another twelve years on, I still regard as a privilege.

Combing through 100 editions to compile *A Century of Wisden* was a compelling prospect, offering the opportunity to increase my understanding of *Wisden*'s history, tradition and content. The task itself, reading thousands of pages, and scanning tens of thousands more, was initially daunting but ultimately hugely rewarding. Every edition revealed gems that often surprised, sometimes amused and always enthralled me. Unfortunately the restrictive but challenging discipline of choosing just one extract from each edition inevitably led to the exclusion of many wonderful items that would easily fill several volumes of a similar anthology.

What soon became apparent is how many modern-day issues are in fact recurring topics in cricket history. The deterioration of basic skills, debatable Laws and gamesmanship are familiar themes that appear among this book's earlier extracts. Yet in other respects the game has changed beyond recognition. The contrast between the decline in schools cricket in the later years of the century and the problems highlighted in the 1924 *Wisden* – of schoolboy cricketers being adversely affected by over-zealous media attention – provides a stark example of the way in which past and present differ.

The choice of extracts did not involve any attempt to judge the best in each edition. As well as being subjective, that would have been as invidious a task as having to decide whether Warne is a better cricketer than Tendulkar. Instead I have attempted to select a wide range of extracts, so that when read in chronological order they provide a pleasing change of themes. I have also tried to ensure that as many examples as possible of *Wisden*'s content – match reports, comment, records, reviews, schools cricket, obituaries, eccentricities, etc. – are represented. As well as celebrating *Wisden*'s considerable achievement of producing a new edition every year of the twentieth century, *A Century of Wisden* demonstrates the great variety of information that the Almanacks contain, from the trivial to the most serious matters in cricket.

Some extracts chose themselves. Sydney Southerton's 1934 review of the Bodyline series, an astute analysis and perhaps the definitive contemporary verdict, was essential. As was E. W. Swanton's 1946 account of how cricket transcended the appalling suffering of his fellow prisoners-of-war on the Thai–Burma railway, which remains a remarkable and uplifting story. My intention was to include the Cricketer of the Year feature for each of *Wisden*'s Five Cricketers of the Century. In the 1964 edition, however, when Sobers was a Cricketer of the Year, John Arlott reviewed *Beyond a Boundary* by C. L. R. James, another of those pieces that demanded inclusion. Fortunately, the 1967 *Wisden* has a special feature on Sobers, which avoided at least one agonising decision. By way of contrast, a 1947 match report records the outstanding performance at Lord's by a thirteen-year-old schoolboy, Michael (Colin) Cowdrey. It is reports like this, along with the fine writing, the reminiscences and the statistics, that make *Wisden* a unique book of record.

The editing of each extract has been kept to an absolute minimum; it has been done only to provide clarity. In some cases, it has been necessary to remove sections of an article either to focus on a specific theme, or simply to keep the overall length in check. There are inconsistencies of style, but as they represent the changing styles throughout the century and so give a period flavour, they have been retained. The overriding intention has been to reproduce the selected text as it originally appeared.

Finally, I would like to express my gratitude for the substantial help I received from a number of my colleagues, in particular Karen Hewat, who keyed in the entire text, Christine Forrest, whose experience working with four *Wisden* editors made her an invaluable copy editor, and Nigel Davies, *Wisden Cricket Monthly*'s accomplished art director, who transformed the manuscript into a book. I am also indebted to the support and assistance given by Hugh Chevallier, Graeme Wright, Lawrence Booth, Gordon Burling and my wife, Sally. My sincere thanks to them all.

Christopher Lane
January 2000

Wisden Editors
in the 20th Century

Sydney Pardon	(1891)–1925
Stewart Caine	1926–1933
Sydney Southerton	1934–1935
Wilfrid Brookes	1936–1939
Haddon Whitaker OBE	1940–1943
Hubert Preston	1944–1951
Norman Preston MBE	1952–1980
John Woodcock OBE	1981–1986
Graeme Wright	1987–1992
Matthew Engel	1993–2000

page xcvi

The Highest Individual Score on Record

Clifton College – Clarke's v North Town

A Junior house match at Clifton College, begun on Thursday the 22nd of June [1899] and completed on the following Wednesday, is noteworthy for having produced the greatest score known to have been made by a single player in a game of any description. The hero of the occasion, A. E. J. Collins, was batting for six hours and fifty minutes, his innings being continued in unequal instalments during five days. His hits included a six, four fives, thirty-one fours, thirty-three threes and 146 twos. The previous best score was that of A. E. Stoddart, who made 485 for the Hampstead Club against the Stoics in 1886. It is remarkable that it was in a Clifton College game that E. F. S. Tylecote made his score of 404 in 1868.

Clarke's

Collins not out	628	Spooner b Monteath		0
Champion c Monteath b Rendall	27	Leake b Monteath		32
Gilbert b Crew	9	Raine b Monteath		14
Sudely c Davis b Sainsbury	8	Redfern c Fuller-Eberle b Crew		13
Sheriff b Crew	6	Extras		46
Galway b Crew	11			
Whittey c and b Monteath	42			836

North Town

Monteath run out		4 – c and b Gilbert	4
Crew b Collins		10 – c Champion b Gilbert	4
Fedden b Collins		10 – lbw b Collins	1
Sainsbury lbw b Collins		0 – lbw b Collins	13
Barstow b Sheriff		32 – b Collins	0
Fuller-Eberle c Galway b Collins		8 – b Sheriff	15
Rendall b Sudely		9 – b Collins	8
Lindrea b Collins		1 – b Sheriff	11
Ratcliff not out		6 – c Champion b Sheriff	0
Robinson b Collins		0 – c Raine b Sheriff	0
Davies b Collins		4 – not out	0
Extras		3 – Extras	5
		87	61

pages 343–346

Gentlemen v Players

The Lord's Match

Played at Lord's, Monday, Tuesday, Wednesday, July 16, 17, 18, 1900. The Gentlemen v Players match at Lord's in 1900 was certainly the most remarkable game of the whole season, and in every way worthy of comparison with the memorable match under the same title on the same ground in 1898. It presented two points that were quite without precedent in the long series of Gentlemen v Players matches. R. E. Foster followed up his record innings in the University match by making two separate hundreds, a feat never before performed at Lord's or elsewhere for either Gentlemen or Players, and the Players, though set to make 501 in the last innings, won the game by two wickets. Never before in a match of such importance – and only once indeed in the whole history of first-class cricket – has a total of over five hundred been obtained in the fourth innings. The one previous occasion – also at Lord's ground – was in 1896, when Cambridge were set to make 507 against the MCC and succeeded in accomplishing the task.* The performance of the Players was a magnificent one, but they could consider themselves lucky in having sufficient time left them in which to make such a huge score. Under ordinary circumstances the task would have been out of the question.

It was in this way that the opportunity of doing an unprecedented thing presented itself. On the second afternoon the Gentlemen already held what was on paper an overwhelming advantage, and Mr Woods, their captain, wishing to have the Players in before the close of the afternoon, instructed his side to play a hitting game, and be out by a certain time. His instructions were loyally obeyed, and though the Gentlemen's score stood at 238 for three wickets when Foster left, the innings was all over for 339. From lunchtime till the end of the innings 279 runs were scored in two hours and twenty minutes. No one was disposed to criticise Mr Woods at all severely, some people going so far as to say that if the Gentlemen could not win with a lead of 500 runs they did not deserve to win at all. This was all very well,

---

* Since 1900, there have been only three more instances in first-class cricket of a side making 500 or more in the fourth innings to win a match.

but the fact remained that there was only one possible way by which the Gentlemen could lose the match, and that their captain adopted it.

If he had not been so anxious for his side to be out before the end of the second afternoon he could have made defeat absolutely impossible, and yet have left his side a whole day in which to win. Of course he could not regard it as at all within the range of probability that the Players would make 500 runs in the last innings, but it is a wholesome rule to take nothing for granted at cricket, and to throw nothing away except under stress of absolute necessity. However, though the Gentlemen suffered a defeat to the risk of which they need not have been exposed, the public profited, the cricket on the last day being quite a marvel of sustained interest. Overnight the Players had lost Albert Ward's wicket for 44 runs, so that on Wednesday morning, with nine wickets to go down, they wanted 457 to win. By wonderful batting the task was accomplished, the honours being divided between Brown, Hayward and Abel. Of the three batsmen Abel made the smallest score, but in the opinion of many good judges he played the best cricket.

Quite early in the day victory for the Players was seen to be possible, a great stand by Brown and Abel putting them in a flattering position. Abel joined Brown at 81, for two wickets, and when lunch time came the score had reached 242, and the two batsmen were still together. So far Brown had made 106 and Abel 94. On the game being resumed Abel seemed certain of his hundred, but he was a little too anxious, and after getting one boundary hit he attempted a big pull off a short-pitched ball from Jessop, and was easily caught at forward short leg. In this way the third wicket went down at 246, Abel having in a couple of hours scored 98 out of 165. When he left it wanted five minutes to three, and the Players with seven wickets to fall required 255 runs to win. Brown, who had been playing a masterly game all the morning, was then joined by Hayward, and again the good bowling of the Gentlemen was mastered.

Hayward had been unwell and away from the ground on the previous day, but having quite shaken off his indisposition he played superbly. For close upon an hour and a half the two batsmen stayed together, and the total was up to 348 when at last Brown's innings was ended by a catch at cover slip. He had one or two narrow escapes of being bowled and might, with his score at 127, have been caught on the leg side by Jessop off one of Jephson's lobs, but all the same he played great cricket. He hit one five (four for an overthrow), twenty-nine fours, two threes and nine twos, and was batting for four hours and threequarters. Brilliant cutting was perhaps the best feature of his game. His 163 is the highest innings ever hit for the Players against the Gentlemen at Lord's, beating by 24 runs the great score made by William Gunn in 1898.

When Brown left an interval of a quarter of an hour was taken for tea, the Players with six wickets in hand wanting 153 to win. A fresh start was made at twenty-five minutes to five, and except that Carpenter failed, things continued to go well for the batting side, victory seeming absolutely certain so long as Hayward and Lilley stayed together. However, Lilley left, sixth wicket down, at 448, and at 469 Hayward's splendid innings was closed by a catch by the wicket-keeper, standing back to Kortright's bowling. In as nearly as possible three hours Hayward had scored 111, his play, though a little unequal in quality, being for the most part admirable. At his dismissal the Players wanted 32 to win with three wickets to fall, and the issue remained in doubt. With sixteen added John Gunn was bowled, but on Rhodes joining Trott the end soon came. At half past six the score stood at a tie, and on Woods taking the ball Rhodes made the winning hit, a wonderful match ending in favour of the Players by two wickets.

We have described the closing stage of the game at considerable length, the cricket being so extraordinary in character. As regards the rest of the match it must suffice to pay proper tribute to the magnificent batting of Foster, and to the excellent services rendered to the Gentlemen in different ways by Fry, Mason, and Jessop. On the second morning Mason and Jessop, with Kortright to help them at the finish, bowled in such capital form that the Players' first innings was finished off for 136, after 66 runs had been scored overnight for two wickets. The performance was the more remarkable as there was nothing the matter with the wicket.

Foster's first innings at 102 not out was in many ways a remarkable effort. So keen was he to do well in this, his first Gentlemen and Players match that, sternly restraining all desire to hit, he was at the wickets nearly half an hour before he made his first run. He was not out six at lunchtime, but on starting afresh he played a very different game, carrying his score to 102 in less than two hours. As a matter of record, it may be added that he hit fifteen fours, three threes, and nine twos. His second innings was from first to last astonishingly brilliant, but was marred by a palpable chance to John Gunn at mid-off when he had made 40. He completed his first fifty runs in little more than an hour, and then hit away in such tremendous form that when at last Brown caught him in the deep field in front of the pavilion, he had only been at the wickets an hour and threequarters. In that time he scored 136 out of 195, hitting in his wonderful innings, twenty-four fours, two threes, four twos and twenty-six singles. Not often, except by such a hitter as Jessop, have first-rate professional bowlers been treated more lightly. Under ordinary circumstances, a batsman who scored 68 and 72 for the Gentlemen at Lord's would stand out very prominently, but Fry on this particular occasion was quite overshadowed by Foster. It should be said for him, however, that in the second innings he played a most unselfish game, caring nothing for his own success when he saw that Foster had a chance of making his second hundred.

Gentlemen

Mr A. O. Jones c Ward b Trott	9	– b Rhodes	5
Mr C. B. Fry b Rhodes	68	– hit wkt b Ward	72
Mr C. L. Townsend run out	30	– b Rhodes	22
Mr R. E. Foster not out	102	– c Brown b Trott	136
Mr J. R. Mason b Trott	2	– c Lilley b Trott	27
Mr D. L. A. Jephson lbw b Rhodes	9	– not out	18
Mr G. L. Jessop c Lilley b Rhodes	18	– b Trott	18
Mr S. M. J. Woods c Lilley b Rhodes	7	– c Carpenter b Ward	0
Mr E. Smith c Rhodes b Gunn	26	– c Brown b Trott	16
Mr C. J. Kortright b Gunn	4	– sub b Trott	12
Mr H. Martyn c Brown b Gunn	3	– c Quaife b Trott	4
B 15, l-b 4	19	B 5, l-b 4	9
	297		**339**

Bowling: *First Innings*—Rhodes 30–4–93–4; Trott 27–11–66–2; Mead 21–5–58–0; Gunn 17.3–3–61–3. *Second Innings*—Rhodes 15–2–51–2; Trott 20.2–0–142–6; Mead 14–1–57–0; Gunn 7–3–23–0; Ward 10–3–39–2; Quaife 1–0–18–0.

Players

R. Abel b Jessop	30	– c Jones b Jessop	98
A. Ward c Jones b Mason	16	– c Martyn b Jessop	4
T. Hayward b Jessop	8	– c Martyn b Kortright	111
W. G. Quaife c Foster b Jessop	9	– lbw b Jones	29
J. T. Brown, sen. c Foster b Mason	18	– c Jones b Smith	163
H. Carpenter run out	14	– b Woods	9
A. A. Lilley b Mason	10	– b Mason	30
A. E. Trott c Foster b Mason	9	– not out	22
J. Gunn c Martyn b Kortright	4	– b Kortright	3
W. Rhodes not out	1	– not out	7
W. Mead b Kortright	4		
B 9, l-b 4	13	B 13, l-b 8, w 1, n-b 4	26
	136	**(8 wkts)**	**502**

Bowling: *First Innings*—Kortright 12.4–4–30–2; Jephson 4–0–9–0; Mason 17–7–40–4; Jessop 14–5–28–3; Jones 5–0–16–0. *Second Innings*—Kortright 18–4–60–2; Jephson 14–2–46–0; Mason 34–11–92–1; Jessop 28–8–74–2; Jones 23–4–69–1; Woods 19.5–3–70–1; Smith 18–3–57–1; Townsend 2–0–8–0.

Umpires: J. Wheeler and J. Phillips.

pages lxxxvi–xc

Leg-Break Bowling in 1901

By D. L. A. Jephson

When the annals of our game come to be chronicled in some great book, the extraordinary growth of this leg-break bowling, or "tosh", as we were wont to call it, will find a prominent place in the year of grace 1901 … During the past five months of cricket it has proved itself to be an easier method of getting rid of many a great player than the old fashioned, done-to-death, wide-on-the-off theory. They can smile for a month, these batsmen, at a ball a foot off the off stump, vary the flight and the pace as you may, but they fall one after another, sooner or later as the case may be, before the bowlers of the slow leg-break.

And so, as we watch these players, what do we see? The bat in the hand of many flashes round as an old-time flail, as a barren windmill that for ever grinds and produces nothing, or we see them, bat uplifted, watching the ball as it strikes their padded legs. Yet, impotent as the majority of batsmen seem in the face of this attack, these bowlers hold but secondary places in that list, the weekly publication of which is such a curse to many a cricketer – the average list …

Every first-class county of today is equipped with a slow leg-break bowler … First and foremost, C. M. Wells, the finest amateur slow bowler on his day I have ever seen. He is the only one that can bowl without the plethora of short legs and of long legs scattered promiscuously on the on side – he bowls the leg-break from the palm of the hand, and he bowls the off-break with but the slightest variation of action. All the other leg-break bowlers … use only the finger break, varied at intervals with a fast straight, or I should say presumably straight, ball, which in three out of five cases counts four. They cannot or do not bowl a similar ball at the same pace with an off-break. In all probability the most successful slow leg-break bowler that we shall ever see was A. G. Steel. Personally, I never remember him at his zenith, my years are too few in number, but I played him at Cromer some seven years ago … and I saw as good bowling from a bowler's point of view as I wish to see – the same length, the same flight, and the ball going six inches either way.

Of Trott it can be said when he bowls leg-breaks that none bowling today can beat him in the amount of spin. In the Gentlemen v Players match at The Oval this past season he bowled L. G. Wright round his legs, *and he was not standing in front,* but swinging the bat like the barren windmill that forever grinds and produces nothing! So from Trott with swift stages we pass to Bosanquet. With his fast bowling it is not my lot to deal; of his slow leg-breaks I can say this, that though his length is often eccentric he possesses the unique capability of delivering a ball with every semblance of a leg-break, which on striking the pitch turns inches from the off. Whether this can be done at will, or whether it is the gift of the blind goddess, I cannot tell – enough, he bowls it …

In conclusion, we who stand beneath the tottering pillars, we who "bowl" the underhand leg-break – the so-called "lob", or the so-called "grub" – "One ball one un" artists, as they call us, in the garbled language of the fair – crave a moment's attention. By himself stands Simpson Hayward, for he "flicks" the ball as we have all seen many a wrathful billiard player do when returning the white from a most unexpected pocket – it spins and spins and breaks sharply from the off, and it sometimes hits the wicket. There are two more, Wynyard and myself, and we both bowl in the old, old way, and we bowl with a persistence born of tentative success – occasionally we hook a fish, and great is our rejoicing. We are both fond of this bowling, I particularly so, and when on many a ground throughout the country there has arisen on every side the gentle sound of "Take him orf!" "Take him orf!" were it not that the side ever comes before oneself I would bowl, and bowl, and bowl, until at eventide the cows come home.

pages lxii–lxix

The Second-Class Counties
and
The Law of "Leg-Before-Wicket"

By Sydney Pardon

During the season of 1902 the Second-class Counties gave in their competition matches – at the request of the Marylebone Club – a trial to the suggested law of "Leg-Before-Wicket", carried by a large, though insufficient, majority at the Annual Meeting of the MCC at Lord's in May, 1901. The Proposed law read: "If with any part of his person (except the hand), which is between wicket and wicket, he intercept a ball which would hit his wicket, 'Leg-Before-Wicket'." The change from the existing rule is the removal of the restriction as to the ball having to pitch in a straight line between wicket and wicket. Wishing to publish in *Wisden* the opinions of those who had subjected the proposed rule to the test of actual play I wrote to the various counties concerned, asking at the same time what was thought of the new method of scoring points adopted in the competition. In reply I received the following letters.* It will be seen that the proposed alteration in the law of "Leg-Before-Wicket" met with comparatively little favour.

* *Eleven letters were published, including the following, some of which have been edited for the purpose of this book.*

Dear Sir,

I have to acknowledge receipt of your favour on the subject of … the proposed alteration to the law of LBW … I do not believe the proposal has had any effect whatsoever upon altering the decision of the matches but, however desirable it may be to prevent batsmen from leg play, as the rule stands it is most objectionable. We had two cases during last season of unsatisfactory decisions, and I feel sure cases like these must have occurred elsewhere and are likely to continue. It is almost impossible for any man to calculate with certainty the angle of any break, and why place this extra duty upon the umpire? I shall certainly vote against the rule for next season, as I think it undesirable to increase the responsibility of the umpire, especially in the direction of doubt. Besides, he is constantly worried with appeals, and general unpleasantness may be caused thereby.

I am, Yours faithfully,

R. W. ALLEN, BEDFORDSHIRE COUNTY CLUB

Dear Sir,

With regard to the LBW question. I stood umpire on two days; in Dorsetshire match one day, and in the Glamorgan match one day – owing to the non-arrival of the MCC umpires – and my opinion is that it is much easier for an umpire to decide the question of LBW under the rule tried by us, but there were a number of appeals, as I don't think the rule is thoroughly understood. Some players seem to think it does not matter where the leg (or part of the body) is so long as the leg stops the ball from hitting the wicket – they don't know that "any part of the person" *must* be between wicket and wicket.

I don't think this rule could ever work in country matches where country umpires are employed, as I am sure it would end in a row.

Yours in haste,

Colonel J. FELLOWES, Hon. Sec., DEVONSHIRE COUNTY CLUB

Dear Sir,

With regard to the working of the LBW rule tried by the Minor Counties this year, I think there can be no doubt that it was an entire failure. I take it the object of the new rule was to help the bowler on fast true wickets and so prevent drawn matches; unfortunately on such wickets the new rule is absolutely innocuous; it does not help the leg-break bowler, as unless one is almost treading on one's wicket one's leg is not in a line between wicket and wicket when hit by the leg-breaker; while on the plumb-wicket the off-break bowler can't do enough for the new rule to help him.

The fact appears to be that the new rule only helps the bowlers when no such help is required, and, such being the case, all who have tried it will be relieved to see it dropped in second-class, and glad that it was never adopted in first-class cricket.

Yours faithfully,

J. H. BRAIN, GLAMORGAN

Dear Sir,

Judging from the remarks I heard during the season, I should say the new LBW rule was decidedly unsatisfactory. It seems to have been a mistake to have made it experimental as a man taking part in second-class county matches had to adopt a different style of play, i.e., he would be out to a stroke in one of those matches LBW for which in an ordinary game or first-class county match he would be not out. It should have been for all or none. Doubtless batsmen would become accustomed to the new order of things, but it would be easy for a man to forget under which rule he was playing, and it is throwing a tremendous amount of additional responsibility on the umpires. Previous to the new rule complaints have been frequent enough in all conscience as to their incompetency but now they will be tenfold. It seems to me a very difficult question for them to decide, and in view of this arrangement of ours for reporting on the competency and satisfaction given by the umpires in each individual match it will cause a deal of dissatisfaction and probably unintentional unfairness. This little incident will show you what I mean. A certain captain had given me his report, which was "good", of a certain umpire. At the time he had not batted a second time. When he did this umpire gave him out LBW, and he asked me for the report back subsequently and altered it to unsatisfactory. It struck me that every umpire who wishes to get on should make it a *hard and fast rule* never to give a captain out LBW, for, as you know, they never are out and he would always be safe for a good report.

Yours faithfully,

H. M. TURNER, Secretary, OXFORD COUNTY

Dear Sir,

I will endeavour to give you my opinion on the Leg-Before-Wicket rule … I do not consider that it has had a fair trial on account of the number of wet wickets. I have heard it almost universally condemned, but personally I think it a good rule, as anything that will make a batsman play at a ball instead of putting his leg across and not *attempt* to play the ball must be of service to the now hard-worked bowler. Everything is now done for batting and nothing for the bowler.

Believe me, Yours faithfully,

P. J. de PARAVICINI, Captain of THE BUCKS ELEVEN

Dear Sir,

The general consensus of opinion amongst players in this county (whose criticisms I consider of more value than that of spectators), is that it made no practical difference to the game and did not fulfil its purpose in any way.

This is somewhat remarkable as Wiltshire possesses a leg-break bowler of rather more than average ability. The tendency to unnecessary appeals, caused by its adoption for this year, was also to be deprecated.

Yours faithfully,

TREVOR WHEELER, Hon. Sec., WILTSHIRE COUNTY CLUB

page 441

English Team v Eighteen of California

Played at San Francisco, Wednesday, November 26, 1902. Arriving at San Francisco early on the morning of Tuesday, the 25th of November, the Englishmen indulged in a little practice, and on the following day opened their tour with a match against Eighteen of California. Warner won the toss, but he decided to put the local team in first, and this policy was attended with the happiest results. The Californian batsmen could do nothing against

Bosanquet's slow leg-breaks, and in the end Lord Hawke's team, which consisted of twelve men, won by 30 runs and three wickets. Bosanquet received splendid support from Whatman, who stumped no fewer than seven of the home side. When the Englishmen went in Warner and Bosanquet hit brilliantly.

English Team

Mr P. F. Warner c Enderby b Richardson..	52	J. G. Thompson c Stahl b Ward......... 0
Mr C. J. Burnup c Richardson b Ward....	6	Mr J. Stanning b Ward 8
Mr F. L. Fane c Casidy b H. F. Elliot.....	9	Mr P. R. Johnson c H. F. Elliot b Coles... 6
Mr T. L. Taylor c H. R. Elliot b Bowley..	9	Extras 7
Mr E. M. Dowson b Casidy............	8	___
Mr B. J. T. Bosanquet not out	50	(8 wkts) 155

Mr A. D. Whatman, Mr A. E. Leatham and S. Hargreave did not bat.

Eighteen of California scored 125.

Bowling: Hargreave 18–10–17–2; Thompson 10–3–26–3; Bosanquet 32–9–37–11; Dowson 3–1–8–1; Burnup 13–8–15–0.

page 324

W. G. Grace's 126th and Last First-Class Century

London County v MCC and Ground

Played at the Crystal Palace, Monday, Tuesday, Wednesday, July 18, 19, 20, 1904. Poorly represented the MCC suffered defeat at the hands of London County by an innings and 18 runs. The MCC practically lost the match on the opening afternoon, as they were all out on an excellent wicket in less than three hours for 189, and when stumps were drawn London County had got to within 72 of this total without loss. Having thus secured a strong advantage London County never let it slip from their grasp. Everything else in the match was dwarfed by the batting of Grace who gave an exceedingly fine display, hitting with great power in all directions. He made one or two faulty strokes, but gave no actual chance during the five hours and a quarter he was at the wickets. He hit fourteen fours. This was the only occasion in first-class cricket last season on which Grace played a three-figure innings. On the Wednesday Braund and May bowled very well indeed, and the

MCC, who had gone in a second time on Tuesday evening 203 behind, never seemed in the least likely to save the game.

MCC and Ground

A. Hearne c Braund b Ranjitsinhji	42	– b May	6
Mr C. C. T. Doll b Ranjitsinhji	35	– c Bale b Braund	4
Capt. A. Legard lbw b Grace	0	– c Moulder b Braund	17
A. E. Relfe c Ranjitsinhji b Braund	24	– b Braund	15
Mr G. J. V. Weigall c Bale b Ranjitsinhji	0	– c Bale b May	36
Mr A. Worsley b Ranjitsinhji	2	– c May	10
Mr W. P. Harrison, jun. c Ranjitsinhji b May	37	– b May	42
Mr R. E. Lambert run out	30	– b Braund	22
H. R. Butt c and b May	4	– c Braund b May	0
A. Fielder c and b May	2	– not out	13
W. Mead not out	5	– b Braund	2
B 5, l-b 1, w 2	8	B 14, l-b 4	18
	189		185

Bowling: *First Innings*—Braund 19-3-43-1; May 6.4-0-31-3; Ranjitsinhji 25-4-63-4; Grace 15-1-44-1. *Second Innings*—Braund 20.1-3-50-5; May 25-1-86-5; Ranjitsinhji 2-0-8-0; Murdoch 1-1-0-0; Wells 6-1-23-0.

London County

Mr W. G. Grace c Fielder b Lambert	166	Mr L. S. Wells run out	29
Mr W. L. Murdoch c Relf b Lambert	51	L. C. Braund not out	11
Moulder c Butt b Hearne	41	Mr P. R. May b Hearne	22
K. S. Ranjitsinhji b Hearne	8	Bale c Mead b Hearne	16
Mr T. B. Nicholson c Butt b Fielder	8	B 10, l-b 2, w 6	18
Mr B. Jaya Ram b Hearne	7		
Mr P. G. Gale b Relf b Lambert	15		392

Bowling: Relf 39-4-101-0; Fielder 19-1-49-1; Mead 30-6-63-0; Hearne 36-8-101-5; Lambert 23-7-53-3; Legard 3-0-7-0.

Umpires: E. Martin and A. Atfield.

page cxxxiv

Notes by the Editor
(Sydney Pardon)

The Laws of Cricket were allowed to remain undisturbed in 1905, the desire for change, so much in evidence during recent years, having apparently lost its force. The proposition brought forward, with the support of the committee, at the MCC meeting at Lord's in May, to make the last sentence of Law 1 read "The choice of innings shall be decided by tossing, unless otherwise arranged" was beaten on a show of hands by such an overwhelming majority that no purpose would have been served by taking a vote. It was certainly curious that this effort to minimise the effect of luck should have been followed by F. S. Jackson's extraordinarily good fortune in winning the toss in every one of the five Test matches. Still, though Darling's unhappy experience strengthened the case for a modification of the existing rule as regards a series of games between the same sides, I hold strongly to the opinion that the toss, as an essential feature of cricket, should not be tampered with. Apart from all other considerations – such as the delightful uncertainty before a match begins as to which side will bat first – the toss for innings affords the best guarantee that wickets will in all cases be fairly and properly prepared. I would not for a moment suggest that in the case of out and home county matches the knowledge that the opposing team were going in first would in the ordinary way lead to any wrong-doing on the part of the ground-keepers. All the same there would be a danger which the law in its present shape prevents. Very little extra water, or the difference of a few hours in the last time for watering, might make all the difference in the world to the side that had first innings, and even the suspicion of any malpractices of this kind would cause great ill-feeling and might lead to an old-established county match being left out of the following season's programme.

pages 1–2

The Leading Counties in 1906

Never since 1889 when, under the system of scoring points in vogue at that time, Notts, Lancashire, and Surrey tied for first place, has the struggle for the Championship been so exciting as in 1906. After their victory over Yorkshire at The Oval towards the end of July, Surrey looked to have the best chance of success, but in the following week they were beaten by Kent at Blackheath and the result again became quite open. Victory over Surrey in the return at Sheffield seemed to put Yorkshire in a secure position, but in a sensational match at Bristol the prize slipped out of their hands, Gloucestershire beating them by a single run. This put Kent in front, but so close was the struggle that it was necessary for them to avoid defeat in their final match against Hampshire at Bournemouth. They won handsomely after making themselves safe on the opening day and so, for the first time in modern days, became champion county. That they played the finest cricket of the year and fully deserved the distinction they earned was admitted on all hands. Right through August indeed they were regarded everywhere as the strongest side. Notts and Lancashire showed a bold front up to a certain point but never had much hope of finishing at the top of the list. In all 172 matches were played of which 129 were won and 43 left drawn. The excellent proportion of finished matches said much for the simpler methods of preparing wickets now generally adopted. Except at Worcester and Birmingham, the drawn games were due rather to the occasional wet days in a wonderful summer than to excessive scoring.

THE COUNTY CHAMPIONSHIP

	Played	Won	Lost	Drawn	Points	Percentage
1 – Kent...............	22	16	2	4	14	77.77
2 – Yorkshire..........	28	17	3	8	14	70.00
3 – Surrey............	28	18	4	6	14	63.63
4 – Lancashire.........	26	15	6	5	9	42.85
5 – Nottinghamshire.....	20	9	4	7	5	38.46
6 – Warwickshire.......	20	7	4	9	3	27.27
7 – Essex.............	22	9	6	7	3	23.00
8 – Hampshire.........	20	7	9	4	–2	–12.50
9 – Gloucestershire.....	20	6	10	4	–4	–20.00
10 – Sussex............	24	6	12	6	–6	–33.33
11 { Somerset..........	18	4	10	4	–6	–42.85
11 { Middlesex.........	18	4	10	4	–6	–42.85
11 { Northamptonshire....	16	4	10	2	–6	–42.85
14 – Worcestershire......	20	2	8	10	–6	–60.00
15 – Leicestershire.......	22	3	14	5	–11	–64.70
16 – Derbyshire.........	20	2	17	1	–15	–78.94

According to the rule laid down by the MCC, "One point shall be reckoned for each win; one deducted for each loss; unfinished games shall not be reckoned. The county which during the season shall have, in finished matches, obtained the greatest proportionate number of points shall be reckoned champion county."

part II, page 219

Gloucestershire v Northamptonshire

Played at Gloucester, Monday, Tuesday, Wednesday, June 10, 11, 12, 1907. In this game a fresh record was made by Dennett and Jessop in dismissing Northamptonshire for 12 runs. This is the smallest total for a first-class inter-county match, the previous lowest being 13 by Notts against Yorkshire at Trent Bridge, in 1901. Play on the first day was restricted to fifty minutes, Gloucestershire losing four wickets for 20 runs, and, despite some hitting by Jessop, being all out next day for 60. The first innings of Northamptonshire only lasted forty minutes, Dennett, who made the ball turn in a remarkable manner, being practically unplayable. Dennett accomplished the "hat-trick", in dismissing Hawtin, Beasley, and Buswell with successive balls, and should have had four wickets in as many balls, Wrathall dropping a catch offered by East. In Gloucestershire's second innings Jessop and Mackenzie were the only batsmen to overcome the difficulties of the wicket, but Northamptonshire were set 136 to get to win. At their second attempt the visitors again failed before Dennett, who in the course of the day took 15 wickets for 21 runs. Northamptonshire finished up on the second day in practically a hopeless position, wanting 97 runs to win with only three wickets left, but rain came to their rescue. Not a ball could be bowled on the Wednesday, the game having to be abandoned as a draw.

Gloucestershire

H. Wrathall b Thompson	4	– b Thompson	7
Mr E. Barnett lbw b Thompson	3	– b East	0
J. H. Board b Thompson	3	– lbw b Thompson	5
Mr M. G. Salter c Buswell b East	3	– c and b East	3
Mr G. L. Jessop b East	22	– c Hawtin b East	24
Mr R. T. H. Mackenzie b East	0	– c King b East	21
T. Langdon b East	4	– lbw b Thompson	4
J. H. Huggins c Crosse b East	8	– c Buswell b East	3
E. Spry lbw b Thompson	6	– b East	4
Parker not out	2	– not out	8
G. Dennett c Pool b Thompson	0	– b East	0
B 2, l-b 3	5	B 9	9
	60		**88**

Bowling: *First Innings*—Thompson 16.5–7–29–5; East 16–5–26–5. *Second Innings*—Thompson 15–2–43–3; East 14.2–4–36–7.

Northamptonshire

Mr E. M. Crosse c Board b Dennett	4	– c and b Dennett	0
M. Cox lbw b Dennett	2	– c Barnett b Dennett	12
Mr C. J. T. Pool c Spry b Dennett	4	– st Board b Dennett	9
W. A. Buswell st Board b Dennett	1	– c Langdon b Dennett	0
Mr L. T. Driffield b Dennett	0		
G. J. Thompson b Dennett	0	– not out	5
Mr R. W. R. Hawtin lbw b Dennett	0	– lbw b Dennett	8
W. East st Board b Dennett	0	– lbw b Dennett	2
Mr R. N. Beasley b Jessop	1	– b Dennett	0
Mr S. King not out	0	– not out	1
W. Wells c Parker b Jessop	0		
		B 2, l-b 1	3
	12	(7 wkts)	40

Bowling: *First Innings*—Dennett 6–1–9–8; Jessop 5.3–4–3–2. *Second Innings*—Dennett 15–8–12–7; Jessop 10–3–20–0; Parker 5–2–5–0.

Umpires: A. Millward and J. E. West.

Northamptonshire's first-innings score of 12 remained the equal lowest first-class score at the end of the century (see Cricket Records section in the 2000 edition of Wisden*).*

part I, pages 160–161

Lord Hawke and Four Cricketers of the Year

Lord Hawke

The presentation to Lord Hawke at Leeds last July, in celebration of the fact of his having in the previous summer completed twenty-five years service as captain of the Yorkshire Eleven, afforded a happy opportunity of giving his portrait in *Wisden*. There was an idea many years [ago] of including him in a group of county captains, but for some reason the project fell through. Lord Hawke has made many a good score, but it is as captain of Yorkshire for more than a quarter of a century that he will live in cricket history. His unique work in managing for such a length of time a team composed almost entirely of professional players has to a large extent overshadowed his doings as a batsman.

He was intended for the Army, and it was only by chance that he was able to give so much of his time to cricket. He has said himself that his acceptance of the Yorkshire captaincy was the happiest event of his life, and as one who has had the pleasure of knowing him almost from the day he took up his post, I can readily believe that such was the case. The well-being of Yorkshire cricket has since 1882 been his abiding interest; and today, when as a cricketer he must be regarded as something of a veteran, he is just as keen and enthusiastic as in his early manhood.

It was no small responsibility that he took upon his shoulders. The Yorkshire team in the early eighties was full of genius, but the results obtained were not, taking one year with another, commensurate with the individual gifts of the players. There is no unkindness in saying that some of the brilliant cricketers who fought Yorkshire's battles in those days lived their lives rather carelessly and were lost to the game much sooner that they should have been. To take one notable instance, Peate, than whom no left-handed slow bowler ever had a greater command over the ball, had done with first-class cricket at the age of thirty-one, and some other careers were even shorter than his. Taking up the captaincy when he was a very young man, Lord Hawke could not all at once make his influence felt but before many years had passed he succeeded in bringing about a vast improvement.

The full result of his work has been seen in recent years, Yorkshire, beginning with 1893, having come out first among the counties eight times in sixteen seasons. The players who carried off the Championship three years in succession, 1900–01–02, were not more gifted than their predecessors but they were far more consistent. Thanks to discipline and careful living they were able to do their best every day in the season, and in the fact of being always in form could be found the secret of their success. Controlling his team during all these years of success Lord Hawke has had a very pleasant task. There is no inherent difficulty in leading a band of highly-skilled players, everyone of whom thinks first of the side and not of his own personal glory.

Lord Hawke has won the affection and regard of his professionals without for a moment losing his authority. An absolute master he has always used his power wisely. Once circumstances arose that called for swift and severe action. The case will be readily remembered and there is no need to mention names or go into details.* Enough that Lord Hawke deemed it

---

* *The incident referred to involved either Robert Peel or Edmund Peate, both of whose careers were curtailed by disciplinary action. According to the* Who's Who of Cricketers *(by Philip Bailey, Philip Thorn and Peter Wynne-Thomas) Peel, a slow left arm bowler, was "regarded as the best bowler of his type in England. His county career came to a premature end when Lord Hawke dismissed him because of his inebriate habits". Peate's entry reads, "His sudden departure from county cricket whilst in his prime was caused by Lord Hawke's determination to rid the Yorkshire team of its more unruly elements." See also the extract, in this book, from the 1932 edition, "Discipline and Fellowship".*

necessary to drop a great cricketer out of the eleven, and for the well-being of the side as a whole did not hesitate to do so. In every respect, both on and off the field, he has been the Yorkshire professionals' best friend. To him, I imagine, is due the wise provision that nowadays the great bulk of the money derived from benefit matches in Yorkshire is soundly invested so that the players concerned may have something substantial to fall back upon when their cricket days are over. During his captaincy the system of winter pay has been adopted, and he has devised his own plan of rewarding special excellence in batting, bowling, and fielding. On the question of investing the proceeds of benefit matches he felt strongly, as in more than one case he had seen large sums squandered within a year or two of a benefit being given. If necessary, I could write much about Lord Hawke's doings at Eton and Cambridge, and his journeyings to various parts of the world where our national game is played. For the moment, however, I am only regarding him as the good genius of Yorkshire cricket. It so happened he was born – on the 16th of August, 1860 – in Lincolnshire, but by family ties and all associations he is a Yorkshireman.

The four Cricketers of the Year were W. Brearley, A. Marshal, J. T. Newstead and J. B. Hobbs (one of Wisden's *Five Cricketers of the Century).*

part II, pages 392–393

Second-class Counties in 1909

Staffordshire

Hon. Secretary – Mr W. C. HANCOCK, Cocknage Road, Longton, Staffs.

Staffordshire were so good a side that had they finished at the top of their section it is quite likely they would have carried off the Championship for the second year in succession. Once more the chief man of their eleven was Barnes who, by being picked to play for England, conferred distinction upon his county. In the course of the season he accomplished some splendid performances, but nothing he did was so startling as in the match at Stoke against Cheshire, when in the two innings he took fourteen wickets for 13 runs. Bucknell also bowled well, and only just beat Barnes in average. B. Meakin proved a useful batsman, and Briggs, Winser, and Bourne gave valuable help.

STAFFORDSHIRE IN 1909
Played 10 – Won 7, Lost 2, Lost on first innings 1

Championship Position   2nd equal (out of six) in the second-class counties North Division (Notts Second XI won the division)

Summary of Matches

At Stoke, June 28, 29   Staffs (130 and 178-5 dec.) beat
                          Notts Second XI (98 and 34) by 176 runs

At Stoke, July 5, 6   Staffs (118 and 85-6) beat
                          Northumberland (80 and 121) by 4 wickets

At Crewe, July 7, 8   Staffs (202) beat
                          Cheshire (134 and 45) by an innings and 23 runs

At Wakefield, July 14, 15 Staffs (118 and 76) lost to
                          Yorks Second XI (179 and 16-0) by 10 wickets

At Newcastle, July 19, 20 Staffs (404-7 dec.) beat
                          Northumberland (101 and 164) by an innings and 139 runs

At Sunderland, July 21, 22 Staffs (223 and 22-2) beat
                          Durham (164 and 77) by 8 wickets

At Nottingham, July 28, 29 Staffs (146 and 44) lost to
                          Notts 2nd XI (78 and 114-5) by 5 wickets

At Stoke, August 2, 3   Staffs (151) beat
                          Cheshire (29 and 14) by an innings and 108 runs

At Stoke, August 4, 5   Staffs (190 and 75-8) lost to
                          Yorks 2nd XI (244) by 54 runs on 1st innings

At Stoke, August 11, 12   Staffs (315 and 12-0) beat
                          Durham (167 and 156) by 10 wickets

Batting Averages

	Innings	Not Outs	Runs	Highest Score	Average
Mr B. Meakin	5	1	195	122	48.75
Mr P. Briggs	15	0	480	101	32.00
Mr C. L. Winser	6	1	150	65	30.00
Mr E. H. Bourne	11	0	327	81	29.72

Bowling Averages

	Overs	Maidens	Runs	Wickets	Average
A. Bucknell	154.2	63	240	40	6.00
S. F. Barnes	224	73	515	76	6.77

part II, pages 299–301

Eton v Harrow

Played at Lord's, Friday, Saturday, July 8, 9, 1910. Eton and Harrow have been meeting on the cricket field for over a hundred years, but they have never played a match quite so remarkable as that of 1910. Indeed in the whole history of cricket there has been nothing more sensational. After following their innings Eton were only four ahead with nine wickets down, and yet in the end they won the game by nine runs. The nearest parallel to this finish that one can recall was one between Lancashire and Oxford University in 1888. On that occasion the county followed on, and managed to win although when their eighth wicket fell they were still 17 runs behind. The struggle between the two public schools last season will be known for all time as Fowler's match. Never has a school cricketer risen to the occasion in more astonishing fashion. When Harrow went in with only 55 to get, Fowler took command of the game, secured eight wickets – five of them bowled down – for 23 runs and brought off what might fairly be described as a forty to one chance.

Until the second afternoon was far advanced the match proved one-sided to a degree. On the first day, Harrow, going in on a soft, but by no means difficult pitch, ran up a total of 232, and when bad light caused stumps to be drawn, five of Eton's best wickets had fallen for 40 runs. By far the best batting for Harrow was shown in different styles by Wilson and Hillyard. In first and out fifth wicket down at 133 Wilson took two hours and a quarter to get his 53, his play all the time being very patient and watchful. Hillyard, more vigorous in his methods, scored 62 in an hour and threequarters, among his hits being a six to square leg and half-a-dozen fours. On Saturday morning, Eton's first innings was soon finished off for 67, and a follow-on against a balance of 165 was involved. At first things went so badly that half the wickets were down for 65, no one being able to get the ball away on the slow pitch.

The first change in the game came with the partnership between Fowler, and Wigan, 42 runs being added for the sixth wicket in fifty minutes. When Wigan left, Boswell, who had been last man in the first innings, joined Fowler and another good start was made, threequarters of an hour's play producing 57 runs. Still despite Fowler's heroic efforts – his 64 was the highest innings in the match – the position was reached of Eton being only four runs ahead with a wicket to fall. Then began the cricket which will for ever make the match memorable. Kaye joined Manners, and so finely and fearlessly did Manners hit that in less than twenty-five minutes 50 runs were put on, the total being carried from 169 to 219. A remarkable catch in the slips at last brought the innings to an end, Hopley just reaching the ball and turning it to Jameson, who held it a few inches from the ground. There can be no doubt that Earle, the Harrow captain, who had made many changes in the early part of the innings, was at fault in keeping himself and Hillyard on too long.

In the case of any ordinary match the ground would have been half empty before the Eton innings closed, but an Eton and Harrow crowd is a law to itself and when Harrow went in with 55 to get about 10,000 people watched the cricket. Whatever their feelings, they must have been glad they stayed as

Harrow

Mr T. O. Jameson c Lubbock b Fowler	5	– b Fowler	2
Mr T. B. Wilson b Kaye	53	– b Fowler	0
Mr G. W. V. Hopley b Fowler	35	– b Fowler	8
Mr T. L. G. Turnbull lbw b Fowler	2	– c Boswell b Fowler	0
Mr G. F. Earle c Wigan b Steel	20	– c Wigan b Fowler	13
Mr W. T. Monckton c Lubbock b Stock	20	– b Fowler	0
Mr J. M. Hillyard st Lubbock b Fowler	62	– c Kaye b Fowler	0
Mr C. H. B. Blount c Holland b Steel	4	– c and b Steel	5
Mr A. C. Straker c Holland b Steel	2	– b Fowler	1
Mr O. B. Graham c and b Steel	6	– not out	7
Hon. R. H. L. G. Alexander not out	2	– c Holland b Steel	8
B 18, l-b 2, n-b 1	21	B 1	1
	232		45

Bowling: *First Innings*—Fowler 37.3–9–90–4; Steel 31–11–69–4; Kaye 12–5–23–1; Stock 7–2–12–1; Boswell 8–4–17–0. *Second Innings*—Fowler 10.2–2–23–8; Steel 6.4–1–12–2; Kaye 3–0–9–0.

Eton

Mr R. H. Lubbock lbw b Earle	9	– c Straker b Hillyard	9
Mr C. W. Tufnell b Hillyard	5	– lbw b Alexander	7
Mr W. T. Birchenough c Hopley b Graham	5	– c Turnbull b Jameson	22
Mr W. T. Holland c Hopley b Hillyard	2	– st Monckton b Alexander	5
Mr R. St L. Fowler c Graham b Jameson	21	– c Earle b Hillyard	64
Mr A. I. Steel b Graham	0	– c Hopley b Hillyard	6
Mr D. G. Wigan c Turnbull b Jameson	8	– b Graham	16
Mr A. B. Stock lbw b Alexander	2	– lbw b Earle	0
Hon. J. N. Manners c Graham b Alexander	0	– not out	40
Mr K. Lister Kaye c Straker b Alexander	0	– c Jameson b Earle	13
Mr W. G. K. Boswell not out	0	– b Earle	32
B 10, w 1	11	B 2, w 3	5
	67		219

Bowling: *First Innings*—Earle 12–9–4–1; Hillyard 19–9–38–2; Graham 9–7–3–2; Jameson 4–1–4–2; Alexander 4.1–1–7–3. *Second Innings*—Earle 17.3–3–57–3; Hillyard 23–7–65–3; Graham 8–12–33–1; Jameson 9–1–26–1; Alexander 14–4–33–2; Wilson 2–2–0–0.

Umpires: J. Moss and J. P. Whiteside.

they may never see such a finish again. Probably Harrow made a mistake in having the heavy roller put on. At any rate Fowler was able at once to bowl his off-break with deadly effect. He bowled Wilson in the first over; at eight he bowled Hopley; and at the same total, Turnbull, the left-handed hitter, was caught in the long field. Earle seemed likely to win the match easily enough for Harrow, but after he had hit up 13 runs, a catch at slip sent him back at 21. Without the addition of a run, Monckton was bowled and Hillyard well caught low down at short mid-on. In this way, as the result of half an hour's cricket, six wickets were down for 21, Fowler having taken them all. Blount was caught and bowled at 26 by Steel, who had just gone on for Kaye, and then Jameson, who had been batting for nearly forty minutes without getting a run, was so badly hurt that for a few minutes the game had to be delayed. With victory in sight, the Eton team played the keenest possible cricket, nothing being thrown away in the field. A yorker bowled Straker at 29, and, after Graham had hit a three, Jameson was bowled by Fowler. It was not to be expected that Graham and Alexander would get the 23 runs still required, but they made a desperate effort, carrying the score to 45 or only ten to win. Then a catch low down in the slips got rid of Alexander and a wonderful match was over. The scene of enthusiasm at the finish was quite indescribable. From the time he went on at 21, Steel with his leg-breaks gave Fowler excellent support and the Eton fielding all round was magnificent.

part II, page 283

The MCC in 1911

The 124th Annual General Meeting of the Marylebone CC was held in the pavilion at Lord's on Wednesday afternoon, May 3rd. The Earl of Londesborough (the retiring president) took the chair.

The annual report, which was unanimously adopted, stated that in 1910 the Club consisted of 5,219 members – a decrease of 29 from the previous year – of whom 4,657 paid, 353 were life members, and 386 were abroad.

The Club played 173 matches in 1910, 96 being won, 37 lost, and the remainder drawn.

During the season 124,275 people passed through the turnstiles at Lord's, as against 199,318 in 1909.

The Right Hon. W. H. Long MP, Lord Hawke, Messrs H. E. Murray-Anderdon, and C. Marriott retired from the committee by rotation, the vacancies being filled by the Earl of Londesborough, Viscount Brackley, Dr Russell Bencraft, and Mr P. F. Warner. The vacancy caused by the death of the Earl Cawdor had been filled previously by the appointment of the Hon. F. S. Jackson.

The drainage of the ground has been thoroughly overhauled, and it is hoped that the effect of the works will be to encourage a more rapid run off of storm water. Close attention has been given to the removal of the plantain roots.

Candidates elected as cricketers on promises to play in MCC matches who have not fulfilled their obligations will have another opportunity next season of showing their willingness to play for the Club before Rule 10 is put into operation.

In consequence of the wet season there was a loss on the working of the refreshment department in 1910 of £140 0s. 4d.

Owing to complaints, the sale of daily and evening papers in the pavilion will be discontinued.

part I, pages 122–126

To mark the 50th edition of Wisden Cricketers' Almanack,
*the editor included a tribute to the founder instead of the regular Five
Cricketers of the Year feature.*

John Wisden

Born September 5, 1826; died April 5, 1884.

Wisden played his first match for Sussex, against Kent at Brighton, in July 1845, and his last, against the MCC and Ground at Brighton, in August

1863. After 1863 he did not take part in first-class cricket. He made his first appearance at Lord's in 1846. His first Gentlemen v Players match was in 1848 and his last in 1859. He and James Dean founded in 1852 the United All-England Eleven, whose famous matches with the All-England Eleven began in 1857. In conjunction with George Parr, Wisden took an England Eleven to Canada and the United States in 1859 two years before the first English team, with H. H. Stephenson as captain, went to Australia.

Personal Recollections

SIR KENELM DIGBY writes: I am glad to have the opportunity of noting down a few reminiscences of John Wisden, who was engaged as professional bowler at Harrow School during the four years 1852–1855. As those were the years in which I was a member of the Harrow eleven and captain for the last three of them, I was during the cricket season brought into close and daily connection with Wisden. I have the pleasantest recollection of his quiet, modest, and unassuming character, his unfailing good temper, and his keenness in and enjoyment of his work, his genial disposition which made him a great favourite with all the present and former members of the school with whom he came in contact…

From time to time it was necessary to give him leave to be absent for some great match, in which his services could not be dispensed with. It was, it must be remembered, the day of round-arm bowling, when the raising of the arm above the level of the shoulder was prohibited. The alteration of this rule has, it seems to me, largely altered the characteristics of first-class bowling. Wisden had a perfect delivery; with a short but rapid run, a graceful and easy sweep of the arm, moderate pace, hardly a loose ball, varying his pace occasionally, but always "on the spot", he was unsurpassed as the standby of a side in first-class cricket.

SIR SPENCER PONSONBY FANE writes: I knew Jack Wisden very well and played with or against him for about ten years in the important matches of those days, for which I was able to get away from the Foreign Office, such as Gentlemen and Players, North and South, Kent and England etc. He was a very fine and accurate bowler, perfect length, but with little work, except what the ground gave it. He was a fast medium, but I think he was classed as a fast bowler – and played on that side in the match, Fast v Slow. He was a delightful bowler to play against, but required very careful watching, for he was apt to send in occasionally a very fast shooter, then so fatal on Lord's Ground. I have no recollection of his bowling a "yorker", called a "Tice" in those days – a mode of attack not in vogue at the time. I believe he was the first of the players to play in a straw hat, instead of the white topper worn by the older players. He was a good field and an excellent bat, which was rather exceptional for a bowler at that time, when bowlers were not expected to be very able performers with the bat. He was a genial, pleasant, and respectable fellow in every way, liked and respected by everyone with whom he came in contact.

THE REV. H. B. BIRON writes: The first time I saw Wisden play was on the old ground at Canterbury just beyond the Barracks. This was before the present St Lawrence Ground was in use. I was then a boy at school and I never imagined then that eleven years afterwards I should be playing against him for Kent, or that after another 55 years I should be asked to give a few remembrances of this famous cricketer on the 50th Anniversary of the invaluable *Cricketers' Almanack* which bears his name … Early in his cricketing career he was called the "Little Wonder", a title which, given him by Bob Thoms, he bore through his life. In his time the wickets were not of the "billiard table", or, as I have heard it called, the "bread and butter" type of the present age, consequently the bowlers of the past had a great advantage over those of the present time – but the pitch and precision of Wisden's bowling would have made him difficult even in the present day, and I have but little doubt that his ingenuity would have risen to the occasion as the wickets became easier. Indeed, he lived to see a great improvement in the grounds, but he was a deadly trundler to the end…

But he did not shine only as a bowler; for so short a man he was a powerful hitter, and a good bat all-round. The centuries, which in these days are as common as blackberries, were very rare in Wisden's time, but he scored 100 against Kent in 1850 – his innings including four sixes, and these against Willsher, than whom a better or more difficult bowler never lived – and 148 against Yorkshire at Sheffield in 1855, when he met such clever trundlers as Ike Hodgson, Crossland, Wright and Chatterton, a formidable quartette indeed – a fact which I can personally assert. In the Kent v England Match at Canterbury in 1853 I saw him make a drive for *seven* all run out, the ball travelling nearly to the entrance gate. The only boundaries then were three or four tents. I have sometimes wondered, when in the present age I see batsmen resting for breath after the very rare four run out, how they would feel after running a hit for seven. Have the Sybaritic luncheons anything to do with this? But it was not only as a cricketer but as a man that the memory of Wisden may be cherished … May John Wisden's memory be kept alive in the cricket world for another 50 years at least, when perhaps one of my great grandchildren may write another *In Memoriam* in the 100th Edition of *John Wisden's Cricketers' Almanack*.

part I, pages 125–126

Hayward's Hundred Hundreds

In the course of the season of 1913 Tom Hayward had the satisfaction of rivalling W. G. Grace's feat of making a hundred three-figure scores in first-class cricket. He and W. G. are, so far, the only batsmen who have reached the number. Happily the time has not yet come to deal with Hayward's splendid career as a whole. So far as one knows he has no present thought of giving up the game, and while he can bat as he did on many occasions last summer there is assuredly not the least necessity for his retirement. The change that has come over modern cricket in the way of an extended programme of first-class fixtures is brought home to us by the fact that Hayward made his hundredth century in his twenty-first season. W. G. Grace began to play first-class cricket in 1865 – the year following his first appearance at Lord's – and it was not until 1895 that his hundredth hundred was obtained. Between the two batsmen, therefore, there was a difference of just ten years. W. G. made fifty-one of his hundreds for Gloucestershire, and Hayward, with many more county matches, no fewer than eighty-six for Surrey. In Gentlemen and Players matches, on the other hand, W. G. beginning at Lord's in 1865 and finishing at The Oval in 1906 made fifteen hundreds, as against Hayward's seven. Hayward, who is, perhaps, not likely to be chosen for the Players again, was first picked against the Gentlemen at Lord's and The Oval in 1895 – two years after he came out for Surrey. Carrying comparison a little further, both batsmen can point to a couple of hundreds for England against Australia in this country. W. G. made 152 at The Oval in 1880 – the first Test match in England – and 170 on the same ground in 1886. Hayward's two were both obtained in 1899 – 130 at Manchester and 137 at The Oval.

It is only a matter of fancy, but if asked to name the finest innings in Hayward's career one would be inclined to select the never-to-be-forgotten 130 at Manchester. The circumstances were quite exceptional. Winning the toss on a fast wicket England made a shocking start, but Hayward saved his side, following up an hour or more of rigid defence by a most brilliant display of hitting. In 1906 Hayward made four hundreds for Surrey in one week – 144 not out and 100 against Notts at Trent Bridge, and 143 and 125 against Leicestershire at Leicester. In the same year he obtained the record aggregate of runs in first-class cricket in one season, 3,518, and equalled

C. B. Fry's feat in 1901 of getting thirteen hundreds. As everyone knows, Hayward was preceded, at some considerable distance of time, as the best professional bat in England by the uncle after whom he was named. The first Tom Hayward, who died in 1876, when the present player was only five years old, damaged a great reputation by lingering on in first-class cricket when his day was over, but from 1859 to 1863, and for a few years afterwards, he was right at the top of the tree.

part I, page 206

Notes by the Editor

(Sydney Pardon)

Writing in the early days of the New Year it is impossible to take other than a gloomy view with regard to the immediate future of cricket. Never before has the game been in such a plight. One may take it for granted that, in any circumstances, county cricket, as we have known it for the last forty years or more, will be out of the question this season, but in the happy event of the War coming to an end at an earlier date than the experts expect, we are sure to see plenty of games of a less competitive character. Indeed, as all the fixtures were provisionally made last summer, the counties might try something in the nature of a modified programme. However, it is idle to speculate in January as to what will happen in May or June. I hope no attempt will be made to close the game down entirely. All the counties are asking their members to keep on with their subscriptions, and in return matches of some kind should from time to time be played on the various grounds. Cricketers have made a splendid response to the call to the colours. They cannot all go to the front; some of them have duties that must keep them at home. To my mind, it would be a great misfortune for any county ground to be closed for the whole summer. I had thought of preparing for *Wisden* a list of the cricketers who have joined the Army, but the number is so great that I could not be at all sure of accuracy. Any accidental omission might have involved protest and correction. After the War, whenever that may be, cricket will, no doubt, go on as before, but it will naturally take some time for the game to recover completely from the blow it has received.

pages 84–85 and 88

Obituary: W. G. Grace

By Sydney Pardon

William Gilbert Grace

Born at Downend, near Bristol, July 18th, 1848
Died at his home, Fairmount, Eltham, Kent, October 23rd, 1915

In no branch of sport has anyone ever enjoyed such an unquestioned supremacy as that of W. G. Grace in the cricket field. In his great days he stood alone, without a rival. Not even George Fordham and Fred Archer as jockeys, or John Roberts as a billiard player, had such a marked superiority over the men who were nearest to them in point of ability. Whatever may be in store for the game of cricket in the future it seems safe to say that such a player will never be seen again. A rare combination of qualities went to the making of W. G. Grace. Blessed with great physical advantages, he united to a strength of constitution that defied fatigue a devotion to the game which time was powerless to affect. When he was in his prime no sun was too hot and no day too long for him. It is on record that when, for a cricketer, he was no longer young, he spent the whole night by the bedside of a patient, and on the following day stepped on to the Clifton College ground and scored over 200 runs.

Mr Grace's career in the cricket field – almost unexampled in point of length – can be sharply divided into two portions. His early fame as a batsman culminated in the season of 1876, when in the month of August he scored, in three successive innings, 344 against Kent at Canterbury, 177 against Notts at Clifton, and 318 not out against Yorkshire at Cheltenham. Soon after that, having passed his examination at Edinburgh as a surgeon, he thought of gradually retiring from cricket and settling down, like his elder brothers, to the busy life of a general practitioner. As a matter of fact, he did for many years hold a parish appointment at Bristol, a *locum tenens* doing his work in the summer months. There can be little doubt that his change of plans was mainly due to the appearance in England in 1878 of the first Australian eleven. Those whose memories go back to that now somewhat distant time will remember the tremendous sensation caused by the victories of that eleven, and in particular by Spofforth's bowling, and Blackham's wicket-keeping. Englishmen realised, with an excusable shock of surprise, that in the cricket field there were serious rivals to be faced.

Mr Grace had never been in such poor batting form as he was in 1878, and on the few occasions that he met the Australian bowlers he did nothing in the least degree worthy of his reputation. I have no exact knowledge on the point, but I feel tolerably certain that the success of the Australians revived Mr Grace's ambition. At any rate, the fact remains that, though the most brilliant part of his career had ended before the invasion of 1878, the Australians found him for the best part of twenty years the most formidable of their opponents. This second part of his career as a batsman began towards the end of the season of 1880. Following some fine performances for Gloucestershire he played, as everyone will remember, a great innings of 152 at The Oval in the first match in this country between England and Australia. Even then, however, though only in his 33rd year, he laboured under one serious disadvantage. In the four years following his triumphs of 1876, he had put on a lot of weight and was very heavy for so young a man.

He said himself at the time that he was never in better form than in those closing weeks of the season of 1880 and that, but for lack of condition, he would have made many more runs. Against increasing bulk he had to battle for the rest of his cricket life. For a long time he retained his activity to a surprising extent, but as the years went on his once splendid fielding gradually left him. He kept up his batting, however, in a marvellous way, the success of what one may call his second period in the cricket field reaching its climax when in 1895 he scored a thousand runs in first-class cricket in the month of May. His batting at that time has never been approached by a man of the same age; he was nearly 47. In 1896 he was still very good, but after that the years began to tell on him, and in 1899, when he moved from Bristol to the Crystal Palace, he played at Trent Bridge his last match for England against Australia. Still, though he had now done with Test matches, he went on playing first-class cricket for several seasons, his career practically ending with the Gentlemen and Players match at The Oval in 1906. The finish was worthy of him as, on his 58th birthday, he scored 74, batting up to a certain point with much of the vigour of his younger days.

Personally, W. G. struck me as the most natural and unspoiled of men. Whenever and wherever one met him he was always the same. There was not the smallest trace of affectation about him. If anything annoyed him he was quick to show anger, but his little outbursts were soon over. One word I will add. No man who ever won such world-wide fame could have been more modest in speaking of his own doings.

W. G. Grace was one of 396 obituaries in the 1916 edition. With very little cricket being played during the First World War, the 1916 to 1919 editions contained less than half the usual number of pages. A large proportion of these consisted of obituaries of cricketers who were killed in the War, which the editor, Sydney Pardon, refers to in his preface to the 1917 edition.

page 13

Preface

By Sydney Pardon

The fifty-fourth edition of *Wisden's Almanack* is of necessity rather a mournful volume. Its chief feature is a record of the cricketers who have fallen in the War – the Roll of Honour, so far as the national game is concerned … Some names may have been overlooked but I am assured that the list – carried up to the end of 1916 – is the most complete that has yet appeared. Apart from the War death has been very busy among cricketers, the well-known men who passed away during the year including Alfred Lubbock, A. W. Ridley, Frank Penn, C. E. Green, Thomas Horan of the first Australian eleven, James Round who though he never got his Blue at Oxford kept wicket for the Gentlemen of England, and Henry Perkins – for over twenty years secretary of the MCC. To all these I have endeavoured, within the limited space at my disposal, to do justice … Last year the wisdom of publishing *Wisden* in War time seemed very doubtful, but the experiment was more than justified, a small edition being sold out in a few days. As a natural result the proprietors had this year no hesitation in going on. At the time of writing the outlook for the game is as dark as possible, another blank season as regards first-class cricket being to all appearance certain. So far supporters of the various county clubs have for the most part been very loyal, but this year some further falling off in subscriptions is almost inevitable.

pages 152–153

As there was no first-class cricket played in England during the First World War, the editor chose five schoolboy bowlers as the portraits in the 1918 edition. One of these five was Harry Calder.

School Bowlers of the Year

H. L. Calder

Calder, the son of an old Hampshire cricketer, came to Cranleigh from South Africa in 1915, and at once got a place in the school eleven. He has been head of the bowling averages in each of his three years. He bowls fast medium with an easy action and a good delivery, and he has a useful slower ball which he developed in 1916, and which he mixes in cleverly with his faster ones. He possesses also the cardinal virtue of length, which means that he is seldom mastered and he keeps the batsman playing most of the time. He has too a dangerous "yorker" on the leg stump which swings in to the batsman at the last moment. He played in several of the holiday games and certainly created a most favourable impression. At The Oval on one occasion, he got eight wickets for 21.

When, in 1994, Wisden tried to track down the oldest surviving Cricketers of the Year to invite them to the Wisden dinner, it was found that there was no record of Calder's death – nor of his adult life. Eventually Robert Brooke traced him, aged 93, to a rest home in South Africa. Calder, who had turned to tennis and golf rather than cricket, had never even known until then that he was a member of the game's elite. But he was "delighted" to hear the news, 76 years late.

pages 29–30

In the early years of the century, Wisden *annually published the following appendix to the Laws of Cricket which set out the regulations for Test matches in England.*

Board of Control of "Test" Matches at Home

(Formed at the request of the Counties, by the MCC, in 1898.)

To consist of the President of the MCC (in the chair), five of its Club Committee, and one representative from each of the ten First-Class Counties that came out at the top of the last season's list.

The constitution of the Board to remain unchanged until after the accounts of the season have been passed.

1. **PLAY**. – In all Test matches play shall begin on the first day at 11.30 a.m.; on the second and third days at 11 a.m. Stumps shall be drawn at 6.30 p.m.
2. **UMPIRES**. – The Umpires shall be appointed by Ballot and shall be paid £10 per match.
3. **DISTRIBUTION OF PROFITS**. – All moneys taken at Stands and Enclosures at the Test Matches shall, together with the Gate Money in respect thereof, less the Opponents' half of the gross Gate Money and less such expenses as are authorised by the Board, be placed in the hands of the Board for distribution as follows: 30 per cent to the grounds where the matches are played, in equal shares; 10 per cent to the Counties that take part in the Second Division of the County Championship; and 60 per cent to be divided equally among the First-Class Counties and the MCC. But should there be a loss on these matches, such loss shall be divided among the said First and Second-Class Counties and the MCC in the proportion of their respective interests.
4. **SELECTION SUB-COMMITTEE**. – A Sub-Committee of three shall be appointed by the Board to select England teams. Such Sub-Committee shall appoint a Chairman, who shall have a casting vote. The said Committee of three shall in each match select the Captain.

5. **TRUSTEES.** – Two Trustees shall be appointed to whom all payments subject to distribution, as aforesaid, should be made.

6. **COLLECTIONS.** – No collection shall be allowed on any ground during a Test match.

7. **EXPENSES.** – The expenses to be deducted from the gross Gate Money (or in Test matches between Australia and South Africa from the stand money) shall include players (including reserve men), police, umpires, scorers, gate and ground attendants, printing, advertising, luncheons, match balls, and any other items specially sanctioned by the Board.

8. **PLAYERS.** – The remuneration of players shall be £20 per match; of reserve men £10.

9. **AMATEURS.** – Amateurs' expenses to be allowed are railway fares and a sum at the rate of 30s. per diem, not exceeding five days for each match.

10. **LUNCHEONS.** – The amount to be allowed for luncheon will be £10 per diem.

11. **SCORERS.** – Scorers shall be paid £5 per match.

12. **ADVERTISING.** – The sum to be allowed for advertising shall not exceed £30 for each match.

13. **TEA INTERVAL.** – There will be a tea interval at 4.30 p.m. daily during the Test matches, unless at that time 9 wickets of the batting side have fallen, or an interval has occurred since luncheon. In the event of there being no interval, drinks can be sent out on the field at the request of the Captain of the fielding side.

14. **NEW BALL.** – Umpires should inform the batsman when a new ball is about to be used.

part I, page 276

Notes by the Editor
(Sydney Pardon)

The season of 1919 proved, beyond all question or dispute, that cricket had lost nothing of its attraction for the public. Indeed, one may go further than that. Despite a break of four years and the fact that at all grounds the charge for admission – in view of the entertainment tax and vastly increased expenses – was doubled, county matches drew far larger crowds than in ordinary seasons before the war. The faint-hearts who, without evidence on the point, had jumped to the conclusion that cricket would never again be its old self, were utterly confuted. Even the hopeful spirits, among whom I include myself, were agreeably surprised, things turning out much better than they had expected. Such being the pleasant state of affairs in the first year of peace, I trust we shall hear no more about the need for drastic alterations in the game. Looking back on the events of the season it is quaint to think that we were asked to shorten the boundaries, to penalise the batting side for every maiden over played, to banish the left-handed batsman, and to limit to three, or at most four, the number of professionals in every county eleven. All these fatuous suggestions and others just as foolish were, it will be remembered, put forward quite seriously. Happily we shall not be worried by them again. It is only right here to pay tribute to the steadfast confidence of Lord Harris. In the darkest days of the war he expressed his conviction that when peace came back cricket would have all its old charm for the English people. Everything he said was amply justified last summer.

part II, page 282

Northamptonshire v Surrey

Played at Northampton, Wednesday, Thursday, Friday, August 25, 26, 27, 1920. Though beaten by eight wickets in a match which produced 1,475 runs – a record in county cricket – the Northamptonshire players had good reason to be pleased with themselves. Scores of 306 and 430 against Surrey were immeasurably above their ordinary form. Surrey's huge total was the more remarkable as Hobbs contributed only three runs to it. The hitting on the second afternoon was some of the fiercest of the season, Fender actually getting his hundred in thirty-five minutes. Peach and Ducat also played in dazzling style.

Northamptonshire

Mr W. Adams b Rushby	3	– c Hobbs b Fender	31
Mr A. P. R. Hawtin c and b Fender	34	– b Rushby	5
R. Haywood c sub b Hitch	15	– c Peach b Fender	96
C. N. Woolley c Wilkinson b Fender	58	– lbw b Hitch	42
F. Walden c Hitch b Lockton	128	– b Rushby	63
Mr S. G. H. Humphrey b Ducat	24	– b Hitch	31
W. Wells c Strudwick b Hitch	4	– c Rushby b Shepherd	71
Mr R. O. Raven b Ducat	4	– lbw b Shepherd	28
V. Murdin b Shepherd	15	– c Strudwick b Shepherd	4
A. E. Thomas not out	8	– c Ducat b Hitch	30
B. Bellamy c Hitch b Fender	11	– not out	13
L-b 2	2	B 9, l-b 6, n-b 1	16
	306		**430**

Bowling: *First Innings*—Hitch 24–6–90–2; Rushby 25–10–66–1; Lockton 20–5–53–1; Shepherd 6–1–17–1; Fender 21.5–1–69–3; Ducat 9–4–9–2. *Second Innings*—Hitch 28.2–2–137–3; Rushby 27–5–68–2; Lockton 10–0–34–0; Shepherd 13–5–27–3; Fender 29–1–118–2; Ducat 8–1–23–0; Peach 4–2–7–0.

Surrey

J. B. Hobbs c Bellamy b Murdin	3	– b Walden	54
A. Sandham c Hawtin b Woolley	92	– b Thomas	6
Mr C. T. A. Wilkinson b Woolley	43		
T. Shepherd c Bellamy b Woolley	9	– not out	42
H. A. Peach not out	200		
A. Ducat c Bellamy b Thomas	149	– not out	11
Mr P. G. H. Fender not out	113		
B 9, l-b 1	10	B 2, l-b 5	7
(5 wkts dec.)	**619**	(2 wkts)	**120**

W. Hitch, Mr J. H. Lockton, H. Strudwick and T. Rushby did not bat.

Bowling: *First Innings*—Wells 31–6–133–0; Murdin 22.4–0–162–1; Thomas 23–0–142–1; Woolley 26–3–116–3; Humphrey 4–0–36–0; Haywood 4–0–20–0. *Second Innings*—Murdin 9–1–37–0; Thomas 14–3–24–1; Woolley 9.3–2–26–0; Walden 4–0–26–1.

Umpires: J. Moss and T. M. Russell.

Modern-day research has shown that Fender scored his hundred from between 40 and 46 balls. It remained the fastest ever authentic first-class hundred at the end of the century (see Cricket Records section in Wisden 2000*).*

part I, pages 228–237

*The following curiosities were included in a survey
of England v Australia matches.*

England v Australia

A Survey of Matches

- G. L. Jessop, at Leeds in 1909, in returning a ball brilliantly, strained a muscle at the base of his spine so severely that he had to be taken to his hotel on an ambulance. He was unable to play again during the season.

- Whilst fielding at Leeds in 1921 in Australia's first innings the Hon. L. H. Tennyson split his left hand and was obliged to have four stitches inserted. With the hand bandaged he batted most pluckily, scoring 63 and 36, his first innings lasting seventy-five minutes and containing ten fours. G. Brown, injured while wicket-keeping, batted an hour and a quarter in great pain for 46.

- Whilst batting at Nottingham in 1921, Tyldesley (E.) was struck on the left cheek by a fast ball from J. M. Gregory: he collapsed dazed to the ground, and the ball rolled on to his wicket.

- A. Ducat, batting for England at Leeds in 1921, had the shoulder of his bat knocked off on to the wicket, removing a bail. The ball was caught.

- In the Australian innings at The Oval in 1921, E. A. McDonald, while batting, thought he had been bowled and accordingly retired. He had almost reached the pavilion when the English captain, the Hon. L. H. Tennyson, having ascertained that the bail had been removed by the wicket-keeper (Brown), called McDonald back to continue batting.

- A. Cotter made a straight drive out of the ground off Blythe, at Manchester, in 1909.

- At The Oval, in 1888, J. J. Ferris was stopped bowling for having changed ends more than twice, which by Law 14 (since repealed) he was not allowed to do.

- In bowling R. B. Minnett at Adelaide, in 1911-12, F. R. Foster smashed the middle stump.

- In England's first innings at Manchester in 1921, W. W. Armstrong was inadvertently allowed to bowl two overs in succession. (There was an adjournment between them.)

- The All-British Cable transmitted news of the close of Australia's first innings in the first match at Sydney, in 1903-04, in record time, the message having been sent in the astounding time of three and a half minutes from the ground to London by the Pacific-Anglo.

- On the second day of the match at Manchester in 1921 – there had been no play on the first – the Hon. L. H. Tennyson wished to declare the English innings closed at ten minutes to six with the score 341 for four wickets. The teams left the field and, after an interval of twenty minutes, England continued batting, it being realised it was too late in the day for a declaration.

- G. J. Bonnor was caught, at long-on 115 yards from the wicket by G. F. Grace, at The Oval in 1880. The same batsman was caught and bowled at Lord's in 1884 by G. Ulyett, off a ball driven back with the force of a cannon shot.

- The rival captains in the 1905 rubber, the Hon. F. S. Jackson and J. Darling, were both born on November 21, 1870.

- In the match at Sheffield, in 1902, C. Hill threw in from the outfield a ball which, after breaking the nearer wicket, passed on and disturbed the other.

- During Australia's innings of 551 at The Oval, in 1884, W. G. Grace fielded in every position. Whilst keeping wicket he caught W. E. Midwinter off a lob from the Hon. Alfred Lyttelton.

- England, set 85 to win at The Oval in 1882, were beaten by seven runs. The third wicket did not fall until 51, and several good batsmen were to go in. F. R. Spofforth was bowling at his best, and nervousness seized some who were reckoned on for runs. One spectator dropped dead from excitement, and another unconsciously gnawed away the handle of his umbrella.

- At Melbourne on March 15, 1877 … Charles Bannerman scored 165 (retired injured) and a collection made on the ground for him realised £165.

- On the third day of the game at Adelaide, in 1907-08, the temperature was 102.2 in the shade and 150 in the sun; on the fourth 106.7, and 151.7 respectively, and later 111.4 and 156.9; and on the sixth 107.6 in the shade and 151.9 in the sun. On the fifth day of the match at Adelaide, in 1920-21, the temperature in the sun was 150 and on the sixth day 152.

- During the final stages of the match at Manchester in 1902, a local printer, anticipating an English victory, issued an *In Memoriam* card which was withdrawn from sale with all speed as soon as it became known that Australia had won by three runs. At the top of the card appeared a representation of a funeral coach, under which were two verses "In Memory of the Australians".

- At Sydney, in 1882-83, the Australian captain, W. L. Murdoch, protested against E. J. Barlow using large spikes in his boots, on the ground that they tore up the wicket. The Hon. Ivo Bligh requested Barlow to remove the spikes but remarked that F. R. Spofforth, who had spikes in the heels of his boots, cut up the pitch quite as much as Barlow did.

part II, page 271

Warwickshire v Hampshire

Played at Birmingham, Wednesday, Thursday, Friday, June 14, 15, 16, 1922. This was the sensational match of the whole season, at Birmingham or anywhere else, Hampshire actually winning by 155 runs after being out for a total of 15. That their astounding failure in the first innings was just one of the accidents of cricket, and not due in any way to the condition of the ground, was proved by their getting 521 when they followed on. The victory, taken as a whole, must surely be without precedent in first-class cricket. Hampshire looked in a hopeless position when the sixth wicket in their second innings went down at 186, but Shirley helped Brown to put on

85 runs and then, with Livsey in after McIntyre had failed, the score was carried to 451. Brown batted splendidly for four hours and threequarters and Livsey made his first hundred without a mistake.

Warwickshire

L. A. Bates c Shirley b Newman	3	– c Mead b Kennedy	1
E. J. Smith c Mead b Newman	24	– c Shirley b Kennedy	41
Mr F. R. Santall c McIntyre b Boyes	84	– b Newman	0
W. G. Quaife b Newman	1	– not out	40
Hon. F. S. G. Calthorpe c Boyes b Kennedy	70	– b Newman	30
Rev. E. F. Waddy c Mead b Boyes	0	– b Newman	0
Mr B. W. Quaife b Boyes	0	– c and b Kennedy	7
J. Fox b Kennedy	4	– b Kennedy	0
J. Smart b Newman	20	– b Newman	3
C. Smart c Mead b Boyes	14	– c and b Boyes	15
H. Howell not out	1	– c Kennedy b Newman	11
L-b 2	2	B 6, l-b 4	10
	223		158

Bowling: *First Innings*—Kennedy 24–7–74–2; Newman 12.3–0–70–4; Boyes 16–5–56–4; Shirley 3–0–21–0. *Second Innings*—Kennedy 26–12–47–4; Newman 26.3–12–53–5; Boyes 11–4–34–1; Brown 5–0–14–0.

Hampshire

A. Bowell b Howell	0	– c Howell b W. G. Quaife	45
A. Kennedy c Smith b Calthorpe	0	– b Calthorpe	7
Mr H. L. V. Day b Calthorpe	0	– c Bates b W. G. Quaife	15
C. P. Mead not out	6	– b Howell	24
Hon. L. H. Tennyson c Calthorpe b Howell	4	– c C. Smart b Calthorpe	45
G. Brown b Howell	0	– b C. Smart	172
J. Newman c C. Smart b Howell	0	– c and b W. G. Quaife	12
Mr W. R. Shirley c J. Smart b Calthorpe	1	– lbw b Fox	30
Mr A. S. McIntyre lbw b Calthorpe	0	– lbw b Howell	5
W. H. Livsey b Howell	0	– not out	110
G. S. Boyes lbw b Howell	0	– b Howell	29
B 4	4	B 14, l-b 11, w 1, n-b 1	27
	15		521

Bowling: *First Innings*—Howell 4.5–2–7–6; Calthorpe 4–3–4–4. *Second Innings*—Howell 63–10–156–3; Calthorpe 33–7–97–2; W. G. Quaife 49–8–154–3; Fox 7–0–30–1; J. Smart 13–2–37–0; Santall 5–0–15–0; C. Smart 1–0–5–1.

Umpires: A. J. Atfield and B. Brown.

part I, pages 286–287

Public Schools Cricket in 1923

Until the 1938 edition, when the editor, Wilfrid Brookes, revamped the Almanack, the high profile of public schools cricket was reflected by the annual inclusion of a lengthy feature, towards the front of the book, examining public schools cricket in the previous year. In writing about the schools in 1923, H. S. Altham concentrated on two matters, the first being poor field placing, and the second as follows.

The second point upon which I have been asked to say something is a much more delicate question, and I do so with considerable diffidence. There is a growing feeling in a good many quarters that school cricket, and indeed school athletics generally, is suffering from an excess of publicity. On the principle that the reading public really determine the contents of any paper, this publicity is perhaps surprising but it is none the less a fact. Eton and Harrow, and to a less degree Winchester and such schools as appear at Lord's, have been more or less accustomed to having their prospects discussed, their performances criticised and their personalities described: but of recent years the process has extended to practically every school of athletic standing: few school cricketers of outstanding performance escape altogether the ever-widening arc of its limelight, and "close-ups", whether by camera or pen, seem to meet a growing demand in not merely the purely sporting papers. Of course, the schools nearest London are most favoured or hardest hit.

Now it may be objected that the remedy lies in the schools own hands – to shut the door if they think fit, and intimate politely that they are not at home to the Press. As a matter of fact cricket fields for the most part have no doors, and moreover most schools are perfectly ready, and indeed anxious to have the scores of their matches recorded and, on big occasions at least, the play and players described, for the sake of a widely scattered, but still intensely interested, circle of old boys. No amount of publishing of score sheets can do much harm: figures, more or less, tell cricket truth, and the elation of seeing three of them opposite one's name in print generally provokes Nemesis to provide a salutary and effective antidote. The crux lies in the match reports, and in the periodical reviews of contemporary school performances which are becoming increasingly common in the London Press. I am not suggesting for a moment that the writers – many of them players of distinguished experience – have not the best interests of the game, and of amateur cricket in particular, at heart: it is their occasional methods that seem open to question.

A school cricketer, worth his salt, should be able to stand both praise and criticism, but it is very important that both should be judicious and based upon unmistakable evidence, and there does seem to be a growing tendency to write up school cricketers into a class to which they do not yet belong, to use superlatives when positives are adequate, to compare a boy to some great cricketer on the strength of a single innings or even of one or two strokes. As for the criticism, it will, I think, be generally agreed that except for slackness or breaches of the spirit of the game, this should be temperate and should err on the side of generosity: but what is more important is that the critic should be very chary indeed of advocating change in method unless he is quite sure of his ground. There have been cases – and recently – of good school cricketers paying more attention to comments in the press than to responsible advisers at home – and with disastrous results. Finally I record, as at least deserving of consideration, the opinion of one school coach of long experience, that in reporting two-day school matches experts, especially those whose names naturally carry great weight, should so far as is possible content themselves with description until the match is over and abstain from such criticism, whether destructive or constructive, as may possibly unsettle individuals, especially the captains, for the second day's play.

part I, pages 225–228

The Googly: The Scapegoat of Cricket

By B. J. T. Bosanquet

Bosanquet, who played seven Tests for England between 1903 and 1905, is regarded as the man who invented the googly.

The visit of the South African team has revived interest in the googly. Poor old googly! It has been subjected to ridicule, abuse, contempt, incredulity, and survived them all. Nowadays one cannot read an article on cricket without finding that any deficiencies existing at the present day are attributed to the influence of the googly. If the standard of bowling falls off, it is because too many cricketers devote their time to trying to master it, instead of carrying on with the recognised and hallowed methods of bowling. If batsmen display a marked inability to hit the ball on the offside, or anywhere in front of the wicket, and stand in apologetic attitudes before their wicket, it is said that the googly has made it impossible for them to adopt the old aggressive attitude and make the old scoring strokes.

But, after all, what is the googly? It is merely a ball with an ordinary break produced by an extra-ordinary method. It is quite possible and, in fact, not difficult, to detect, and, once detected, there is no reason why it should not be treated as an ordinary "break-back". However, it is not for me to defend it. Other and more capable hands have taken it up and exploited it, and, if blame is to be allotted, let it be on their shoulders. For me is the task of the historian, and if I appear too much in the role of the "proud parent", I ask forgiveness. In view of many conflicting statements, it may be of interest if I recapitulate the inception and development of the googly.

Birth of the Googly

Somewhere about the year 1897 I was playing a game with a tennis ball, known as "Twisti-Twosti". The object was to bounce the ball on a table so that your opponent sitting opposite could not catch it. It soon occurred to me that if one could pitch a ball which broke in a certain direction and with more or less the same delivery make the next ball go in the opposite direction, one would mystify one's opponent. After a little experimenting I managed to do this, and it was so successful that I practised the same thing with a soft ball at "Stump-cricket". From this I progressed to a cricket ball, and about 1899 I had become a "star turn" for the luncheon interval during our matches at Oxford. That is, the most famous batsman on the opposing side was enticed into a net and I was brought up to bowl him two or three leg-breaks. These were followed by an "off-break" with more or less the same action. If this pitched on the right place it probably hit him on the knee, everyone shrieked with laughter, and I was led away and locked up for the day.

Recognition

During this and the following year I devoted a great deal of time to practising the googly at the nets, and occasionally bowled in unimportant matches. The first public recognition we obtained was in July 1900, for Middlesex v Leicestershire at Lord's. An unfortunate individual (I believe it was Coe) had made 98 when he was clean bowled by a fine specimen which bounced four times. The incident was rightly treated as a joke, and was the subject of ribald comment, but this small beginning marked the start of what came to be termed a revolution in bowling.

From then on progress was slow but sure. We achieved marked success at Nottingham in August, and attracted a certain amount of notice, and my old friends Gregor McGregor and "Plum" Warner were fully alive to future possibilities. At that time I myself always endeavoured to convey the impression that the result was unintentional and accidental, as I did not wish batsmen to be too much on their guard. I even persuaded "Plum" not to write about it, which he nobly refrained from doing for nearly a year! By that time, however, human nature had to be served, and, following on other successes I obtained, he and others began to write it up, and considerable attention was attracted to it as a new development.

The Secret

At this stage I would like to say that it was in reality nothing new in itself. Many leg-break bowlers (including Attewell and E. R. Wilson to my knowledge) had dismissed batsmen with balls which, intended to break one way, had done the opposite. The sole difference was in achieving this result at will; and although leading cricketers and the more knowledgeable critics appreciated that this could be done, it was some time before the ignorance and prejudice of others was overcome. The Googly after all (bowled by a right-handed bowler to a right-handed batsman) is nothing more nor less than an ordinary off-break. The method of delivery is the secret of its difficulty, and this merely consisted in turning the wrist over at the moment of delivery far enough to alter the axis of spin, so that a ball which normally delivered would break from leg breaks from the off. That is all there is to it.

To revert to ancient history, from the moment it became generally recognised that a ball could be bowled which left the batsman in doubt as to which way it would break, the fun began. I must confess that in the beginning I persevered with the Googly chiefly because I found that the lot of an average fast-medium bowler on a county side was not a happy one. It generally meant being put on under a sweltering sun, on a plumb wicket, when the other bowlers had failed and the two batsmen were well set. If one was lucky enough to get a wicket, the original bowlers resumed, and unless the same conditions recurred one was not wanted again. If the wicket was difficult, one was never thought of. As a result, partly from a natural disinclination to work hard on hot days (how much more pleasant to walk slowly up to the wicket and gently propel the ball into the air), and partly, I hope, from a sneaking ambition to achieve greater things, I persevered with the Googly. It took any amount of perseverance, but for a year or two the results were more than worth it, for in addition to adding to the merriment of the cricketing world, I found that batsmen who used to grin at the sight of me and grasp their bat firmly by the long handle began to show a marked preference for the other end!

Puzzled Australians

Contemporary history has recorded the progress of the Googly from this period onwards, and I do not propose to enlarge any further on my personal connection with it. There are a few incidents, however, which stand out vividly.

There was the first time it was bowled against the Australians – at Lord's late one evening, in 1902 – when I had two overs and saw two very puzzled Australians return to the Pavilion. It rained all next day, and not one of them tumbled to the fact that it was not an accident. The first Googly ever bowled in Australia, in March 1903; Trumper batting, having made 40 in about twenty minutes. Two leg-breaks were played beautifully to cover, but the next ball (delivered with a silent prayer), pitching in the same place, saw the same graceful stroke played – and struck the middle-stump instead of the bat! W. Gunn stumped when appreciably nearer my wicket than his own! Arthur Shrewsbury complaining that "it wasn't fair". These are a few impressions.

There are two or three bright patches I can recall, as, for instance, in 1904 when in three consecutive matches I got five wickets in each innings v Yorkshire, six in each v Notts, and seven in each v Sussex (including Fry and Ranji). There was one week in 1905 in which I had eleven wickets v Sussex at Lord's (and got 100 in each innings. The double feat is still a record); and during the next three days in the first Test match at Nottingham I got eight out of nine wickets which fell in the second innings, the last man being out just before a thunderstorm broke – and even then if Trumper could have hobbled to the wicket it meant a draw! This recalls the fourth Test match at Sydney in 1904, in which at one period in the second innings I had six for 12, and then got Noble leg-before, and never appealed. The last man was in, and the match won, and there were reasons!

I have the balls used in these two matches, both presented to me by my old friend Dick Lilley, the best wicket-keeper in a big match we have known. There is a good story of Lilley (whom I last saw pigeon-shooting at Monte Carlo in 1914!) in the Gentlemen v Players match at The Oval, in 1904. I got a few wickets in the second innings. Then one of the "Pros" came in and said: "Dick's in next; he's calling us all a lot of rabbits; says he can see every ball you bowl. Do try and get him, and we'll rag his life out." Dick came in. I bowled him two overs of leg-breaks, then changed my action and bowled another leg-break. Dick played it gracefully to fine leg, and it removed his off-stump! I can still hear the reception he got in the dressi   ~oom.

If the preceding lines seem egotistical let the following be my excuse. Last year a great pal of mine, with whom I have played a lot of cricket, said at a dinner-table: "I know old Bose invented the Googly and that sort of thing, but did he ever get any wickets?" I can truthfully say that after 1905 he didn't, and one over subsequently bowled at Harrow elicited about a quarter of a column of ribald comment in a newspaper, which finished the Googly so far as I am concerned, and I had better finish this article.

part I, pages 291–292

The 1926 edition was the last in which Wisden's *theme of Five Cricketers of the Year was varied. In this edition the new editor, Stewart Caine, named just one Cricketer of the Year – the great Jack Hobbs, who had been one of the Cricketers of the Year in 1909.*

Cricketer of the Year

Cricketer of the Century: Jack Hobbs

Great as his successes had been since he first appeared for Surrey in 1905 when, with scores in his first two matches of 18 and 88 against the Gentlemen of England and 28 and 155 against Essex, he showed himself at once a batsman of remarkable ability, John Berry Hobbs surpassed himself in the summer of 1925. Never previously had he made 3,000 runs in one season or headed the batting averages, but he accomplished both those feats, his aggregate amounting to 3,024 and an average of 70.32 placing him above all his rivals. He seized the occasion, too, of the Gentlemen and Players match at Scarborough to put together the highest innings of his career, beating his previous best – 226 for Surrey against Nottinghamshire at The Oval in 1914 – with 266 not out. Furthermore, whereas until last summer the largest number of hundreds he had obtained in one season was eleven – his total in 1914 and again in 1920 – and the record for any batsman was thirteen – made by C. B. Fry in 1901 and equalled by Tom Hayward in 1906 and by Hendren in 1923 – he eclipsed those performances by reaching three figures on no fewer than sixteen occasions.

These achievements, however, notable as they were, counted for little compared with Hobbs's triumph in first equalling and then heading the number of centuries which stand to the credit of W. G. Grace. That the "Grand Old Man's" record of 126 hundreds was likely to go, Hobbs speedily demonstrated. So far from the strain of the Australian tour having any ill effects upon his powers, he jumped into form at once, playing such wonderful cricket that at the end of a dozen matches he had ten centuries to his name. A few small scores ensued but an innings of 140 for the Players at Lord's being immediately followed by one of 105 against Kent at Blackheath, Hobbs by July 20 was within one of Grace's total. Then came what must have been a nerve-wracking time even for one so well-balanced as Hobbs. He found himself the most talked of man in England, pursued by interviewers and photographers, and day after day, while the coveted century eluded his powers, he was referred to – whatever score he made – as having "failed again". For the time being the performances of one individual were, in many quarters, actually allowed to overshadow the game as a whole. Hobbs managed to survive all the embarrassing attentions showered upon him but, according to those watching him closely, he became rather weary-looking during the four weeks which elapsed before August 16 when with an innings of 101 against Somerset at Taunton he at last equalled Grace's record and on the following day beat it with 101 not out.

Grandly as Hobbs batted in 1925 there yet were times when something seemed to have gone out of his game. He who had often in the past shaped in the first over as though he had batted for an hour generally found it necessary to play himself in with some care, as, perhaps, was not surprising now that he is in the "forties". Yet, whatever might be noticed at the start of one of his innings, once he had settled down he was usually as adventurous as of old. Certainly he had not to drop any of his special strokes although many of these demand supreme quickness of foot and wrist.

That Hobbs, during the forthcoming season, may show himself in something like the form of last summer will be the fervent prayer of all followers of the game. The great occasion is at hand and we look to him to "speak with the enemy at the gate". It would be a glorious climax to an historic career were he, by his batting, to play the outstanding part in so long-delayed a triumph of England over Australia. Curiously enough while more than 2,000 runs (including nine centuries) stand to his credit in Test matches with Australia, he has played only ten innings for England against Australia in this country. He did quite well in 1912, scoring 224 runs in four innings, but in 1921 he figured in only one of the five encounters and, attacked with appendicitis during the progress of the struggle, he did not bat.

In view of that disappointment a real triumph for him next summer would be singularly appropriate. Certainly it will not be his fault if he cannot give of his best for he has been at much pains during the winter to keep himself in condition. Still, whatever the next few months may have in store – whether success or failure attends his efforts – Hobbs will go down to posterity as one of the greatest figures in cricket history. A masterly batsman under all conditions, possessed of exceptional grace of style, remarkable in the variety of his strokes, ready to run any risk for his side, and a superb field, he has been at once the wonder and delight of all cricketers of his generation.

part I, pages 289–291 and 299–301

Obituary: F. R. Spofforth

SPOFFORTH, MR FREDERICK ROBERT, one of the most remarkable players the game has ever known, was born at Balmain, Sydney, on September 9, 1853, and died at Ditton Hill Lodge, Ditton Hill, Surbiton, Surrey, on June 4, aged 72 … From his earliest days cricket had the greatest possible fascination for him, and whilst still quite a small boy at Eglington College, Sydney, he determined, through seeing the success met with by George Tarrant, of Cambridge, to become as fast a bowler as possible. Later he studied the methods of Southerton and Alfred Shaw, and resolved, if possible, to combine the styles of all three men. He had played with success in good class matches before he ever bowled a ball in England, but his great days may be said to date from May 27, 1878, when he had so much to do with the wonderful victory gained, in the course of a single day, by D. W. Gregory's team over a very strong MCC side at Lord's. From that day forward, Spofforth was always regarded as a man to be feared, even by the strongest teams. He probably never did anything better than to take fourteen wickets for 90 runs in the Test match at The Oval in 1882, when Australia gained their first success – by 7 runs – in an International game on English soil. It is to be regretted that when he came over with the teams of 1878 and 1880 so few eleven a side matches were played, for he was presumably then at about his best, and his energies were expended for the most part in mowing down wickets in games against odds. For the former side he obtained 764 wickets at a cost of 6.08 runs each, and for the latter 763 for 5.49 apiece.

Spofforth was a member of the Australian Teams of 1878, 1880, 1882, 1884 and 1886 … in Tests against England he obtained 94 wickets for 18.41 runs each. In his own country he represented both New South Wales and Victoria, the former by birth and the latter by residence, and in really big cricket, both at home and abroad, took 1,146 wickets with an average of 13.55.

In minor matches he naturally did many very remarkable things. Thus, in an up-country game in Australia, in 1881-82, he bowled down all twenty wickets of his opponents; for the Australian Team of 1878 he took nine wickets in twenty balls against XVIII of Hastings, and for that of 1880, twelve in eighteen against XVIII of Burnley; while twice for Hampstead he obtained all ten wickets in an innings of Marlow on his opponents' ground – for 20 runs in 1893, and for 14 a year later. In the game of 1893, his day's figures were seventeen for 40. When he made his first appearance for Hampstead he was in his thirty-eighth year, yet he took as many as 951 wickets for the Club for 7.50 runs each. In 1894 he claimed 200 wickets for the side for an average of 5.90.

Recollections of Mr F. R. Spofforth

By Lord Harris

I was talking to Mr Noble early in the season at The Oval, and he told me that Spofforth was seriously ill, and then put to me the astonishing question, "Was he a great bowler?" It was about equivalent to asking if W. G. was a great bat. "About the best I ever played," was my reply; "but did you never see him?" It was another shock to find that Noble, with whom I had never played, had never seen him bowl. Later on I went down to see Spofforth, and we had a chat about old times; he was keenly interested in past as well as present times, but as I left the room he said, "The doctors say I shall see the first Test match but I made my reputation in May; you knocked me out in May; and I shall go out in May." He actually passed away in the first days of June.

Now what he described as my "knocking him out" was a very curious coincident. If anyone cares to look at the Cricket Records of 1885 and 1887, he will find in Australians v Gentlemen of England, at Lord's, in 1884: F. R. Spofforth absent 0, and absent 0, and in 1886, F. R. Spofforth retired hurt 0, and that he did not bowl at all in the second innings.

I have recorded in A Few Short Runs, and I can but repeat that on each occasion I hit a ball back which injured his right hand; and he always said that he was never the same bowler after the second injury. He followed up his ball very far, and as I probably jumped in, he was very close, too close to put his hand in exactly the right place; else he was ordinarily a very good field to his own bowling, but so full of nerves, that a hard blow made more difference to him than to many.

An amusing illustration of this sensitiveness occurred at Canterbury in 1886, in Kent v Australians. I was in with G. G. Hearne, who would always run at a nod from me. Old Spof had been rather upset about the wicket-keeping; a ball was thrown in badly from long field, which hurt him; he went dancing about wringing his hand, and at last danced on the opposite side of the wicket to where the ball was lying close to the wicket, and we ran, much to the amusement of the crowd.

It is a common misconception, amongst those who did not see or play him, that he was a very fast bowler. He may have been in Australia before his first visit to England, in 1878, but he was far too knowledgeable on our slower wickets, and 1878 was little better than a mud lark, to depend on pace. He could bowl a very fast ball, and did, as often perhaps as once an over; but what he depended on was what he termed the "judgment" ball; medium pace, but with great variety of pace, and therefore of flight, and a strong break from the off. He could break slightly from leg, I believe, though I cannot remember his doing so; and the rumour went round amongst us who had to face him for the first time, that if he was going to break from the off, he held the ball at the tips of his fingers; if from leg, in the palm of his hand. In my opinion what deceived the batsman was that he came up at a great pace and then bowled a much slower ball than his pace up to the wicket led one to expect. Consequently the batsman played rather too quickly, cocked the ball up a bit, and he was so close up, and judged the direction the ball would come off the bat so well, that he brought off the catch and bowl very frequently; and if it did not come off in his direction, the break would take it round to silly mid-on, where Boyle was waiting for and seldom missed it. Indeed, with Spof bowling, Blackham at the wicket, and Boyle at short leg, the forward type of play on slow wickets almost certainly led to disaster. That he was a great bowler cannot be disputed, his performances on the tours he took part in were astonishing.

There were two signs which pretty clearly indicate what the public thought of him; his title "The Demon" Bowler; and that he was singled out amongst cricketers for a cartoon in *Vanity Fair*. In after years there were quite a number of cricketers similarly honoured by that paper, but in his day it was a rarity.

I have said that he came up to the wicket very fast, and he followed up straight down the wicket, thus, left foot on or about the popping crease, right foot well on to the half volley pitch, and then both feet plump on the awkward pitch; and when wickets were soft, he undoubtedly made a mess of the pitch. In those days, we were not so particular as cricketers are now; we took such happenings as the "rubs" of the game; but in his case we used to remonstrate, and Spof's indignation was deep seated and high voiced. "Look at my heels, no spikes," was his retort; which was true, but the heels were high.

At Sydney in 1878-79, we had made a very good start. I was in, and could not imagine why they did not put Evans, a most accurate bowler, on to bowl at the hole Spof had made. At last they did, and I said to Murdoch, who was keeping wicket, "This innings is over," and we were out for some 40 more. Evans kept on finding the broken spot. He was much more thought of than Spofforth in Australia, and was a much better cricketer all round; but was not successful when he came home, partly due to ill-health. Spofforth was of no great worth as a bat, and was never conspicuous in the field; he seemed to concentrate on his bowling, and I think did really study his opponents' weak points, and work at them; and in after years it was interesting to get him to talk about his performances, which, when we met at Lord's, he was quite ready to do.

I was playing for ten years abroad and at home against those great medium pace Australian bowlers, Allan, Garrett, Palmer, Giffen, Turner, and Ferris, as well as Spofforth, and I have of course also played such great English medium pace bowlers as Alfred Shaw, Watson, Jim Lillywhite, Lohmann, C. T. Studd and W. G. Grace, and I am quite satisfied and always have been, that Spofforth was the most difficult of them all, because he concealed so well the pace of the ball. What he could have done on the easy wickets of the present day, no one can say, but I am sure he could have adapted his bowling to them; and does it matter? What we must judge performances by are the circumstances and conditions of the time when they were done, and taking those as the criteria, I do not see how any bowler can be held to be better than was F. R. Spofforth.

part II, page 681

Highest Innings Total

Victoria v New South Wales

Played at Melbourne, December 24, 27, 28, 29, 1926. In this match Victoria set up a new record in first-class cricket, their total of 1,107 beating that of 1,059 obtained by the same State against Tasmania in the 1922-23 season. Throughout the innings which lasted ten hours and a half, runs came at a great pace. A brilliant opening partnership between Ponsford and Woodfull produced 375 runs in three hours and threequarters and the former player and Hendry added a further 219 for the second wicket in just under two hours. Ponsford hit thirty-six fours in a memorable display. The brightest of some wonderful batting was that of Ryder, who, by powerful driving, obtained six sixes and thirty-three fours and scored 295 out of 449 in rather more than four hours. New South Wales, with a weak team, were outplayed from the start and suffered defeat by an innings and 656 runs.

New South Wales

N. E. Phillips c Blackie b Liddicut	52	– lbw b Kartkopf	36
G. Morgan c Love b Liddicut	13	– c King b Liddicut	26
T. J. E. Andrews st Ellis b Hartkopf	42	– b Liddicut	0
A. F. Kippax b Liddicut	36	– b Hartkopf	26
A. D. Ratcliffe c Ryder b Liddicut	2	– c Morton b Hartkopf	44
A. Jackson c Ellis b Blackie	4	– not out	59
J. R. Hogg not out	40	– c Hendry b Liddicut	13
A. A. Mailey b Ryder	20	– c Morton b Hartkopf	3
N. Campbell lbw b Blackie	0	– c Ryder b Hartkopf	8
R. McNamee b Ryder	8	– b Liddicut	7
H. McGuirk b Ryder	0	– b Hartkopf	0
Extras	4	Extras	8
	221		**230**

Bowling: *First Innings*—Morton 15–4–45–0; Liddicut 21–7–50–4; Ryder 9–1–32–3; Blackie 16–3–34–2; Hendry 3–2–1–0; Hartkopf 17–1–57–1. *Second Innings*—Morton 11–0–42–0; Liddicut 19–2–66–4; Blackie 5–1–16–0; Hartkopf 16.3–0–98–6.

Victoria

W. M. Woodfull c Ratcliffe b Andrews	133	A. E. V. Hartkopf c McGuirk b Mailey	61
W. H. Ponsford b Morgan	352	A. E. Liddicut b McGuirk	36
H. L. Hendry c Morgan b Mailey	100	J. L. Ellis run out	63
J. Ryder c Kippax b Andrews	295	D. D. J. Blackie not out	27
F. L. Morton run out	0	Extras	27
H. S. B. Love st Ratcliffe b Mailey	6		
S. King st Ratcliffe b Mailey	7		**1,107**

Bowling: *First Innings*—McNamee 24–2–124–0; McGuirk 26–1–130–1; Mailey 64–0–362–4; Campbell 11–0–89–0; Phillips 11.7–0–64–0; Morgan 26–0–137–1; Andrews 21–2–148–2; Kippax 7–0–26–0.

Victoria's innings of 1,107 remained the highest first-class innings total at the end of the century (see Cricket Records section in the 2000 edition of Wisden).

part II, pages 670–671

Bradman's First-Class Debut

South Australia v New South Wales

Played at Adelaide, December 16, 17, 19, 20, 1927. A keenly-fought match ended in exciting fashion, South Australia, despite some splendid bowling by McNamee, getting home by one wicket. Bradman joined the select band of cricketers who have made a century in their first Sheffield Shield match and Kippax – twice compelled to retire owing to illness – and Phillips also put together three-figure scores for New South Wales. Owing much to the sound cricket of their early batsmen, South Australia made a creditable response, Schneider, the diminutive left-hander, batting attractively in partnerships with Harris and Richardson which realised 140 and 128 for the first and second wicket respectively. The rest of the game saw the bowlers with the upper hand. Grimmett, taking eight wickets for 57, had chief share in the cheap dismissal of New South Wales in the visitors' second innings. Set 189 to win, South Australia had seven men out for 131 but Lee and Grimmett batted steadily when the issue hung in the balance.

New South Wales

N. E. Phillips b Whitfield	112	– lbw b Grimmett	11
G. Morgan b Scott	11	– b Grimmett	34
T. J. E. Andrews c Williams b Grimmett	58	– b Scott	20
A. F. Kippax c Alexander b Williams	143	– c and b Grimmett	0
A. Scanes c Williams b Schneider	44	– c Whitfield b Grimmett	26
W. A. Oldfield c Hack b Grimmett	12	– c Richardson b Grimmett	4
D. Bradman c Williams b Scott	118	– b Grimmett	33
F. Jordan lbw b Scott	1	– lbw b Grimmett	0
S. C. Everett st Hack b Grimmett	5	– c Harris b Scott	8
A. A. Mailey b Scott	0	– c Schneider b Grimmett	5
R. L. A. McNamee not out	1	– not out	1
B 2, l-b 5, w 1, n-b 6	14	B 1, l-b 1, w 1, n-b 5	8
	519		**150**

Bowling: *First Innings*—Scott 19.6–1–99–4; Whitfield 17–3–43–1; Grimmett 31–1–160–3; Williams 11–0–70–1; Lee 17–1–76–0; Schneider 6–0–39–1; Alexander 3–0–14–0; Johnson 1–0–4–0. *Second Innings*—Scott 17–3–46–2; Whitfield 7–1–26–0; Grimmett 21.7–5–57–8; Williams 2–0–13–0.

South Australia

K. J. Schneider c and b Mailey	108	– lbw b McNamee	11
G. W. Harris c and b Andrews	77	– b McNamee	18
V. Y. Richardson b Jordan	80	– b McNamee	0
W. C. Alexander st Oldfield b Mailey	42	– b Andrews	49
E. A. Johnson st Oldfield b Andrews	0	– b Mailey	0
H. E. P. Whitfield b Jordan	15	– run out	17
A. Hack c Morgan b Everett	45	– b McNamee	6
P. K. Lee st Oldfield b Mailey	28	– not out	27
C. V. Grimmett not out	43	– c Oldfield b McNamee	32
J. D. Scott c Phillips b Everett	0	– c Phillips b Mailey	14
N. L. Williams b Everett	21	– not out	0
B 8, l-b 12, n-b 2	22	B 4, l-b 11	15
	481	(9 wkts)	189

Bowling: *First Innings*—Everett 26.7–4–92–3; McNamee 22–11–34–0; Jordan 21–1–65–2; Mailey 50–9–143–3; Andrews 18–0–86–2; Phillips 7–0–22–0; Morgan 3–0–17–0. *Second Innings*—Everett 3–0–16–0; McNamee 29.2–12–53–5; Jordan 4–0–13–0; Mailey 28–2–79–2; Andrews 6–1–13–1.

Umpires: G. A. Hele and J. J. Quinn.

part I, pages 44–45 and 309–310

Experimental Laws
for County Championship Matches

Meeting at Lord's on Friday, April 26, 1929, the Advisory County Cricket Committee received the report upon certain suggested cricket reforms of a Special Sub-committee consisting of Lord Harris, Hon. F. S. G. Calthorpe, J. W. H. T. Douglas, P. T. Eckersley, G. A. Faulkner, A. E. R. Gilligan, N. Haig, V. W. C. Jupp, Hon. R. H. Lyttelton, C. T. A. Wilkinson, and Captain W. A. Worsley ... Of the five changes proposed the following were carried:

No. 1 "That the wicket be one inch wider and one inch higher than that provided for in Law 6" ;

No. 2 "That the striker be given out LBW under Law 24, even though the ball may have first hit his bat or hand"; and

No. 5 "That a maximum of seven minutes' actual rolling be made the rule instead of ten minutes."

The remainder were not carried.

These recommendations, which were experiments to be tried in inter-County matches only in 1929, had the consent and approval of the MCC.

Notes by the Editor

(Stewart Caine)

The summer of 1929 will always be remembered for the introduction of a larger wicket into use in matches connected with the County Championship. For years past the need for something which would lessen the supremacy of the bat over the ball had become more and more pronounced and, after much consideration, a special sub-committee of the Advisory County Cricket Committee came to the conclusion that the endeavour to meet the difficulty should – at any rate for one season – take this shape. The experiment, it may at once be said, proved very popular. Players and umpires alike agreed that the game benefited by the change, and when the summer came to an end, supporters of the alteration could point to the fact that in a championship programme, almost identical with that of 1928, the number of unfinished games had fallen from 122 to 89. Admittedly the proportion of matches not played out remained far too high, even allowing for the vagaries of the British climate, but on the reduction, such as it was, there existed matter for satisfaction and certainly encouragement to make further trial of the alteration. As a consequence the Committee decided to recommend that next summer the larger wicket should be used not only in matches between the First-Class Counties but in the Minor Counties competition as well, so 1930 should furnish an exhaustive test of the merits of the new departure. Last season the change, being specially laid down as applying only to County Championship matches, did not find favour at either Oxford or Cambridge and the experience of the South Africans with it was limited to one occasion – the concluding engagement of the tour – but it was tried in some games by the MCC. Whether in the coming season the higher and wider stumps shall make their appearance at the Universities has probably not yet been settled, but there exists every reason to assume that the Australians will insist – as they, of course, have every right to do – upon playing their games with the smaller-sized wicket prescribed by the Laws.

Another suggestion by the special sub-committee given a trial last season was one by which a batsman even if he "snicked" the ball, could, provided the ball pitched in a line between wicket and wicket, be out LBW. Over this experiment no such practical unanimity of approval prevailed. Batsmen generally, indeed, expressed their disapproval but a majority of umpires, although the number in favour was not so pronounced as in the matter of the larger wicket, came to the conclusion that the game had benefited by the regulation. The sub-committee, very properly attaching much weight to the opinions of the first-class umpires, thereupon decided to recommend a further trial and, the proposal being approved by the MCC, the new leg before rule, as well as the larger wicket, will again obtain in the contests for the County Championship. Another innovation introduced last year that will again apply to the county competition – one which, whatever the fate of the other experiments, may very well become a Law of the game – is the reduction of the time for rolling the pitch from ten to seven minutes.

The big question, of course, is whether the larger wicket has come to stay.* If the hearty reception given to it last year is followed by a further chorus of support at the end of the forthcoming season the probabilities must be that, eventually, Law Six will undergo the alteration necessary to provide for the change. It is possible, of course, that a wet summer, with a big proportion of games fought out on rain-affected pitches and batsmen unable to hold their own, may cause opinion to veer round in favour of the old dimensions but at the moment the chances appear all in favour of the larger wicket becoming in the not distant future an official implement of the game. Certainly anything, if not unduly drastic, calculated to bring more matches to a definite issue must be given favourable consideration even if it entails a change from what has obtained for more than a hundred years. At the same time it is by no means certain that the object in view – the reduction of scoring to normal limits – might not be brought about by the more natural preparation of wickets, the use, as suggested by the sub-committee, of grass producing a thicker mat, and the disuse of liquid manures. Of that return to old practice and conditions, however, there exists little likelihood when county club committees – naturally enough in view of their heavy commitments – are so anxious there should be plenty of run-getting. So for the moment, at least, the matter must be left, with the hope that the larger wicket may realise the expectations of its sponsors in improving the bowler's chances.

Upon this question of the larger wicket an interesting point was raised a little while ago by F. C. Cobden, the famous bowler, who, in the University match of 1870, when Oxford, with three wickets to fall, wanted only three runs to win, performed the "hat-trick", and so snatched an extraordinary victory for Cambridge by two runs. Mr Cobden – now 80 years of age – contended that the new departure, if it became a law, would create a dividing line between "two histories of the game". The change

---

* The larger wicket, 28 inches high and 9 inches wide, was officially adopted and is currently defined in Law 8.

would scarcely need to be regarded in so serious a light as that, but the batsman making a hundred with the larger wicket to defend could urge with some measure of reason that his achievement was greater than a three-figure innings put together under the conditions at present laid down by Law Six. To most men, when really well set, however, the actual dimensions of the wicket, probably, mean very little.

part I, pages 283–285

Cricketer of the Year

Cricketer of the Century: Donald Bradman

Donald George Bradman, who, coming to England for the first time met with greater success as a batsman than any other Australian cricketer who has visited this country, was born at Cootamundra, a small up-country township in New South Wales on August 27, 1908. While still a child he accompanied his parents when they moved to Bowral, some fifty miles from Sydney. Although not his birth-place, therefore, Bowral enjoys the distinction of giving the first insight into the game to a young man, who at the present moment is one of the most remarkable personalities in cricket. When it is considered that Bradman made his first appearance in a big match only just over three years ago – to be exact it was at Adelaide in December, 1927 – his rise to the very top of the tree has been phenomenal. Yet in that particular encounter, his first for New South Wales in the Sheffield Shield series of engagements, he showed clearly he was someone out of the common by scoring 118 and 33. Later on in that season in Australia he put together 73 against South Australia and not out 134 against Victoria and those performances stamped him as a future representative batsman. Sure enough, he got his place in the Australian team a year afterwards when the MCC side, under A. P. F. Chapman, were in that country. He did not justify expectations in a Trial match in October but in the same month he scored 131 and not out 133 against Queensland. Subsequent scores for his State included 71 not out against Victoria, 340 not out in the return with Victoria and 175 against South Australia. Meanwhile, he had secured a place in the Australia Eleven at Brisbane but, dismissed for scores of 18 and 1, was passed over for the next Test. It was obvious a bad mistake had been made in leaving him out and, chosen for the third match at Melbourne, he put together 79 and 112. At Adelaide in the fourth Test in which England were successful by 12 runs he scored 40 and 58, being run out in the second innings when he and Oldfield looked like winning the match for Australia, while in the concluding Test match – the only one in which Australia were successful during that tour – he obtained 123 and not out 37, being in with Ryder at the finish.

By this time he had, of course, firmly established himself, and it did not need another even more successful season in 1929-30 to make his inclusion in the team for England a certainty. He put together many fine scores in Sheffield Shield matches and at Sydney in the first week in January eclipsed everything else by an astonishing innings of 452 not out for New South Wales against Queensland. This score – the highest individual ever hit in first-class cricket – occupied him only 415 minutes and included forty-nine fours. A month before this, playing in the trial match prior to the team for England being selected, he put together for Woodfull's Eleven against Ryder's Eleven 124 and 225, while on the journey to England he hit up 139 against Tasmania. In Sheffield Shield matches that season he averaged over 111, or more than twice as many as any other cricketer in the tournament, with an aggregate of 894 runs.

Already, therefore, he had in a very short space of time accomplished wonders but his triumphs were far from being at an end, for in England he left further records behind. In the second innings of his first Test match in this country at Trent Bridge he made 131, following that with 254 at Lord's, 334 at Leeds and, after failing at Manchester, putting together 232 at The Oval. With his big innings at Leeds he beat the record individual score in Test matches between England and Australia which had stood since 1903-04 to the credit of R. E. Foster, with 287 at Sydney. Without a not out to help him, an aggregate of 974 runs in seven innings gave him an average of over 139 for the five Test matches and in the course of the summer he altogether played 11 three-figure innings for his side, six of these being over 200.

Just as they did during the last tour of the Englishmen in Australia, so, at the present time, opinions differ as to the merit of Bradman's abilities, judged purely from the standpoint of the highest batsmanship. Certain good judges aver that his footwork is correct; others contend the reverse is the case. Both are right. For a fast, true wicket his footwork, if not on quite such a high plane as that of Charles Macartney, is wonderfully good. When the ball is turning, however, there are limitations to Bradman's skill. As was observed by those who saw him on a turning wicket at Brisbane and on one nothing like so vicious at Old Trafford last summer, this young batsman still has something to learn in the matter of playing a correct offensive or defensive stroke with the conditions in favour of the bowler. Still, as a run-getter, he stands alone. He does not favour the forward method of defence, much preferring to go halfway or entirely back. His scoring strokes are many and varied. He can turn to leg and cut with delightful accuracy but above all he is a superb driver. One very pronounced feature of his batting is that he rarely lifts the ball and as he showed English spectators so frequently last season, and particularly against England at Lord's, he will send two consecutive and similar deliveries in different directions. In grace of style he may not be a Trumper or a Macartney but his performances speak for themselves. Over and above his batting he is a magnificent field and, like all Australians, a beautiful thrower. Occasionally he has met with success as a bowler but while his powers as a run-getter remain with him there is no need for him to cultivate the other side of the game.

Bradman first learned his cricket in pick-up matches at the Bowral Intermediate High School, and when he went to Sydney in 1926 at the invitation of the State Selectors for practice at the nets he was a somewhat uncouth, uncultured batsman. Still, he made 37 in a Trial match and then played in the Southern Districts country team. He reached first grade cricket in Sydney for the St George Club in 1926 and, as has already been told, proceeded thence into the New South Wales eleven. After he left School, where he was entirely self-taught in batting, he played for the Bowral club and, with scores of 234 and 300, had an aggregate of 1,318 and an average of 109. In the one match he played for them in 1926-27 he scored 320 not out. Not yet 23, Bradman should have years of cricket in front of him and, judging by what he has already accomplished, there would seem to be no limit to his possibilities.

The other four Cricketers of the Year in 1931 were C. V. Grimmett, B. H. Lyon, I. A. R. Peebles and M. J. Turnbull.

part I, pages 258–260

*The following extract is taken from Lord Hawke's article
"Fifty Years of Yorkshire County".*

Discipline and Fellowship

That, when captain, I had to act decisively and promptly in the case of two
professionals who I desire shall remain nameless, is well known in the
world of cricket.* I had to act as I did in the best interests of the Club and,
as I believe then and believe still, of the game everywhere. I bore, and bear,
them no malice. That they reciprocate this feeling I know. My action, I
believe, worked for the good of the game and the sobriety of its players, and
not only in my own county. In the days of which I now write the trouble was
not the player but the hangers-on, who, mainly for the sake of being seen
talking to a famous cricketer, pestered professionals with their attentions
and, worse still, by their offers of wholly unnecessary drinks. I am glad to
think, however, that this evil has grown so much less as to be almost
stamped out, and am proud to think I may have done something to help in
such a matter.

Here I must add something about the origin of the tea interval. Prior to
its introduction onlookers were used to seeing odd players leave the field for
a few minutes, the fielding side continuing one short. Those absences were
sometimes not beneficial only to the tea trade! The authorities weighed up
this matter, with the desirable result that there was introduced a regular tea
interval at a fixed hour. It is very rare now for a player to leave the field
under any pretext, and that is, I think, one point at least to the credit of the
tea interval.

In regard to discipline generally, I am a strong believer in the right kind
of friendship between the captain and the professional members of a county
eleven. Between that and the kind of familiarity which only breeds
contempt and therefore naturally weakens the playing power of an eleven
by undermining the absolute authority – and it must be absolute – of the
captain, there is a very wide margin. I believe I am the only captain who
held an annual party for the whole county eleven at his own residence. To

---

* *See footnote to the extract from the 1909 edition, page 17.*

myself and my family this was always one of the jolliest days of the year, and I only hope my "boys" enjoyed themselves at Wighill Park as much as we did. An amusing incident occurred at our little family party in 1906, after the season when we had lost the Championship by one run, our last wicket falling LBW. We were, of course, discussing the Championship when one of my sisters turned to Ringrose, who was next to her, and remarked, quite innocently: "Who *was* it who was leg before, *do* tell me?" Poor Ringrose! It can surely not be possible for anyone to blush a deeper pink than he did, as he had to own up that he was the culprit.

I must give now a few of the facts and figures concerning what I may call the behind the scenes management of the County Club in my time.

Our professionals are handed a small printed brochure which gives in full all the facts of our "Regulations relating to Players". In these the position with regard to match fees and talent money is plainly set forth, showing that professionals who have got their county caps get £2 more per match, away or in Yorkshire, than is paid to players who have not yet won their cap. The fee is at present £15 away and £11 at home for those with caps. For an Australian or South African match the professional receives £12, and in all cases £1 extra per won match. Twelfth man is paid the same, but no fee for a match won. It is a hard and fast rule with us that a professional on gaining his cap joins the Cricketers' Friendly Society. A similarly definite rule is that professionals are not permitted to write to the press in any form whatsoever. We have made a solitary exception in the case of articles on "hints how to play", etc., by Sutcliffe. But I think we are on sure ground in putting out of the way of our professionals the temptation to be paid for signing their names to articles which they do not always actually write.

In the matter of bonuses we have instituted in my time the system whereby players who have played regularly for five years get a bonus of £250 if their services are no longer required. If they have played for more than five but less than ten years, our Committee guarantees them not less than £50 for each subsequent year above five. We reserve the right to grant permission to our players to go on foreign tours and, if they go, they have to insure themselves against accident or illness.

part I, pages 302–304

In his obituary in the 1958 Wisden, Frank Chester was described as "the man who raised umpiring to a higher level than had ever been known in the history of cricket". By the end of the century, only Dickie Bird (66 matches) and David Shepherd (49) had umpired in more than Chester's 48 Tests.

The Umpire's Point of View: Some Experiences and Suggestions

By Frank Chester

Imagine the feelings of an umpire just appointed to the list, anxious to "make good" and denied admission to a ground at which he had been instructed to officiate. That was my experience in 1922 at Northampton. It all occurred because of my youthful appearance – I was little more than twenty-five at the time. When I told the gateman I was one of the umpires, he treated it quite as a joke. "You have made a mistake," he said, "this is a first-class match." Happily, he consented to fetch the club secretary, and after explanations and apologies the twenty-five-year-old umpire was passed through.

Since then I have umpired regularly each season – we get an average of twenty-two matches each year. Sound eyesight and good hearing are, of course, the first essentials but knowledge of cricket and – more important – knowledge of the Laws of the Game is imperative. Don Bradman has said that he considers our umpires the best in the world, but it must be remembered that we have a big advantage because more cricket is played in England than anywhere else.

People have asked me, "Why don't the Selectors take some of you umpires on their Committee when they are picking the England team? You are on the field all through the matches in which you are acting as umpires, you see everything that goes on and can spot the good players." That suggestion is not for me to discuss here, even if we certainly get an excellent view of all that happens. Umpires are often asked whether they have any suggestions to make regarding the game, as well as for an opinion on various experiments tried in recent years. That is a gesture which all umpires appreciate.

At the time of writing, everyone seems to be discussing our bowling in

Australia – the so-called "leg-theory" bowling. If it is of the character described in the cables, I do not agree with it; it is sure to make cricket a good deal slower and may keep people away. It is said our bowlers are aiming to hit the leg stump, but to hit the wicket you do not pitch halfway and there is a danger the practice may lessen interest in the game.

The bowler to whom the term "leg-theory" was first applied used to bowl the swinger. The best player I ever saw do this was A. Jaques, the Hampshire amateur (killed in the War) between 1912 and 1914 when I played for Worcestershire.* He could swing an old ball. He stood 6ft 3in in height and bowled medium pace, placing nearly all his field on the on side and pitching on the wicket or outside the leg stump. As he could make the ball swing in and also get on an off-break, he cramped the batsmen so much that many of them lost patience and were out. W. T. Greswell, of Somerset, was another very good "leg-theory" bowler.

Still, spin bowlers get most of the wickets nowadays, not those who swerve. Freeman, Sam Staples, Parker, V. W. C. Jupp, Goddard, Verity, James Langridge and Mitchell (Derbyshire) generally finish with well over 100 wickets each season. We should not hear so much of pitches being over-prepared if we had more spin bowlers. In my opinion, pitches are no better now than they were during my playing career. I could mention some county grounds where the pitches before the War were much better than they are at the present time. It was a big help to the bowlers when the larger wicket was adopted. With the new stumps in use, I have seen a large number of batsmen out from balls which, before the alteration in the size of the stumps, would have just missed the mark. Also, the experimental rule regarding LBW and "the snick" has been a very good one, and, I think, has come to stay.

Why do not bowlers make more use of the bowling crease? The late J. W. H. T. Douglas used the crease more than any other bowler I have seen and I am told that Walter Brearley used to bowl from varying places between the stumps and the return crease. Suggestions have been put forward that a new ball after 150 runs have been scored should be allowed. This would certainly help bowlers of the fast and fast-medium pace and swing bowlers, but personally I do not favour such a change. Cricket is just as popular as ever. It is the uncertain weather we get during the summer

---

* Qualifying for Worcestershire at the age of sixteen and a half, Frank Chester a year later – in 1913 – scored 698 runs, playing three innings of over a hundred, and took forty-three wickets. Wisden of 1914 said of him: "Very few players in the history of cricket have shown such form at the age of seventeen and a half." The following season, he scored 924 runs, making 178 not out against Essex at Worcester. A very promising career was interfered with by the War, Chester being badly wounded and so prevented from playing further cricket.

months that keeps so many people away. When we get a good summer the "gates" are always better.

Perhaps in the near future special rules for certain grounds will disappear. I should like to suggest that definite times for the luncheon and tea intervals be in force everywhere. The hours of play – 11.30 to 6.30 – are ideal.

While it may not be considered within the province of an umpire to suggest tampering with the rules, there is one matter which I think merits very close consideration. Where a batsman, not out overnight, is not present on the ground to resume his innings next morning and the two minutes grace has lapsed, he can according to the existing laws bat with the consent of the opposing captain. Surely, unless an unanswerable explanation or excuse is given, the batsman should be ruled out without the captain of the opposing side being approached on the point. An incident touching on this rule occurred last season.

Another curious occurrence at a match in which I was standing umpire took place some years ago. A batsman deliberately ran after a ball and kicked it; then he started to run. I informed the batsman he could not run and no runs were allowed, but afterwards I was "called over the coals" and told there was no law whereby a man should not kick the ball. My defence of the action was that this was unfair play and that, had it occurred again, I should, had I been appealed to, have given the batsman out for impeding the wicket-keeper.

It has often struck me as curious how in some matches one of the umpires is constantly dealing with appeals while the other man receives hardly any. I remember one match in particular, at Dover, when the late Harry Butt was my colleague. Altogether, he gave twelve batsmen out, but meanwhile I did not have an appeal made to me. Butt called to me jokingly, "It is about time you earned your money."

Out in Australia, I have read, umpires are using special "over" watches. Umpires scarcely need anything so elaborate. Personally, I use stones to count, some umpires use a special machine with six levers, others coins and some their fingers. Whatever the method is, it becomes automatic. There is nothing else automatic about an umpire's job. We need to be very much on the alert the whole time.

part I, pages 332–335

*The 1932-33 Ashes series in Australia was notorious
for the England team's use of what became known as the bodyline tactic.*
Wisden *commented as follows.*

The Bowling Controversy

By Sydney Southerton

During the last few tours of MCC teams in Australia, and the visits of the
Australians to this country, one could not fail to detect a subtle change taking
place in the conduct of Test matches – reflected unfortunately in the style of
play of the cricketers themselves. The *result* of the contests was given a
prominence out of keeping even with the importance of Test matches, and
the true sense of perspective stood in danger of disappearing altogether.

There is no need to enter into some of the reasons for the hostility with
which D. R. Jardine in particular and certain of his team were received by
the huge crowds in Australia. Animosity existed and was fanned into flame
largely by the use of the term "bodyline" when Larwood and others met
with such success against the leading Australian batsmen. To such an extent
had real bitterness grown that the storm burst during the Third Test match
at Adelaide. The dispatch of the petulant cablegram by the Australian Board
of Control even placed the completion of the tour in jeopardy. Saner
counsels prevailed and, although tension existed for months afterwards, the
MCC for their part never lost their grip of the situation and, what was even
more important, refused to be stampeded into any panic legislation.
Whatever individual opinions were held at the time the MCC Committee,
as a whole, naturally stood by the captain of their team in Australia. They
had heard only one side of the question.

And now, what of this fast leg-theory method of bowling to which not
only the Australian players themselves, but a vast majority of the people of
Australia took such grave exception? With the dictum of the MCC that any
form of bowling which constitutes a direct attack by the bowler on the
batsman is contrary to the spirit of the game everyone must unquestionably
concur. D. R. Jardine, on his return to England, stated definitely in his book
that the bowling against which the Australians demurred was not of this

description and Larwood, the chief exponent of it, said with equal directness that he had never intentionally bowled at a man. On the other hand, there are numerous statements by responsible Australians to the effect that the type of bowling adopted was calculated to intimidate batsmen, pitched as the ball was so short as to cause it to fly shoulder and head high and make batsmen, with the leg side studded with fieldsmen, use the bat as a protection for their bodies or their heads rather than in defence of the wicket or to make a scoring stroke. Victor Richardson, the South Australian batsman, has said that when he took his ordinary stance at the wicket he found the ball coming on to his body; when he took guard slightly more to the leg side he still had the ball coming at him; and with a still wider guard the ball continued to follow him. I hold no brief either for Jardine or Larwood or for Richardson, Woodfull or Bradman; but while some of the Australians may have exaggerated the supposed danger of this form of bowling I cling to the opinion that they cannot all be wrong. When the first mutterings of the storm were heard many people in this country were inclined to the belief that the Australians, seeing themselves in danger of losing the rubber, were not taking defeat in the proper spirit always expected from honorable opponents. I will confess that I thought they did not relish what seemed to me at that stage to be a continuous good length bombardment by our fast bowlers on to their leg stump. This idea I afterwards found was not quite correct.

There is nothing new in leg-theory bowling. The most notable exponent of it in recent years was Root, of Worcestershire; to go back to just before the War A. Jaques, of Hampshire, often exploited it with success; and to delve deeper into the past an Australian – no less than the famous Spofforth himself – would at times bowl on the leg-stump with an off-break and two fieldsmen close in on the leg side. Root and Jaques were, however, medium-paced bowlers while Spofforth, even if he had a very destructive fast ball always at command, could not truthfully be classified as a fast bowler consistent in the pace of say Larwood, Knox, Richardson, Lockwood, or Kortright. Moreover, Root, Jaques and Spofforth almost invariably bowled a good length, so that the ball could be played either in a defensive manner or with the idea of turning it to leg, and when the batsman made a mistake in timing or in placing he usually paid the penalty by being caught.

That type of bowling, however, is very different from the kind sent down at top-speed with the ball flying past the shoulders or head of the batsman who has only a split second in which to make up his mind as to whether he will duck, move away, or attempt to play it with the bat high in the air. Against one sort a perfectly legitimate and reasonable stroke could be played without any apprehension of physical damage; against the other it seems to me that by touching the ball in defence of the upper part of his body or his head a batsman would be almost bound to be out. One would not accuse Hammond or Hendren of being slow on their feet, yet Hendren at Lord's on one occasion was not quick enough to get out of the way and received a crashing blow on his head, while last season at Manchester Hammond, in the Test match against the West Indies, had his chin laid open, and on resuming his innings was caught off a similar kind of ball. We saw in that particular match at Old Trafford what I should conceive to be a somewhat pale – but no less disturbing – imitation of Larwood in Australia, when Martindale and Constantine on the one hand, and Clark, of Northamptonshire, on the other were giving a demonstration of fast leg-theory bowling. Not one of the three had the pace, accuracy of pitch, or deadliness of Larwood but what they did was sufficient to convince many people with open minds on the subject that it was a noxious form of attack not to be encouraged in any way.

Cricketers whose memories go back to the days of the bad wickets at Lord's are, I think, a little too prone to emphasise the fact that W. G. Grace and other famous batsmen of that era were often struck so frequently on the body that after their innings they were covered with bruises, but I should like to suggest that the blows they received were to a large extent caused by good-length balls getting up quickly off the rough turf. I certainly can find no trace in the course of a good deal of research among old reports and comments on these matches that the fast bowlers of those days like Tarrant and Jackson continually dropped the ball short with the idea of making it bounce.

Fast bowlers of all periods have delivered the ball short of a length on occasions – sometimes by accident, and sometimes by intention to keep batsmen on the *qui-vive* – but in modern days some of our bowlers of pace have become obsessed with the idea that it is necessary to do this three or four times in an over. I desire none of my readers to get the impression that I am against fast bowling. Nothing is further from my thoughts. I like to see fast bowling, the faster the better, but I do like to see it of good length and directed at the stumps.

The Australians without any doubt thought that during the last tour they were being bowled at, and small wonder that edging away as some of them unquestionably did they found themselves bowled when, instead of the expected short-pitched "bouncer", occasional good-length straight balls came along and beat them before they were in a proper position to defend their wickets. It is, to say the least, significant that G. O. Allen, whom nobody would place quite in the same class as Larwood, enjoyed many successes and for the most part obtained his wickets by bowling with which we in England are familiar. Surely, with his extra pace, Larwood could have done as well as Allen and so have prevented that bitter ill-feeling which led a good many people in this country to the belief that the winning of the

Ashes had been gained at too great a cost to the relations hitherto existing between England and Australia.

For myself, I hope that we shall never see fast leg-theory bowling as used during the last tour in Australia exploited in this country. I think that (1) it is definitely dangerous; (2) it creates ill-feeling between the rival teams; (3) it invites reprisals; (4) it has a bad influence on our great game of cricket; and (5) it eliminates practically all the best strokes in batting. Mainly because it makes cricket a battle instead of a game I deplore its introduction and pray for its abolition, not by any legislative measures, but by the influence which our captains can bring to bear and by avoiding use of the objectionable form of attack take a great part in wiping away a blot. Early last season I heard Mr Weigall, the Recorder of Gravesend, deliver a great speech at a dinner to the West Indies team, in which in beautifully chosen phrases he exhorted them always to look upon cricket with the idea that the game is of far greater importance than the result. If that lesson is driven home to all our cricketers we shall hear no more of the kind of bowling which so nearly brought about a severance of the cricket relations between England and Australia.

part I, pages 247–252

In editing this article, the order of some paragraphs has been changed.

The Hobbs Era

By Jack Hobbs

My career in first-class cricket having, after a very happy period, reached its end, I gladly comply with the request of the Editor of *Wisden's Almanack* to jot down some personal impressions which may be of interest to present and future readers of the book.

The honour has been done me of referring to the period of my active participation in important cricket as "The Hobbs Era", and I should like to say at once how mindful I am of this distinction … The era covers first-class cricket from 1903 to 1933. The War came to rob all of us of four solid years of the game, and although I played a little last summer I think that I really finished in 1933 when at 50 years of age after, roughly, 30 seasons at The Oval, I was beginning to feel that the strain of the game day after day was getting just a little too much for me. There was also the fact that younger players were knocking at the door, and that it did not become me, having had a longer innings than most cricketers of modern days, to stand in the way of promising recruits who wanted to feel that their positions in a county eleven were secure. So even though I scored one century last season I still fall short by three of the two hundred I had fondly hoped to obtain. Records after all are ephemeral; they are only made to be beaten by somebody else, and … someone will come along one of these days and surpass the 197 hundreds which now stand to my credit.

Before my time there were other epochs in our great game. The days of top-hats, when Alfred Mynn, the "Lion of Kent" and other famous men were in their prime, are now far distant. Then came the Grace period when that marvellous batsman stood out head and shoulders above everybody else; the Hon. F. S. Jackson, Ranjitsinhji, G. L. Jessop, Tom Hayward, C. B. Fry, A. C. MacLaren, George Hirst, J. T. Tyldesley, Victor Trumper, M. A. Noble and others too numerous to mention were contemporaries in what has been described as the "Golden Age" of cricket. It will be seen therefore that my own follows in a natural sequence in this recurring cycle.

As to whether during the past thirty years cricket generally has been better or worse than those periods to which I have referred is not perhaps for me to say. Cricket was at its very best in that Golden Age when almost every county had one, if not two or three outstanding personalities either as batsmen or bowlers.

I do not agree, however, with the oft-repeated statement that cricket nowadays is not what it used to be, and I would ask why, when in the ordinary affairs of every-day life as well as in most other games we have gone ahead, cricket should be singled out as an example of deterioration in all-round form and skill? … It should not be overlooked that there were several county enclosures before say 1900 where the wickets were really good, and one has only to look up the records to find that big scores were made at The Oval before swerve bowlers came into existence, and when length, allied to spin, was the first consideration. All wickets were not bad, as many people seem to think. The one important difference between those of my early times and those of the present is that you very, very rarely see a real "sticky" wicket nowadays. Over-preparation is the cause of this, and probably the system in use at certain centres of covering the pitch completely before the match has also had something to do with it. That, however, brings you to another consideration, that of finance. Many county clubs are often hard put to it to make both ends meet.

Efforts have been made more than once, because of the heavy

programmes and constant play day after day, to limit first-class matches to two days. I am not altogether opposed to this; in fact I would ask: why not two-day matches of one innings each? That would give a lot of our professionals a much needed rest and, as far as I can see, the main argument against this would come from professionals themselves because they would not be able to earn quite as much as they do now.

I think the development of the County Championship in regard to the number of counties now competing is rather to be regretted. There are too many counties – some of them, I am afraid, not quite up to the best standard – and we in England have got a false opinion of the strength of our cricket. The trouble is that, against the weaker counties, players get plenty of runs and wickets and they are thought at once to be Test match cricketers. It is much harder now to pick a team for a Test match than it was thirty years ago. The field of choice is so much wider and the all-round standard consequently more on a level – especially in the County averages.

I have always regarded it as curious that while most of the changes in cricket in my thirty years have been in favour of the bowler, such as the smaller ball and the wider wicket, bowling generally, in my opinion, has deteriorated. There are very few outstanding bowlers of real class today, and I remember that just after the War, when admittedly things had changed a good deal, bowlers opened for their sides who weren't considered prior to 1914. Everyone nowadays seems to want to bowl the in-swinger. This is absurd, for my experience is that this particular ball is not so dangerous as the one which goes away from you. It has led to what I should call "negative cricket". Bowlers adopting this method try rather to keep the batsman quiet than to get him out. The result of this is that back-play has developed to a large extent and on-side play has increased out of all proportion, to the detriment of off-side batting. But then it must be remembered that it is very difficult indeed to drive an in-swinging ball on the off side, and with bowlers keeping just short of a length, as modern bowlers do, the natural tendency of a batsmen, at any rate since the War, has been to step back and play the ball to the on … In my early days youngsters were taught to play forward, and it was the accepted theory that one only played back when the wicket was soft and the ball was turning. Now, batsman play back on a hard wicket … consequently, young bowlers, seeing that this type of attack cannot be driven to the off, very rarely try to make themselves spin bowlers pure and simple. I know, of course, that it is not given to everyone to keep such a perfect length as J. T. Hearne or Albert Relf used to. They would bowl all the afternoon and scarcely give you six balls that you could hit with safety.

There is one point about the improvement in batting to which I should like to draw attention, and that is that it is not confined to those in the first half of the order. Even in my early days we seldom expected or saw the last four men stay very long. Nowadays Numbers 8, 9, 10 and 11 all come in, not so much to have a wild swipe, but to play for runs; and they very often obtain them. This, of course, may be considered to be partly due to the difference in bowling. Back-play, too, has been the means of driving the off-spinner largely out of the game, and figures clearly show that batsmen, even when allowance is made for a great deal of extra cricket which they play, generally get far more runs now than they used to do.

Before my time it was considered rather *infra dig* to hook a ball round to the leg side. Nowadays, batsmen will step right across and hook a ball from wide of the off stump round to square leg. Hammond is the great exception. He won't hook. He considers it a dangerous stroke and I remember once, the first time I saw him, he persisted in playing balls which the ordinary batsmen would have hooked, hard back either to mid-on or mid-off. But then Hammond, as a batsman, is a law unto himself. He can step right back and force the short ball to the off, but not many men possess such power of wrist and forearm, and quickness on the feet, to be able to do that.

We saw last season one noticeable feature about the batting of the Australians in the power they put into their strokes. When young, they are taught first to hit the ball; we in England are taught defence. The wickets in Australia are, of course, easier as a general rule than ours. They are the same pace and the ball comes along at a uniform height. Because of this Australian batsmen are for the most part more confident.

I have already said that one of the most notable changes in cricket with regard to bowling has been the introduction of "swing" or "swerve". No doubt long before my time bowlers were able to, and probably often did, make the ball swing, but it was not known then how this was brought about and quite likely when it occurred bowlers put it down to an extra strong current of air or some outside influence of a similar kind. The secret of being able to make a ball move about in the air was acquired during my era and at the present time almost anybody with any knowledge of bowling can send down swingers of one sort or the other. It is all a question of how the ball is held in the hand at the moment of delivery and bowlers of this description now come under the general heading of "seam-up bowlers". Shortly after I began to play first-class cricket came the googly, known in Australia as the "bosie" because it was first discovered by B. J. T. Bosanquet. The South Africans were quick to realise the deadliness of this ball once a command of length had been gained. On the matting wickets in their country they soon perfected it and in G. A. Faulkner, A. E. Vogler, Gordon White and R. O. Schwarz they produced the finest array of googly bowlers ever seen together in one team. W. G. Grace did not, I think, play in an important match against googly bowling but obviously he must have been so very good that he, like many of us later on, would have mastered it.

He would have played every ball on its merits.

While on the question of bowling I am definitely of the opinion that during my career the art of flighting the ball has steadily deteriorated. We have nobody now so good at this as Colin Blythe. He was one of the world's greatest bowlers of his type, and, unlike most of the present-day exponents, was never afraid of being hit. Of fast bowlers the only ones of recent years at all comparable with those giants of the past have been Larwood and McDonald. Being a member of the same county side I only played against N. A. Knox in Gentlemen and Players matches and games of a similar description, when he was probably past his best, but I think he was the best fast bowler I ever saw. He brought the ball down from such a great height that he could often make good length deliveries rear up straight.

It is a little difficult to say definitely if fielding has improved. Individually it may not have done, but collectively I think it has. Thirty years ago, the positions of mid-on and short leg were both known as "Mugs' Corner". The captain looked round and almost invariably put his two incompetent fieldsmen in those places. I have never agreed that mid-on's was an easy job. You have to watch the batsman and anticipate his stroke, and you have to be quick off the mark when you field there. Only in recent years have we awakened to this fact, while men like "Bill" Hitch made short leg an honorable position in which to field. Hammond is my ideal fieldsman. He would be great anywhere, and Mitchell of Yorkshire runs him very close. No matter where they are put these two men can be right at the top, and it has often struck me that Hammond's fielding would very likely have been far more extensively talked-of had he been an outfielder, while it is certain he would do wonderful work at cover point. With regard to the placing of the field there can be no question at all that this has engaged the attention of captains to a far greater degree than it used to and consequently it is better. The Australians, for instance, have developed the study of this to such an extent that they are now much better than we in England at placing their fieldsmen to stop runs, and the increase in on-side strokes by batsmen has led to two or three men being placed on the leg side when in my early days there was only one. This is not meant as a reference to "bodyline" bowling. My views on that are well known. I deplore its introduction. I think it has done great harm to the game, because it fosters a spirit foreign to the traditions of cricket and which certainly never existed when I first came on the scene.

part I, pages 352–353

Miscellany

- At the end of March, a strip of turf from Melbourne was laid on the practice-ground at Lord's as an experiment to see how it fared in the English climate, with a possibility that such turf might be used to obviate the wearing of bowlers' footholds.

- Hot drinks were served in the morning on the field in many matches during a very chilly May.

- A plague of "leather-jackets" (larvae of the crane-fly) infested the Lord's wicket in the 1934-35 winter, causing many bare patches on the wicket-table. A section of the ground was returfed during the following autumn.

- A "bad light" signal, a form of radiovisor, erected at Lord's was considered "too mechanical for a sporting game" and dismantled.

- Two first-class umpires, A. Morton and A. Young, could not, owing to illness, fulfil their duties last summer. Substitutes had to be found. Morton died in December.

- Hours of play were adjusted in some county games to enable players chosen for Test matches to avoid all-night journeys.

- The Silver Jubilee of King George V coincided with his completion of fifty years as an honorary member of MCC. In the MCC minutes of July 6, 1885, appears the following: "It was proposed by Lord Winterton, seconded by Lord Bessborough and unanimously resolved that Prince George of Wales be elected an Honorary Member of the Club."

- Hours of play in the Oxford v Cambridge match were extended in order to increase the possibility of definite results. The game began at 11.30 a.m. each day and play continued until 7 p.m. with the option of an additional half hour on the third day.

- Owing to inadequate score-boards at Wells, where first-class cricket was played for the first time, details of bowling changes, etc., in the Somerset v Worcestershire match were announced by loud-speaker.

- In the Surrey and Essex match at The Oval, one of the umpires signalled as the players left the field at the end of the day that a batsman was out. The decision, challenged on the ground that it had been made after the drawing of stumps, led to MCC drafting a special addition to Law 50.

- A special signal to indicate decisions under the experimental LBW rule* was devised by Mr W. Findlay, secretary of MCC, and first used in the MCC v Surrey match. After giving the decision "Out", the umpire raised his right hand, palm upwards.

- Sunnucks, of Kent, was the first man to be given out in a county cricket match under the new rule.

* *On page 340, the experimental LBW rule is explained as follows: "In regard to LBW … the only new instruction is that the Striker is out to a ball which pitching on the off side of the Striker's wicket would have hit the wicket had it not been intercepted by part of the Striker's person which was* between wicket and wicket *at the moment of impact."*

part I, pages 249–255

Recollections of Oxford Cricket: Some Memorable 'Varsity Matches

By H. D. G. Leveson Gower

The Editor of *Wisden* has paid me the compliment of asking me to give some reminiscences of Oxford Cricket – a compliment that I naturally appreciate very much and an invitation that I readily accept. Perhaps my chief qualification to do this is that since the beginning of this century I have had the pleasure of getting up "Teams" against the Universities, both at Oxford and Cambridge, for over twenty years at Eastbourne, and the last three years at Reigate. While there is always a certain amount of responsibility and at times anxiety in collecting sides, the reward is great, for it has enabled me year after year, not only to keep in touch with the different generations of 'Varsity cricketers, but also to retain the friendship of those who were good enough to play for my "Elevens".

My reminiscences of Oxford cricket date back to 1893 for although, before I "went up", I had with keen and boyish delight followed the fortunes of the University Matches at Lord's since the early 1880s, it was when I got my Blue in 1893 that I may be said to have become intimately connected with Oxford cricket … Of the four University Matches in which I took part, those of 1893 and 1896 provided "incidents". In 1893 C. M. Wells and in 1896 E. B. Shine gave away eight runs while bowling, to prevent Oxford following on. Being captain at Oxford in 1896 I was naturally very interested in the decision reached by Frank Mitchell in giving orders to E. B. Shine to bowl no-balls to the boundary in order to prevent my side from going in again. In my opinion the reception he and his team received from the members of MCC and when his team went in to bat from the "spectators", was quite unjustifiable. His motive, no doubt, was to do what he thought was best to ensure victory; whether his policy was sound or not was entirely a matter for him as captain to decide. Personally, I should not have done it; I do not say this because we won. The moral effect of following on in a University Match is great, and the Cambridge Eleven had not had an over-strenuous time in the field. Of all the players on both sides only G. J. Mordaunt and myself took part in both these "incident matches".

I may perhaps be excused for going rather fully into the match of 1896. Naturally it is the ambition of a captain to win his 'Varsity match, and once again Dame Fortune did not forsake me. I had the luck at the last moment of making the right choice for the last place in my side. I left the selection till the morning of the match. G. O. Smith and G. B. Raikes, both old Blues, were the candidates. I had practically made up my mind to play Raikes. He was a good all-round cricketer – useful bowler, very good slip and a sound bat. What made me alter my mind was this: when I inspected the wicket I did not think that another bowler, unless an exceptional one, would make the difference, and I decided to play the better bat of the two, G. O. Smith. Experience had taught me that you can never have too much batting in a 'Varsity Match. I took the risk of going into the field against a powerful Cambridge batting side with only four bowlers. It meant that I should have to work these extremely hard. F. H. E. Cunliffe and J. C. Hartley, my two chief bowlers, sent down no fewer than 88 and 92 overs in the match respectively. The last choice won me the match by a superb 132 when we were set 330 runs to win. Thus, G. O. Smith followed the example of Lord George Scott in 1887, for Oxford, and Eustace Crawley, of the Cambridge Eleven, in the same year. The former contributed 100 and 66; the latter 33 and 103 not out; both were last choices. P. F. Warner had a most unusual experience in this 1896 match, being run out in both innings.

Another incident during this game that I recall is a personal talk I had with an onlooker, who apparently came to watch the 'Varsity Match like one might The Derby, to spot the winner with advantage to himself. During the lunch interval on the last day, when I was none too happy of our prospects of victory – three good wickets were down for just over 70 – this spectator approached me and said, "I'm afraid Oxford's prospects of victory are very poor. What do you think?" My answer, given rather abruptly, was "We shall win all right." "What?" said my interrogator, "are you sure? I have been laid 8 to 1 against Oxford, shall I take it?" "Certainly," I said, anxious to get away from this rather adhesive person. Ten days afterwards I received a registered envelope with a sapphire pin enclosed – and the following letter: "Thank you so much for your very valuable information. I collected a very nice sum but I knew it was a certainty as it came from 'The Horse's Mouth'."

It is a long time since a 'Varsity match yielded a close finish. The two runs win by Cambridge in 1870 and the six runs success of Oxford in 1875 are now very distant memories. In the last decade the only thrill that one remembers was when, a few years ago, the last two Oxford men managed to stay in until the finish and had the minor satisfaction of annoying their opponents though they could not defeat them. During the present century the nearest approaches to a level result were the matches of 1908 and 1926. In the former game Oxford got home by only two wickets, while in the other, the margin in favour of Cambridge was 34 runs.

Often enough we have seen reversal of public form. The side supposed to be the weaker nearly always confounded the prophets not only by winning, but by winning easily. In 1881 Cambridge, with A. G. Steel, Ivo Bligh, the three brothers Studd and other great players, had what looked like an invincible side. Steel, practically on his own one may say, had already beaten Oxford three times and was confidently expected to do so a fourth time. But the side failed completely against the fast bowling of Evans, the Oxford captain, and were beaten by 135 runs. In 1895 Oxford, with a splendid eleven, were never in it from start to finish and lost by 134 runs.

Let us examine finally University cricket as a stepping-stone to Test cricket. If we restrict our enquiry to matches against Australia and South Africa, as being contests in which for many years we have in this country chosen absolutely our best teams, we find that since 1880, when we first played Australia over here, 63 amateur cricketers have appeared in England elevens. Of these, 33 have been Oxford or Cambridge Blues. The distinction of being selected while still in residence at the University is uncommon, and only seven of the 33 have enjoyed it. And yet four of the five English teams sent out to Australia since the War have been under the leadership of University players, A. E. R. Gilligan, A. P. F. Chapman, D. R. Jardine and G. O. Allen. If I had to choose a combined University eleven of Blues since 1919 – and what a difficult task! – my nominations would be the following twelve: G. O. Allen, H. Ashton, A. P. F. Chapman, K. S. Duleepsinhji,

A. E. R. Gilligan, E. R. T. Holmes, D. R. Jardine, D. J. Knight, C. S. Marriott, Nawab of Pataudi, G. T. S. Stevens and G. E. C. Wood.

Long may the Universities continue to be the stepping-stone of Cricket – long may University cricketers continue to keep up the high tradition handed down to them by famous cricketers of the past.

page 769

First Women's Test Match

Australia v England

At Brisbane, December 28, 29, 31, 1934. England won by nine wickets. The importance of the occasion, the first Women's Test match, proved too much for the Australians who never recovered from a disastrous start. They lost five wickets for 13 runs and were out in under two hours. Maclagan, the English fast bowler, took full advantage of her opponents' uncertainty and was almost unplayable. By her batting, Maclagan saved England when they went in, for few others showed confidence against the slow bowling of Palmer who spun the ball appreciably. Australia, 107 in arrear, did better in their second innings, thanks to a splendid knock by Shevill, but England were left only 32 to get for victory.

Australia

H. Pritchard hit wkt b Maclagan	4	– c Snowball b Spear	20
R. Monaghan c and b Maclagan	4	– run out	4
N. McLarty c and b Maclagan	0	– c Snowball b Spear	8
E. Shevill b Maclagan	0	– not out	63
K. Smith c Spear b Maclagan	25	– b Valentine	12
H. Hills retired hurt	2	– absent ill	
M. Peden b Taylor	1	– c Partridge b Spear	11
L. Kettels c Partridge b Maclagan	9	– b Spear	0
A. Palmer c Partridge b Maclagan	1	– b Partridge	4
P. Antonio c Partridge b Taylor	0	– b Spear	5
F. Blade not out	0	– c Child b Hide	4
Extra	1	Extras	7
	47		**138**

Bowling: *First Innings*—Maclagan 17–11–10–7; Taylor 14.3–8–9–2; Spear 8–7–2–0; Hide 4–0–6–0; Turner 4–1–7–0; Partridge 2–0–12–0. *Second Innings*—Maclagan 28–12–31–0; Taylor 19–6–30–0; Spear 34–24–15–5; Hide 21–7–26–1; Turner 13–7–14–0; Partridge 5.3–2–6–1; Valentine 5–1–9–1.

England

M. Maclagan b Palmer		72	– b Antonio	9
B. Snowball c Shevill b Antonio		15	– not out	18
M. Hide c Kettels b Palmer		9	– not out	6
M. Child c McLarty b Palmer		5		
J. Partridge b Palmer		0		
B. Archdale not out		32		
D. M. Turner c McLarty b Palmer		2		
J. Liebert b McLarty		1		
M. I. Taylor c McLarty b Smith		0		
M. Spear b Palmer		9		
C. Valentine b Palmer		0		
Extras		9	Extra	1
		154		**(1 wkt) 34**

Bowling: *First Innings*—Blade 10–2–24–0; Smith 13–2–32–1; McLarty 10–4–12–1; Antonio 15–1–41–1; Palmer 13.2–4–18–7; Kettels 8–2–8–0; Shevill 4–1–10–0. *Second Innings*—McLarty 2–0–4–0; Antonio 5–1–20–1; Palmer 6–1–9–0.

pages 48–51

Cricket Conundrums

By A. E. R. Gilligan

Whenever I have given cricket talks in different parts of England, I have always devoted at least a quarter of the time to the many cricket problems and difficulties caused by wrong interpretation of the rules. During my experiences, I have collected quite a useful list of cricket conundrums which I shall discuss in this article.

First of all, I remember being asked rather an important question at a meeting some twelve years ago: "Why doesn't the MCC legislate for many of the doubtful points arising from the Laws of Cricket?" I promised that I would put this problem before the Secretary of the MCC himself and accordingly went to see Mr W. Findlay.

His answer was an excellent one, and I can think of no better way of starting my article than by setting it out here and now. He said: "Why should the MCC legislate for doubtful points arising from the Cricket Laws? Our duty is to see that the Rules of Cricket are made to cover only the rightful interpretation of the very spirit of the game, and anything which borders on unfairness can never be legislated for by the premier cricket club."

I think that everyone will agree that Mr Findlay's outlook on so important a question was absolutely correct and that we should not endeavour to get round the rules by what may be termed unfair methods. Therefore I shall try to keep my cricket conundrums on amusing lines, and prove that all of them are covered by the existing rules of the game.

One Ball: Five Men Out

Do you know how five men can be dismissed by one ball bowled? Of course, you must allow a certain amount of licence in this respect, but actually several years ago in a county match when play was due to resume, it was found that one of the overnight not-out batsmen had taken a wrong tube-train, and at half past eleven was miles away from the "scene of conflict".

The umpires, on appeal, ruled that the batsman was "absent" and could not continue his innings. There is the first man out. The next comes in and the bowler delivers a no-ball, which naturally does not count as a legitimate delivery. The striker hits it towards cover-point and calls his partner for a run. His partner, seeing that there is not the slightest chance of a quick single, sends back the striker, who unfortunately slips up and falls to the ground. The ball is returned to the wicket-keeper and No. 2 is run out, still with no legitimate ball being bowled. No. 3 arrives and hits the first ball, a half-volley, with terrific force straight back at his partner, who receives the ball right in the middle of the forehead. The ball bounces in the air and mid-off catches it easily. No. 3 is out, caught; No. 4 is also out – knocked out – and is carried off the field unconscious, and when No. 5 (who is No. 11 on the batting list) comes to the wicket, he finds he has no one with whom to bat. So there you have five men out with one ball bowled.

Who is Out?

Now here is another very interesting poser. Jones is bowling to Smith, with Robinson the non-striker. Smith hits a very hard return catch to the bowler, who just touches the ball and deflects it on to the wicket. Robinson is out of his crease and the ball, without touching the ground, ricochets off the stumps into the hands of mid-on.

Who is out? Is Smith out, caught, or is Robinson run out?

I have asked over a hundred people this riddle and practically 90 per cent give Robinson run out. I put the point to two first-class umpires, Frank Chester and Jack Newman, last season at Hastings, and they replied simultaneously: "Smith is out, caught" ; and that is the correct answer.

What about this one? The striker plays the ball a few yards up the wicket and calls his partner for a sharp single. Mid-off dashes in and the striker, seeing that a run is impossible, turns back to his crease, but in so doing accidentally kicks the ball into his wicket. With the striker well out of his ground, the bails drop off and the umpire gives him out.

The question before you now is: How is the striker out?

When asked for an immediate decision, many people say: "Oh, he is run out." That is wrong, because the ball has not been touched by any of the fieldsmen after the striker has hit it. Others maintain that he is out, hit wicket. Again that is incorrect, because *the ball* has broken the wicket. The correct decision is therefore *bowled* – played on. It is just the same as if the batsman had played the ball on to his foot, from whence it rebounds on to his stumps.

Half Caught?

The subject of another conundrum actually happened in a match in New Zealand. The last two batsmen are in, the last ball of the game is about to be delivered, and two runs are necessary for victory. The bowler runs up to bowl and sends down a good length ball to the striker, who takes a terrific swipe at it, sending the ball a tremendous way in the air. When it has reached the apex of its flight, the ball breaks in two pieces. Mid-on shouts "Mine" and catches half the ball. "You're out," says the fielder. "No, I am not," retorts the batsman. "The other half of the ball is on the ground."

An appeal is made to the umpire, who rightly decides that this particular delivery should not count and sends for another ball, as much as possible like the one which has been discarded, and play is resumed. The bowler is so excited by the occurrence that he sends down a full toss to leg, the batsman hits it straight to the square-leg boundary, and the match is won by the batting side.

This case was sent to the MCC Committee for a ruling, the result being that the umpire's action was unanimously upheld.

Holding On!

I remember George Cox, the old Sussex player, telling me of the following remarkable case which was submitted to him. The batting side require 50 runs for victory and the last two men are together, with the last over of the match to be bowled. No. 11 is a complete "rabbit", but manages somehow or other to survive five balls. As the bowler is running up to bowl the final ball, No. 11 waits till the ball is delivered, throws away his bat and, turning, holds on the bails with his hands. The ball just snicks the off-stump and travels slowly to the slips.

The batsman removes his hands from the bails, picks up his bat and says, "Well, that is a drawn game."

An appeal is made to the umpire, who scratches his head and the batsman, noticing this, declares loudly: "There is nothing in the rules which says a batsman cannot hold his bails on."

"Oh, yes, there is," says the umpire. "I give you out for unfair play, Rule 43." So the match is won by the fielding side.

Some years ago, when giving a cricket talk to the Portsmouth Umpires' Association, I was asked to give an instant decision upon this perplexing problem, and I wonder how many of you can do likewise: "How can a batsman hit the ball twice, yet score runs and not be given out by the umpire?"

Knowing that a striker may be out for hitting the ball twice without any attempt at a run being made – that is to say, he hits the ball a second time before it touches the ground, and is out for obstructing the field – I was momentarily at a loss to give the correct answer. Suddenly, like a flash, I remembered, and said: "If the ball has been struck twice lawfully, in defence of his wicket, and an overthrow is made, the striker is entitled to any runs that follow."

Test Match Contretemps

I have already mentioned that, if the umpires agree that a ball in use is unfit for play, they have the right to allow the substitution of another ball as much as possible similar to the one discarded.

I recall that, in the second Test match between England and Australia at Melbourne in 1925, after only 15 runs were on the board – I was bowling at the time – I noticed that a great piece of leather had come off the ball. I immediately showed the ball to umpire Bob Crockett, who consulted his colleague and a brand new ball was brought out.

Before lunch that day we had no fewer than four new balls with the total no more than 87! When we adjourned, we discovered that, by mistake, a wrong packet of balls had been delivered to the ground and that we had No. 3 grade cricket balls instead of No. 1. It was agreed between Herby Collins and myself to play out the first innings with both sides using the No. 3 grade variety, and it is interesting now to record that we used eight new balls before the score reached 200 and Australia had seven.

pages 741 and 744–745

South Africa v England

Fifth Test Match

At Durban, March 3, 4, 6, 7, 8, 9, 10, 11, 13, 14, 1939. Drawn. Unparalleled in the history of the game this was in many ways an extraordinary match, emphasising that there are no limits to the possibilities of what may occur in cricket; but it ended farcically, for insufficient time remained to finish the "timeless" Test. Although undecided, the final Test left the rubber with England after a magnificent and unequalled performance by W. R. Hammond and his men. Stopped by rain on the tenth day, the longest match ever played produced amazing records and brought personal triumph to Edrich who, after most heart-breaking experiences in Test cricket, established his reputation by hitting a double-century at a time when England needed an almost superhuman effort to avoid disaster.

South Africa set England to make 696 to win and few people imagined the team had a ghost of a chance of averting defeat, much less of scoring such a colossal total. Instead of going in with their tails down the batsmen set about their task in a magnificent manner and proved what can be done when the wicket remains unimpaired. It was an astonishing achievement to get within 42 runs of their objective with five wickets in hand, but, like The Oval Test between England and Australia the previous August, the game developed into a test of endurance. For one thing the pitch was much too good and many batsmen discarded their natural methods and adopted unnecessary caution.

When heavy rain prevented any more cricket after tea on the tenth day the South African Board of Control and the two captains went into conference before issuing a statement that the game had been abandoned because the England team had to catch the 8.5 p.m. train that night (Tuesday) from Durban in order to reach Cape Town in time to make the necessary arrangements for their departure on the *Athlone Castle* on Friday. The date of sailing for England could not be postponed.

South Africa

P. G. Van der Byl b Perks	125	– c Paynter b Wright	97
A. Melville hit wkt b Wright	78	– b Farnes	103
E. A. Rowan lbw b Perks	33	– c Edrich b Verity	0
B. Mitchell b Wright	11	– hit wkt b Verity	89
A. D. Nourse b Perks	103	– c Hutton b Farnes	25
K. Viljoen c Ames b Perks	0	– b Perks	74
E. L. Dalton c Ames b Farnes	57	– c and b Wright	21
R. E. Grieveson b Perks	75	– b Farnes	39
A. B. C. Langton c Paynter b Verity	27	– c Hammond b Farnes	6
E. S. Newson c and b Verity	1	– b Wright	3
N. Gordon not out	0	– not out	7
B 2, l-b 12, n-b 6	20	B 5, l-b 8, n-b 4	17
	530		481

Bowling: *First Innings*—Farnes 46–9–108–1; Perks 41–5–100–5; Wright 37–6–142–2; Verity 55.6–14–97–2; Hammond 14–4–34–0; Edrich 9–2–29–0. *Second Innings*—Farnes 22.1–2–74–4; Perks 32–6–99–1; Wright 32–7–146–3; Verity 40–9–87–2; Hammond 9–1–30–0; Edrich 6–1–18–0; Hutton 1–0–10–0.

England

L. Huttton run out	38	– b Mitchell	55
Mr P. A. Gibb c Grieveson b Newson	4	– b Dalton	120
E. Paynter lbw b Langton	62	– c Grieveson b Gordon	75
Mr W. R. Hammond st Grieveson b Dalton	24	– st Grieveson b Dalton	140
L. E. G. Ames c Dalton b Langton	84	– not out	17
W. J. Edrich c Rowan b Langton	1	– c Gordon b Langton	219
Mr B. H. Valentine c Grieveson b Dalton	26	– not out	4
H. Verity b Dalton	3		
D. V. P. Wright c Langton b Dalton	26		
Mr K. Farnes b Newson	20		
R. T. D. Perks not out	2		
B 7, l-b 17, w 1, n-b 1	26	B 8, l-b 12, w 1, n-b 3	24
	316		(5 wkts) 654

Bowling: *First Innings*—Newson 25.6–5–58–2; Langton 35–12–71–3; Gordon 37–7–82–0; Mitchell 7–0–20–0; Dalton 13–1–59–4. *Second Innings*—Newson 43–4–91–0; Langton 56–12–132–1; Gordon 55.2–10–174–1; Mitchell 37–4–133–1; Dalton 27–3–100–2.

pages 55–59

Notes on the 1940 Season

By R. C. Robertson-Glasgow

It is not easy to write notes on our First-Class cricket season of 1940, because no competitive First-Class cricket was played. Nearly all the

County players were occupied in some form of National Service. The war was critical. Our ally France fell; and the British forces were evacuated from Dunkirk. There are those who still think that MCC might have done more to encourage and foster the game. I cannot agree with this view. MCC had given the County Clubs the opportunity to discuss the possibility of organised cricket, and nearly all the Counties in effect decided that such a thing would be impossible.

The military crisis wiped out several matches due to have been played at Lord's, in at least two of which the standard of play would probably have been that of a Test Trial, without the insistence on individuality which often mars such a match as a spectacle. Entertainment, therefore, was left largely to private enterprise. Of teams so raised two stood out far above the others: The London Counties, of whom the originator was Mr C. J. E. Jones and the President Mr J. B. Hobbs, and the British Empire Team, gathered and directed by Mr Desmond Donnelly, with Sir Pelham Warner as President. Both these teams could and did put teams into the field of strong County standard. London Counties relied mainly on Southern professionals of established reputation. Their team sparkled with hitters and known fast scorers. Such players as Frank Woolley, Wellard, Jim Smith, Watt, Hulme, Watts, and Todd often scored runs at an almost unbelievable pace, and so gave pleasure to many County folk to whom previously these cricketers had been but names in the newspapers. Both this Club and the British Empire Team did very good work for war charities.

The British Empire players appeared always as amateurs. Besides playing very good cricket, by which they raised over £1,200 for the Red Cross Fund, they brought to the public notice at least two club cricketers of more than ordinary ability, L. F. Parslow and W. M. F. Bebbington … R. P. Nelson, the Northamptonshire captain, played seven innings for the club, heading the averages with 299 runs at 49.83 an innings. He has since been killed by enemy action, while serving as a Second Lieutenant in the Royal Marines; a source of grief to his many friends, who will remember a character of charm and sincerity. Like many quiet men, he was a determined fighter …

Essex, always enterprising, had arranged a long programme of one-day matches for 1940, but early in the summer the County was declared a Defence Area, which stopped teams from travelling into restricted parts. Six matches were played, and won; and a profit of some £60 was made in the season.

Only in the Leagues did cricket flourish with scarcely diminished strength, and the lack of County Cricket enabled many First-Class players to help various League teams. Here are some who took part: Birmingham League: R. E. S. Wyatt (Moseley); head of the batting averages with 64.5 for 516 runs, highest score 120. Howorth (Walsall); third in the batting averages with 52.84; ninth in the bowling with 60 wickets at 12.5. Merrett (Dudley);

fourth in the batting with 46.21; fourth in the bowling with 80 wickets at 11.47. His score of 197 against Smethwick is the highest individual score ever made in the First Division. His aggregate of 878 runs equals H. O. Kirton's record. Merrett's all-round performance is unrivalled in League history …

Hollies (Old Hill), heading the bowling averages with 99 wickets at 9.92 each, beat the record of Freeman (A. P.), who in 1937 took 98 wickets. Second was Perks, with 94 at 12.14. The Bradford League, too, was full of distinguished cricketers. Paynter, the Lancashire and England batsman, playing for Keighley, headed the batting averages with 1,040 runs at an average of 74.28; and on Whit Monday he set up a record for the Lackholme ground by making 150 not out against Lightcliffe. Other well-known players in the League were: Barber (Brighouse), average 59.62; Place (Keighley), 57.3; Pope (G. H.) (Lidget Green), 42.73 … Constantine (Windhill), 30.50, with an innings of 106 not out in less than an hour … In bowling, T. A. Jaques, formerly of Yorkshire County, came first with 79 wickets at 8.53 each, taking all 10 wickets for 49 against East Brierley.

In the Lancashire League all contracts with professionals for 1940 were cancelled at the outbreak of war. This, combined with some rainy Saturdays, sadly diminished the gates. Church were the champions, R. Parkin, son of the Old England cricketer, and T. Lowe bowling extremely well. League cricket is but very ordinary stuff without the "star" professionals. The gate for the match between Nelson and Burnley, keen rivals, on a fine Saturday, only came to £14. It has been known more than once to reach nearly £250. This cricket must have a showman, such as Constantine. The general standard of play, contrary to the opinion of some who have never seen it, is not high; but the entertainment is concentrated. A "star" player should not only make runs, but make them in a distinctive, even a flamboyant manner. Ordinary merit is insufficient in so very personal an atmosphere. The crowd is better pleased, and so more likely to fill the hat, if a bowler can knock stumps out rather than merely knock them back. All this, which is foreign to the temperament and the habit of the average County Cricketer, is natural in a type of game which is intended to give the greatest possible diversion and excitement in one afternoon of the week. It must sparkle if it is to rival the horses and the dogs.

Enemy action has caused occasional disturbance on well-known cricket grounds. After a night visitation on a certain South Coast ground last summer the following notice was found pinned to the gates: "Local cricketers are as pleased as you. Each peardrop which fell on this ground saved lives and property. We shall carry on. Nothing which falls from the skies will deter us, except RAIN." A good document.

As a study in finance, even satire, it is interesting to note that a few counties have actually gained through the absence of cricket. Expenses have dropped to a minimum, and a large number of subscriptions have been received. As a whole, County members, from devotion and the desire for future pleasures, have continued to subscribe in whole or in part. Mr A. J. Spelling, who is deputising for Major B. K. Castor as Essex Secretary, writes that he has received a large number of letters promising full support after the war. A thousand Hampshire members had sent their subscriptions by December 1940. From Kent, in November 1940, came the news that 1,200 members had continued to subscribe wholly or in part, and that the manager, Mr G. de L. Hough, having been turned down for active service, was successfully working a scheme for Army welfare in East Kent.

The Middlesex Club announced in December 1940 that members had been given the option of paying one guinea instead of two guineas, but those who could afford it had been asked to pay in full. In the following month the annual report showed that the Club had a credit balance of some £735, and that MCC had agreed to reduce the war-time rental from £800 to £350.

From Surrey comes news that The Oval has had its trials; but all records and pictures had been removed before these diversions began. The subscription has been reduced by half. Martin, the groundsman, retires after fifty-one years of excellent service; esteemed by all except, possibly, the bowlers!

Yorkshire arranged no inter-County cricket in 1940, but over £2,000 was raised in matches for the Red Cross Fund.

In Australia, inter-State matches have been played for charity. Don Bradman enlisted in the Australian Royal Air Force, but later was transferred to the Army School of Physical and Recreational Training. On Christmas Day 1940 he was bowled out first-ball in a match at Adelaide. We have not found that secret.

Events allowing, and of them no man can prophesy, there should be far more cricket of good quality than was possible last summer. Sir Pelham Warner has been busy on behalf of Lord's. The Royal Air Force, capable of turning out a very strong side indeed, are due to appear there four times.

And so to a close. If little has been said, little enough was done. We hope for more; much more, and soon. But first a task falls to be completed. *Delendus est hostis.*

February, 1941

page 106

Summer Football

MCC Protest to FA

In May, 1941, the President of MCC, Mr Stanley Christopherson, sent a letter to the Football Association expressing concern at the serious effect which the extension of the football season was having upon cricket, particularly upon games in the North of England and representative matches at Lord's.

The FA replied that in future every effort would be made to ensure the observance by football clubs of the condition upon which the extension was granted, i.e. football clubs to arrange matches to take place at a time which would interfere as little as possible with recognised summer sports, such as cricket.

At the beginning of each of the first two cricket seasons of the war the football season was extended by five weeks until the end of the first week in June. Just before this edition of *Wisden* went to press the football season was again prolonged – until May 31, 1942.

pages 133–134

Middlesex and Essex v Kent and Surrey

At Lord's, August 3, 4, 1942. Drawn. A splendid match, worthy of the players engaged, produced much fine cricket, sensational incidents, and a finish that compensated for the inconclusive result which came after a glorious effort to snatch victory. Trevor Bailey, the Dulwich College captain, put enthusiasm into a Bank Holiday crowd of 22,000 people – 16,693 paid for admission – by dismissing three batsmen in his first over. G. O. Allen gave way at 33 to Bailey, whose second ball beat Bennett; Ames hit 3 to the on, but the seventh delivery got Bridger leg-before and the next sent Todd's middle stump flying. Nichols, bowling Fishlock, claimed the first wicket, and by similarly dismissing Parker he made the score five wickets for 37 before Ames prevented Bailey doing the hat-trick. Carefully nursed by G. O. Allen, Bailey resumed after lunch and bowled Bedser, while Nichols accounted for more seasoned batsmen. By adding 70 in fifty minutes Holmes and Ames checked the collapse, and Evans, with a six to the on from Nichols and six fours, hit up 55 at one a minute while 77 runs were scored and two wickets fell. He and Gover, batting in admirable style, added 65 in thirty-five minutes. Evans drove splendidly and fell to a catch at mid-on, which Haig with his high reach only just grasped.

A stand of 82 by Brown and Edrich gave Middlesex and Essex the upper hand, but Pierpoint bowling fairly fast, straight and a good length, dismissed them and Denis Compton during a spell of eight overs which cost 37 runs. Nichols and Allen increased their side's advantage on Tuesday morning. The arrears of 88 were cleared off before Bennett was second out, but not until E. R. T. Holmes advanced himself in the batting order did Kent and Surrey pull the game round. Going in third wicket down, Holmes justified his policy of taking first innings by giving a superb forcing display at the critical period. The game proceeded without a tea interval, but Holmes received only moderate support until Todd, relying on defence, stayed while 85 runs came in fifty-five minutes. Having scored 114 out of 189 in an hour and threequarters Holmes declared at five minutes past five. Besides driving two consecutive balls from Peter Smith high up into the pavilion, he found the boundary nine times, mainly by drives. Middlesex and Essex were left with a hundred minutes in which to get the 190 runs required for victory.

Accurate bowling and sure fielding kept the runs to 87 when Brown was dismissed, but in Denis Compton Edrich found a partner equal to himself at the forcing game. The two England batsmen brought off every possible run, their judgment and speed between the wickets supplementing audacious stroke play. Holmes changed his pace bowlers so that none of them tired, but only an amazing catch separated the dashing batsmen. Edrich drove a half volley back knee high with tremendous force and Bedser, knocking the ball up with his left hand, caught it with his right. This third wicket put on 68 in thirty-five minutes. Leslie Compton showed the nerve required for the exciting situation, but with only five minutes left 26 runs were needed. Denis Compton hit three boundaries among other strokes, but, jumping in to drive the sixth ball of the last over, he failed in the desperate attempt and was stumped. So the match ended amidst tremendous cheering from eight thousand people, with Middlesex and Essex four runs short of victory. Besides the grand finish he gave to the match, Denis Compton distinguished himself by catching Evans brilliantly at long-on. The match produced £417 for King George's Fund for Sailors (War Fund).

Kent and Surrey

L. B. Fishlock (Surrey) b Nichols	18	– c L. Compton b Bailey	15
J. R. Bridger (Surrey) lbw b Bailey	9	– c Edrich b Sims	41
A. C. L. Bennett (Surrey) b Bailey	3	– c Smith b Allen	27
Flt-Lieut. L. E. G. Ames (Kent) c L. Compton b Allen	34	– c Brown b Bailey	22
Sgt L. J. Todd (Kent) b Bailey	0	– c Sims b Smith	17
Sgt J. F. Parker (Surrey) b Nichols	0	– not out	12
Major E. R. T. Holmes (Surrey) lbw b Nichols	39	– not out	114
Sgt T. G. Evans (Kent) c Haig b Nichols	55	– c D. Compton b Smith	17
Sgt A. V. Bedser (Surrey) b Bailey	2		
CSMI A. R. Gover (Surrey) not out	20		
Sgt F. G. Pierpoint (Surrey) b Allen	1		
B 4, l-b 3, w 4, n-b 1	12	L-b 5, w 1, n-b 6	12
	193	(6 wkts dec.)	277

Bowling: *First Innings*—Nichols 14–3–47–4; Allen 9.1–1–32–2; Bailey 7–1–36–4; Edrich 3–0–26–0; Smith 6–0–40–0. *Second Innings*—Nichols 8–1–25–0; Allen 6–0–28–1; Bailey 8–0–42–2; Edrich 6–0–24–0; Smith 8–0–62–2; Sims 12–1–58–1; Haig 5–0–26–0.

Middlesex and Essex

A. V. Avery (Essex) b Bedser	27	– lbw b Todd	15
Cpl S. M. Brown (Middlesex) c Evans b Pierpoint	58	– lbw b Pierpoint	34
Sqn Ldr W. J. Edrich (Middlesex) c Parker b Pierpoint	46	– c and b Bedser	73
Sgt-Instr. D. Compton (Middlesex) lbw b Pierpoint	10	– st Evans b Bedser	57
PC L. H. Compton (Middlesex) b Gover	33	– not out	4
Sgt-Instr. M. S. Nichols (Essex) b Bedser	51		
T. E. Bailey (Essex) b Parker	0		
Major G. O. Allen (Middlesex) c Ames b Pierpoint	29		
Lieut. P. Smith (Essex) c Todd b Bedser	11		
Capt. N. Haig (Middlesex) b Bedser	0		
J. Sims (Middlesex) not out	1		
B 7, l-b 2, n-b 6	15	B 1, n-b 2	3
	281	(4 wkts)	186

Bowling: *First Innings*—Gover 12–1–45–1; Todd 9–0–48–0; Bedser 19.7–0–72–4; Parker 8–0–31–1; Bridger 3–0–28–0; Pierpoint 10–1–42–4. *Second Innings*—Gover 7–0–54–0; Todd 4–0–23–1; Bedser 6.6–0–44–2; Parker 2–0–22–0; Pierpoint 4–0–40–1.

Umpires: G. Beet and A. Fowler.

pages 104–106

England v The Dominions

At Lord's, August 2, 3, 1943. England won by eight runs. A match remarkable for many changes of fortune and sensational incidents ended at quarter to seven in a narrow victory for England, thanks to Robertson taking the last two wickets in the only over he bowled. Robins won the toss, and

England in uneven batting displays did well enough to warrant the closure of each innings. Denis Compton and Ames checked a poor start by adding 56 and, with Holmes in good form, 71 more runs came quickly, while Bailey, exercising discreet defence, helped the Kent batsman add 112. Compton played a dashing game, but the honours belonged to Ames, who hit splendidly all round the wicket; his chief strokes during two hours forty minutes were two sixes and eleven fours.

After scoring 93 for two wickets, The Dominions collapsed so badly before Denis Compton at the practice ground end, that eight men fell for 22 runs before stumps were drawn, and when Robins in the morning decided that England, although 209 ahead, should bat again, they lost four men for 6 runs – altogether twelve consecutive wickets for 28 under conditions apparently quite favourable to batsmen. Not until Robins joined Holmes did England

England

H. Gimblett (Somerset) c Sismey b Roper	10	– b Roper	0
Capt. J. D. Robertson (Middlesex) b Constantine	33	– c Sismey b Roper	1
L Cpl L. Compton (Middlesex) b Martindale	1	– b Martindale	1
Sgt-Instr. D. Compton (Middlesex) run out	58	– c Miller b Martindale	17
Sqn Ldr L. E. G. Ames (Kent) c and b Clarke	133	– c Sismey b Martindale	13
Major E. R. T. Holmes (Surrey) c and b Clarke	39	– not out	45
Flt-Lieut. R. W. V. Robins (Middlesex) b Martindale	2	– not out	69
2nd Lieut. T. E. Bailey (Royal Marines) not out	30		
L Cpl A. W. H. Mallett (Royal Marines) lbw b Clarke	2		
Sgt T. G. Evans (Kent) b Clarke	5	– b Roper	0
B 5, l-b 5, n-b 1	11	B 3, l-b 1	4

(9 wkts dec.) 324   (6 wkts dec.) 150

Flt-Sgt A. V. Bedser (Surrey) did not bat.

Bowling: *First Innings*—Roper 9-0-51-1; Martindale 10-0-50-2; Clarke 19.7-1-89-4; Constantine 10-0-61-1; Miller 4-1-25-0; Morkel 1-0-6-0; McDonald 8-1-31-0. *Second Innings*—Roper 7-1-36-3; Martindale 9-1-28-3; Clarke 3-0-29-0; Constantine 4-0-32-0; Miller 4-1-21-0.

The Dominions

F/O D. K. Carmody (Australia) c Evans b Mallett	43	– c Ames b D. Compton	9
Lieut. C. S. Dempster (New Zealand) c Ames b Bedser	18	– b Mallett	113
Sgt K. Miller (Australia) c L. Compton b D. Compton	32	– c Evans b Bedser	2
Sgt J. Workman (Australia) c Mallett b Bedser	8	– b D. Compton	16
L. N. Constantine (West Indies) c Mallett b D. Compton	2	– c L. Compton b Bedser	21
Cdt Officer D. P. Morkel (S. Africa) lbw b D. Compton	2	– c and b Bedser	0
E. A. Martindale (West Indies) b D. Compton	4	– c D. Compton b Bedser	0
F/O S. Sismey (Australia) lbw b Bedser	0	– c Bedser b Robertson	70
P/O A. D. McDonald (Australia) lbw b D. Compton	0	– not out	9
C. B. Clarke (West Indies) c and b D. Compton	0	– b D. Compton	52
F/O A. W. Roper (Australia) not out	0	– c Bailey b Robertson	2
B 3, l-b 1, n-b 2	6	B 11, w 1, n-b 5	17

115   351

Bowling: *First Innings*—Bedser 10.6-1-33-3; Bailey 4-0-15-0; Mallett 8-1-26-1; Robins 3-0-20-0; D. Compton 8-2-15-6. *Second Innings*—Bedser 25-1-108-4; Bailey 6-1-31-0; Mallett 9-4-28-1; Robins 12-0-75-0; D. Compton 20-3-60-3; L. Compton 3-0-12-0; Holmes 1-0-14-0; Robertson 1-0-6-2.

recover, and they played such fine cricket that 106 runs came in 55 minutes. Robins, quite in his old dashing style, made the bowling the length he desired by jumping in or stepping back, and audacity brought him a six and ten fours.

The Dominions did not shirk the big task of getting 360 in roughly four hours and a half. Dempster played grandly. Workman proved such a useful opening batsman that he saw the total reach 80, and Carmody, going in second wicket down, gave such assistance that 104 were added. Third out, Dempster scored his 113 out of 187 in an hour and fifty minutes, hitting ten fours by beautiful strokes. After tea Constantine played in his own aggressive style, but from a hard drive Leslie Compton caught him with the left hand at full stretch while leaning on the pavilion rails with feet on the ground. This perfectly fair catch caused much criticism as the ball might have been over the boundary, but Constantine knew the rules and said "That is cricket." With seven out for 218, The Dominions looked well beaten, but Sismey and Clarke put on 108 and the final sensation, with two very good catches, finished the match amidst much excitement. The wicket-keeping by Sismey and Evans was always high-class. On Monday the teams were presented to the Duke of Gloucester before lunch. The exact numbers paying for admission were 23,993 on Monday and 14,217 on Tuesday. The proceeds went to the Red Cross Fund.

pages 46–47

Views and Values

By R. C. Robertson-Glasgow

While the fate of the world was being determined, English cricket was the scene of an interesting little battle, which ended in the rout of the "hustlers" and the triumph of conservatism over the heresy that progress and speed are synonymous. The defeat of the *soi-disant* progressives, with their programme of one-day and time-limited matches for first-class cricket, was a certainty so long as the issue of debate rested with the majority opinion of practicing cricketers. In truth, it was an easy victory, as their opponents for the most part consisted of a few honest, if deluded, zealots, a few showmen, always ready for any change that might bring them into the light of publicity, and a few columnists, who instinctively hammer tradition.

Cricket reform has always attracted the attention of the eccentric. Golfers rest content with an unfinished argument about the weight and size of the ball. Rugby football sometimes regurgitates an ancient question concerning the points-value of a dropped goal. Association has flirted with the notion of one referee for each half of the field. But neither code has so far proposed that a match should consist of fifteen minutes play each way.

The cricket reformers should be more honest about their aims. They talk much about improving cricket, in the same way that some talk about improving the breed of race-horses. But what they are really talking about is money. They are not considering the art and technique of the game. They speak as financiers, not craftsmen. To them "faster, faster" means "richer, richer". They believe that one-day cricket would mean more spectators. I believe it would empty the grounds as surely as the rain. A whole season of it, and there would be a clamour compared with which the sound of the reformer would be as a piccolo among a thousand cymbals.

Note that these crude plans for so many runs in an hour and so many hours for an innings are concerned entirely with the batsman. They are framed on the postulate of standard pitches, standard weather, and standard bowling. Note, too, that they attribute slow scoring to the batsman's ineptitude, never to the bowler's excellence. The "brighter cricketers", for their one-day carnivals, cannot allow for an hour in which survival with twenty runs is a far finer performance than five wickets gone for sixty. They have, literally, no time for the artistry of defence. To them a drawn match is a wasted match, no matter what skill, resource, and endurance, have gone to its achieving.

The three-day match is a thing of hope. It gives time for recovery and surprise; as in that game at Edgbaston in June of 1922, when Hampshire, after being bowled out by Howell and F. S. G. Calthorpe for 15 (Mead 6 not out!), scored 521 in the follow-on and won by 155 runs*. Besides, if cricket were to be reduced and levelled to a thing of one day only, it would lose those pleasures of old acquaintance and social entertainment that raise it above all other games which, so often, are just ninety minutes of mud and energy, a boiled face over a tea-cup or beer-mug, and a hurry for the station. Three days mean three evenings; and, as I look back, if I may, to Somerset scenes, I reflect that, without the three-evening match, I should never have seen Yorkshire's Arthur Dolphin, with his rufous face set off by a whitish apron, selling fried flat-fish in the twilight, at a whacking profit, to the citizens of Taunton; I might never have listened to Sam Woods's nightly conversation on cricket and the world, compared with which all books that have ever been written on sport are like cocoa and hot water; I should never have asked Jack Hobbs how he felt on the Monday morning after sitting out the week-end with

---

* See extract from the 1923 edition, page 38.

six runs wanted to equal W. G. Grace's 126 centuries, and he would never have answered by hooking my third ball that morning to the boundary.

pages 48–51

Cricket Under the Japs

By Major E. W. Swanton, RA

It is strange, perhaps, but true, how many of us agreed on this: that we were never so thankful for having been cricketers as we were when we were guests of the Japanese. There were periods when we could play "cricket" if our antics do not desecrate the word. There were occasions when we could lecture, and be lectured to, about it. It was a subject that filled countless hours in pitch dark huts between sundown and the moment that continued to be euphemistically known as lights-out. And it inspired many a daydream, contrived often in the most gruesome setting, whereby one combated the present by living either in the future or the past.

In the days that followed shortly on the fall of Singapore, before work for prisoners had become widely organised, there was a certain amount of play on the padangs of Changi camp that really deserved the name of cricket. It is true that one never seemed able to hit the ball very far, a fact probably attributable about equally to the sudden change to a particularly sparse diet of rice, and the conscientious labours of generations of corporals in charge of sports gear, for whom a daily oiling of the bats had clearly been a solemn, unvarying rite. These Changi bats must have reached saturation point in the early thirties, and I never found one that came up lighter than W. H. Ponsford's three pounder. However, the pitches were true – matting over concrete – and there were even such refinements as pads and gloves. After most of us had been moved to Singapore City on the first stage of the journey up to Thailand, Lieut.-Colonel A. A. Johnson, of the Suffolk Regiment, promoted some excellent matches with the Australians, whose captain was none other than B. A. Barnett; I cannot write of these from first-hand knowledge, but this was, so to speak, *Cricket de Luxe*, and our jungle cricket bore little outward relation to it.

This first of the camps on the Thai-Burma railway in which we played cricket was Wampo. Christmas Day, 1942, was our first holiday, I think, since our arrival in October, and it was perhaps the fact of our so occupying the afternoon that caused our guards to receive subsequent requests to play cricket with suspicion, as having some religious significance and being therefore good for morale. (It was always the policy to keep prisoners' morale at the lowest level compatible with their being considered able to undertake whatever work was on hand. It was no doubt on this principle that, later on, the Allied chaplains were solemnly and sternly forbidden to pray for victory!)

This particular game was notable, I remember, for what is probably the fastest hundred of all time. It was scored in about five overs by a very promising young Eurasian cricketer called Thoy, who, with graceful ease, kept hitting the tennis ball clear over the huts! Nothing, of course, could have been more popular than the victory of the Other Ranks over the Officers, but the broad lesson of the match was that the merit of any contest depends on the preservation of the balance between attack and defence. (One could not help wondering, earlier in the war, when bombs were raining down on The Oval, whether the Surrey Committee were taking the hint.) For Jungle cricket our bat, surreptitiously made by the carpenter, was obviously too big.

Our cricket for the next twelve months was confined to theory and reminiscence, but lower down the line, at the base camps of Tarsao and Chungkai, various forms of play were improvised, while still later, at Nakom Patom, the hospital camp, the technique was exploited in front of large and happy crowds of men anxious to forget the tiresomeness of dysentery, beri-beri, and malaria.

Cricket at Nakom Patom reached its climax on New Year's Day, 1945, when a fresh, and certainly hitherto unrecorded, page was written in the saga of England v Australia. The scene is not easy to put before you, but I must try. The playing area is small, perhaps sixty yards by thirty, and the batman's crease is right up against the spectators, with the pitch longways on. There are no runs behind the wicket, where many men squat in the shade of tall trees. The sides are flanked by long huts, with parallel ditches – one into the ditch, two over the hut. In fact all runs by boundaries 1, 2, 4 or 6. An additional hazard is washing hung on bamboo lines. Over the bowler's head are more trees, squaring the thing off, and in the distance a thick, high mud wall – the camp bund – on which stands a bored and sulky Korean sentry. (Over the bund no runs and out, for balls are precious.) In effect, the spectators are the boundaries, many hundreds of them taking every inch of room. The dress is fairly uniform, wooden clogs, and a scanty triangular piece of loin-cloth known (why?) as a "Jap-Happy". Only the swells wear patched and tattered shorts. The mound at long-on is an Australian preserve, their "Hill". The sun beats down, as tropical suns do, on the flat beaten earth which is the wicket. At the bowler's end is a single bamboo stump, at the other five – yes, five –

high ones. There is the hum of anticipation that you get on the first morning at Old Trafford or Trent Bridge, though there are no score cards, and no "Three penn'orth of comfort" to be bought from our old friend "Cushions".

The story of the match is very much the story of that fantastic occasion at The Oval in August 1938. Flt-Lieut. John Cocks, well known to the cricketers of Ashtead, is our Hutton; Lieut. Norman Smith, from Halifax, an even squarer, even squatter Leyland. With the regulation bat – it is two and a half inches wide and a foot shorter than normal – they play beautifully down the line of the ball, forcing the length ball past cover, squeezing the leg one square off their toes. There seems little room on the field with the eight Australian fielders poised there, but a tennis ball goes quickly off wood, the gaps are found, and there are delays while it is rescued from the swill basket, or fished out from under the hut. As the runs mount up the barracking gains in volume, and in wit at the expense of the fielders. When at last the English captain declares, the score is acknowledged to be a Thailand record.

With the Australian innings comes sensation. Captain "Fizzer" Pearson, of Sedbergh and Lincolnshire, the English fast bowler, is wearing BOOTS! No other cricketer has anything on his feet at all, the hot earth, the occasional flint being accepted as part of the game. The moral effect of these boots is tremendous. Captain Pearson bowls with shattering speed and ferocity, and as each fresh lamb arrives for the slaughter the stumps seem more vast, the bat even punier. One last defiant cheer from "the Hill" when their captain, Lieut.-Colonel E. E. Dunlop, comes in, another and bigger one from the English when his stumps go flying.

While these exciting things proceed one of the fielders anxiously asks himself whether they will brew trouble. "Should fast bowlers wear boots? Pearson's ruse condemned – where did he get those boots? ... Boots bought from camp funds: Official denial ... Board of Control's strong note ..." headlines seem to grow in size. Then he remembers gratefully that here is no press box full of slick columnists and Test captains, no microphones for the players to run to – in fact, no papers and no broadcasting. The field clears at last. As he hurries off to roll-call he thinks of a New Year's Day six years before when the bund was Table Mountain, the field was the green of Newlands, and he decides that even the South Africans who jostled their way cheerfully back into Cape Town that evening had not enjoyed their outing more than the spectators of this grotesque "Cricket Match".

There was much more "cricket" at Nakom Patom of similar sort, and not a few who came to jeer stayed on to cheer. One was reminded how hitting a moving ball demands the observance of certain principles, whatever the circumstances, while, as for bowling, I defy anyone who does not obey the cardinal rules to pitch six running to a length with a tennis ball.

Talks on Cricket were given at many camps, and there were cricket

"Quizzes" too, wherein a few so-called experts were showered with questions from all sides. These occasions were never lacking in humour, and there were generally enough Australians among the audience to give, as one might say, a bite to the thing. Sometimes the game was presented from a particular angle. Thus Len Muncer, of Middlesex, a sergeant in the Sherwood Foresters, described the life of a cricket professional, while Lieut.-Colonel D. V. Hill, of Worcestershire, showed the game from the point of view of a County captain. Admittedly in a prison camp there was not much in the way of alternative diversion. None the less the interest was wide enough and genuine enough to emphasize what a tremendously strong hold cricket has in England; a hold that among Australians is even stronger.

A few days after the Japanese surrender our camp at Kanburi began to assemble frequently for news bulletins. Emissaries, we heard, were flying hither and thither, instructions and encouragement were being relayed from Governments to POWs; the air was heavy with the most momentous happenings. Moreover, many of those present had had no news of the outside world for months, or longer; yet, no item commanded so much attention as the Test match at Manchester.

I had, by then, already taken my first walk for three and a half years as a free man. We found ourselves in a Thai village on the edge of the jungle. In the little cafe our hosts politely turned on the English programme. Yes, we were at Old Trafford, and a gentleman called Cristofani was getting a hundred. …

pages 217–218

Clifton v Tonbridge

At Lord's, July 29, 30, 1946. Tonbridge won by two runs. Reputed to be the youngest player to appear in a match at Lord's, 13-year-old Michael Cowdrey … contributed largely to the success of his side. When Tonbridge were sent in to bat on a drying pitch, Cowdrey scored one more than the runs made by his colleagues, and in the second innings raised his aggregate to 119. A right-arm spin bowler, mainly with leg-break, he proved deadly in the Clifton second innings and with Kirch, medium, supported by smart fielding, dismissed the last five Clifton batsmen for 33 runs, so snatching a victory. Exton, with length and spin, excelled as a bowler, taking 14 wickets for 125.

Tonbridge

D. S. Kemp lbw b Exton	25	– st Lindsay b Exton	44
G. Bowler b Exton	28	– b Exton	0
M. C. Cowdrey c Lindsay b Exton	75	– c Lindsay b Exton	44
D. K. Horton c Green b Penny	3	– st Lindsay b Bird	51
J. Wrightson c Lindsay b Penny	0	– c Ritchie b Exton	1
G. McNicol c Penny b Exton	0	– c Lindsay b Ritchie	6
A. J. Turk b Penny	0	– c Bishop b Exton	8
M. J. Bickmore c Lindsay b Penny	16	– b Exton	0
J. D. Bickmore c Bishop b Exton	1	– not out	10
J. F. MacMillan b Exton	1	– b Exton	2
P. N. Kirch not out	0	– b Exton	1
B 2, l-b 2, w 3	7	B 5, l-b 3	8
	156		175

Bowling: Ritchie 0 for 14 and 1 for 36; Exton 6 for 64 and 8 for 61; Dickinson 0 for 21 and 0 for 39; Bird 0 for 18 and 1 for 15; Penny 4 for 32 and 0 for 16.

Clifton

T. S. Penny c Cowdrey b MacMillan	25	– absent	
P. M. Crawford c MacMillan b M. J. Bickmore	57	– st Wrightson b Cowdrey	17
M. L. Green c Wrightson b Cowdrey	56	– st Wrightson b Cowdrey	6
R. N. Exton b M. J. Bickmore	9	– st Wrightson b Cowdrey	28
M. F. Bishop not out	44	– not out	45
R. K. Green c Turk b Cowdrey	0	– b M. J. Bickmore	1
D. B. Bird b Cowdrey	5	– lbw b Cowdrey	2
D. C. Dickinson b Kirch	8	– b Kirch	8
R. A. M. Whyte b Kirch	0	– b Kirch	0
I. V. Ritchie b Kirch	0	– c Horton b Cowdrey	0
R. T. M. Lindsay b Kirch	0	– b Kirch	0
B 7, l-b 1, w 2	10	B 6, w 2	8
	214		115

Bowling: Kirch 4 for 20 and 3 for 21; MacMillan 1 for 41 and 0 for 7; M. J. Bickmore 2 for 26 and 1 for 20; Cowdrey 3 for 58 and 5 for 59; Bowler 0 for 33; McNichol 0 for 26.

pages 45–48

The 1947 season was dominated by the remarkable feats of two charismatic cricketers for Middlesex and England.

Compton and Edrich

By R. C. Robertson-Glasgow

They go together in English cricket, as Gilbert and Sullivan go together in English opera. Nor is the analogy so careless as you might suppose. It may be allowable that each or any of these four has been surpassed as executant in his own sphere; that would develop an argument to make any Paper Controller clutch his scanty reserves. But it should not be doubted that, in the art of giving pleasure to an English audience, both pairs lack rival.

In cricket of the first class both D. C. S. Compton and W. J. Edrich have, Providence favouring, at least ten years to go of play and struggle and alliance. As a pair they have yet, at the hour of writing, to quell the fiercest Test attack, in the sense that Hobbs and Sutcliffe quelled it; or as Bradman and Ponsford lorded it over English bowlers here in 1934. In summer, 1947, they scored between them over 2,000 runs against South Africa. To Tuckett and his fellow bowlers, Compton and Edrich became the daily task and, maybe, the nightly vision. In the matter of Australia, fulfilment is awaited.

But, in that territory which lies outside the microcosm of numerals, already they are kings; benevolent kings appointed and acclaimed by like-minded subjects, champions in the fight against dullness and the commercial standard. In their cricket, it is what they are that matters far more than what they have done. They stand, in these eyes at least, for something which has no place prepared in the books of score and record. They are the mirror of hope and freedom and gaiety; heroic in the manner of the heroes of school stories; the inspiration, and quarry, of the young, because, in a game that threatens to become old in the saddest sense, they do not outgrow the habit, the ideals, the very mistakes of youth.

Most cricketers enjoy doing well, though I could name great ones who had a queer way of showing their enjoyment. But Compton and Edrich are of that happy philosophy which keeps failure in its place by laughter, like boys who fall on an ice-slide and rush back to try it again. They give the impression, whether batting, bowling or fielding, that they are glad enough merely to be cricketing for Middlesex or England – "Fate cannot harm me, I have played today." And they seem to be playing not only in front of us and for us, but almost literally with us. Their cricket is communicative. We are almost out of breath at the end of an over by Edrich. We scratch our heads perplexedly at a googly from Compton which refuses to work. We smile with something near to self-satisfaction when, with easy vehemence, he persuades a length-ball from the leg stump to the extra-cover boundary.

That such players should break records is inevitable rather than relevant. Numbers can be such silly things. They excite many and prove nothing, or nothing that matters. Sinatra has had more listeners than Caruso, Clark Gable more letters of homage than Sir Henry Irving. But *homo*, however *sapiens*, cannot feed on artistry alone, and, in cricket, the record-hunt inspires us with as pleasing an insanity as ever took John Peel from the first view-halloo to a death in the morning.

In summer, 1947, records made by the great Surrey and England pair,

T. Hayward and J. B. Hobbs, were knocked down. Compton's 18 centuries in a season beat Hobbs's 16 centuries in a season of twenty-two years before; his 3,816 aggregate beat Hayward's 3,518 scored in 1906. And Hayward was also beaten by Edrich with 3,539. Very well done, too. But let us not therefrom deduce comparisons of skill; for, if we were to try anything in this line, we should have to bring up the subject of modern and ancient bowling, and that would lead us not only far from our brief but also to an inescapable, if unpalatable, conclusion. Let us, rather, flatter by inconclusiveness, and meditate on the analogy that Blackpool with 2,000,000 holiday-makers would not necessarily be an improvement upon Blackpool with 1,468,749.

Touching upon this question of records, I received at the end of summer, 1947, a letter from an Australian, a friend of cricket and of mine. "As one of Compton's admirers," he wrote, "and doubtless all who see or meet him get that way, I hardly expected him to score 18 hundreds in a season. I thought him too good a player for that sort of thing. Am I right in assuming that Denis played his usual cricket and the 18 hundreds just happened in the process?" Well, my Sydney friend *is* right, or very nearly.

Compton cannot help it. He has the habit of batting, as the sun has the habit of journeying from east to west; and the fielders are his satellites. Hardest-worked of them, and most perplexed, is cover-point. Other batsmen of our time have been severer on the stroke. Walter Hammond could leave the nimblest cover motionless or just flickering as by token, could use cover's toe caps as an echoing junction for the boundary; but Compton uses cover-point as a game within a game, tantalises him with delayed direction and vexes him with variety. He is for ever seeking fresh by-products of the

D. C. S. COMPTON IN 1947

Batting

	Tests	Other First-Class Matches	Totals	Runs v South Africa	100s
May	—	832	832	303	3
June	436	157	593	436	2
July	151	495	646	151	4
August	166	1,029	1,195	166	7
September	—	550	550	131	2
Totals	753	3,063	3,816	1,187	18

Bowling

	Tests				Other First-Class Matches				Totals			
	O	M	R	W	O	M	R	W	O	M	R	W
May	—	—	—	—	38	7	111	4	38	7	111	4
June	58	22	98	4	67	20	159	11	125	42	257	15
July	30	3	104	1	100.2	9	357	16	130.2	12	461	17
August	15	4	61	0	253.2	47	862	28	268.2	51	923	28
September	—	—	—	—	74	6	301	9	74	6	301	9
Totals	103	29	263	5	532.4	89	1,790	68	635.4	118	2,053	73

old forward stroke and has not yet, I fancy, come to the end of experiment. He finds it so amusing and so profitable. He outruns the traditional and discovers new truth. Compton is the axiom of tomorrow.

They say his feet are wrong. So, once, were Whistler's hands. They turn up the diagrams and manuals and grumble about the direction of his left leg. But why legs and feet only? I saw him, last summer at Lord's, playing strokes to Kent's Douglas Wright, when his body went one way, his arms the other way, and the ball the same way, past the fielders. It was genius; also contortionism. Dan Leno should have been batting at the other end, Nervo and Knox should have been in the umpires' coats, and Cinquevalli in the scorers' hutch. But, praise be, Compton has limitations, or pretends to have them. He uses the straight and near-straight drive less than most masters. Perhaps such strokes are too obvious; too easy, almost. They interfere with the jokes he hurls round cover-point. Again, he has a playful weakness for the short-arm sweep of the slow leg-break towards square leg and long leg, leading the bowler on to not always frustrated hope of timing error from inconsistency of bounce.

Compton has genius, and, if he knows it, he doesn't care. Edrich has talent; or, more truly, he started with a number of talents and has increased them into riches. Compton, in essence, has not altered from the lad of just eighteen who scored 100 not out at Northampton in 1936 while numbers ten and eleven, Sims and Peebles, admired and defended at the other end. His whereabouts in artistry cannot be doubted. His effect silences question. But Edrich has, as they say, gone through it. He rose, half fell, and rose again, to a place higher and less slippery. The cost and the lesson are expressed in his concentration. With bat and ball he is an all-in cricketer; no funny stuff here;

W. J. EDRICH IN 1947

Batting

	Tests	Other First-Class Matches	Totals	Runs v South Africa	100s
May	—	758	758	200	4
June	296	257	553	296	2
July	256	791	1,047	256	3
August	—	735	735	—	2
September	—	446	446	118	1
Totals	552	2,987	3,539	870	12

Bowling

	Tests				Other First-Class Matches				Totals			
	O	M	R	W	O	M	R	W	O	M	R	W
May	—	—	—	—	191.1	40	519	33	191.1	40	519	33
June	46	14	117	4	84	12	200	6	130	26	317	10
July	88.5	19	253	12	97	13	287	8	185.5	32	540	20
August	—	—	—	—	55.5	12	137	4	55.5	12	137	4
September	—	—	—	—	—	—	—	—	—	—	—	—
Totals	134.5	33	370	16	428	77	1,143	51	562.5	110	1,513	67

no holidays of mind or body. Compton is poetry; Edrich is prose, robust and clear. Far more than Compton, Edrich uses the practical and old-fashioned methods and areas of attack. He likes the straight hit, and that pull-drive which gave old E. M. Grace so many runs and "W. G." so many moments of reflective beard-stroking. Old-fashioned, too, is Edrich's high back-lift in preparation for stroke. He gives the idea of a height and a reach beyond fact. But also he is a hooker, nearly as vicious as his great forerunner, Pat Hendren.

In bowling, though Compton uses the left arm and Edrich the right, they are alike in improvement by use. Edrich began as a muscular slinger, as a but moderate advance on village heroics; then he grew into knowledge of swerve and variety. He is never done with. Others of his kind blaze away for an hour or two, then die into ashes or a mere harmless flicker; but Edrich, near the end of an else fruitless day, flies flat into the attack and unlooses the unanswerable ball. Compton's slow left-hand bowling has about it a certain casual humour. He brings unrehearsed jokes on to the legitimate stage. He can bowl in a Test as if he were trying things out on a friend in the nets. He is still among the joys and errors of experiment. Anything may yet happen.

Both are magnificent fielders and throwers. Edrich has been allotted specialist work in the slips; Compton more often ranges the boundaries, where he may join, for moments of leisure, in that talk which is the salt and salad of cricket.

Both are fitting adornments and exponents of a game that was meant not as an imitation of, but as a refreshment from, the worldly struggle.

pages 221–222

Dubbed "The Invincibles", the Australians who toured England in 1948 are widely regarded as the finest Test team of all time. Under the leadership of Don Bradman, who retired at the end of the tour, they set many records and left lasting memories.

Essex v Australians

At Southend, May 15, 17, 1948. Australians won by an innings and 451 runs. In light-hearted vein, they made history by putting together the highest total scored in a day of six hours in first-class cricket.* Bradman led the run-getting revel on the Saturday. Complete master of the Essex bowlers on a fast pitch, he scored 187 in two hours five minutes, and by a wide variety of orthodox and unorthodox strokes hit thirty-two fours and a five. Brown's 153 occupied three hours and contained seventeen fours. Loxton (fourteen fours and a six) and Saggers (nine fours) also scored centuries. The biggest partnerships were 219 in ninety minutes between Brown and Bradman for the second wicket, 166 in sixty-five minutes by Loxton and Saggers for the sixth, and 145 in ninety-five minutes between Barnes and Brown for the first. Bailey dismissed Brown and Miller with successive balls, but generally the bowlers failed to stem the scoring. Because of injury Bailey did not bat in either innings. Essex, dismissed twice on Monday, first failed against the pace of Miller and the cleverly varied left-arm deliveries of Toshack; then in the follow-on – apart from Pearce and P. Smith, who made a stand of 133 – they broke down in face of Johnson's off-spinners. The attendance and receipts – 32,000 and £3,482 – were ground records.

Australians

S. G. Barnes hit wkt b R. Smith	79	I. W. Johnson st Rist b P. Smith	9	
W. A. Brown c Horsfall b Bailey	153	D. Ring c Vigar b P. Smith	1	
D. G. Bradman b P. Smith	187	W. A. Johnston b Vigar	9	
K. R. Miller b Bailey	0	E. R. H. Toshack c Vigar b P. Smith	4	
R. A. Hamence c P. Smith b R. Smith	46	B 7, n-b 2	9	
S. J. Loxton c Rist b Vigar	120			
R. A. Saggers not out	104		**721**	

Bowling: Bailey 21–1–128–2; R. Smith 37–2–169–2; P. Smith 38–0–193–4; Price 20–0–156–0; Vigar 13–1–66–2.

Essex

T. C. Dodds c Ring b Miller	0	– b Toshack	16	
S. J. Cray b Miller	5	– b Johnson	15	
A. V. Avery b Johnston	10	– c Brown b Johnson	3	
F. H. Vigar c Saggers b Miller	0	– c Johnson b Toshack	0	
R. Horsfall b Toshack	11	– b Johnson	8	
T. N. Pearce c Miller b Toshack	8	– c and b Johnson	71	
R. Smith c Barnes b Toshack	25	– c Ring b Johnson	0	
T. P. B. Smith b Toshack	3	– lbw b Barnes	54	
F. Rist c Barnes b Toshack	8	– b Johnson	1	
E. Price not out	4	– not out	4	
T. E. Bailey absent hurt		– absent hurt		
B 2, l-b 6, n-b 1	9	B 6, l-b 3, n-b 6	15	
	83		**187**	

Bowling: *First Innings*—Miller 8–3–14–3; Johnston 7–1–10–1; Toshack 10.5–0–31–5; Ring 11–4–19–0. *Second Innings*—Miller 10–4–26–0; Toshack 17–2–50–2; Ring 7–3–16–0; Loxton 12–3–28–0; Johnson 21–6–37–6; Barnes 9.4–5–11–1.

Umpires: W. H. Ashdown and D. Hendren.

---

* *The Australians' innings of 721 was completed on the first day, stumps being drawn when the last wicket fell. Essex were the only county to bowl out the 1948 tourists, and at the end of the century 721 remained the most runs scored in a day in a first-class match.*

page 971

*Although some earlier editions had included a cricket bibliography,
the 1950* Wisden *was the first to carry book reviews,
with John Arlott appointed the Almanack's first book reviewer –
a role he continued to fulfil in most editions until his death in 1991.
This is his introduction to the first book review section.*

Cricket Books, 1949

By John Arlott

One might have expected a small output of cricket books in 1949 after the
spate which greeted the Australians in 1948. More than seventy books dated
1949, however, stand before me.

The major problem facing the critic in his assessment of these books
lies in their being directed to different sections of the public and, hence,
having no common denominator of style, aim or method. This rules out all
but the most limited comparative criticism and, simultaneously, demands a
statement of the critical standard to be applied. *Wisden* is largely published
for those interested in cricket and who, we may assume, will be to some
extent sympathetic to almost *any* book on the game. For these readers, a
cricket book must be accurate in its technical and statistical content. Indeed,
such accuracy is an obvious prerequisite of the records and reports which
every game has – as its original chronicles. But cricket has more: it has
produced a body of minor but genuine art which is a vital ingredient in the
unique character of the game.

It is this cultural and imaginative characteristic which gives cricket its
high standing even in the eyes of those who do not value the game as such.
Therefore, those of us who are jealous for the reputation of cricket must be
concerned for the preservation of its creative quality in its books, the
medium where it has most often manifested itself. On the other hand, to
demand of every book on cricket – or, indeed, on any other subject – that it
should be a work of art in its own right, is absurd. Moreover, any balanced
cricket library must contain a considerable body of works whose main bias
is technical, statistical or documentary.

Specialist criticism, of cricket books for cricketers, must resolve upon a balance between technical and literary merits. It seems a first requirement of a book on cricket that it should be accurate and should be presented in an orderly and literate manner. However, those few great books on cricket entitled to the name of literature have gone further: although they may have aimed no higher than our basic requirement, the vital fusion between craftsmanship and experience which is called "art" has taken place within them. The books which achieve this fusion must be given recognition, for, not only do they win respect for their subject, but their quality will outlive their subject-matter.

page 128

1950
The Centenary of
John Wisden & Co Ltd

It seems natural that a message of goodwill to the firm on its centenary from the Prime Minister should have its counterpart in a similar message from the Australian Prime Minister. "Wisden and cricket are synonymous," said Mr Menzies. So it seemed to Mr Oliver Lyttelton, who presided at the firm's centenary luncheon and introduced the principal guest, Mr Harold Wilson, President of the Board of Trade. He, too, appeared to share the same opinion. The many great performers at the game, past and present, who rose to toast the memory of the firm's celebrated founder, at the bidding of that doyen of cricketers, Sir "Plum" Warner, bore witness to the accuracy of Mr Menzies' words.

"Wisden and cricket are synonymous." Let this message from Australia be the tribute of the whole British Commonwealth at once to a famous cricketer, to the great enterprise which he founded, and to the game of cricket wherever it is played.

page 638–639

England v The Rest

Test Trial

At Bradford, May 31, June 1, 1950. England won by an innings and 89 runs. One of the most remarkable representative matches on record finished before lunch on the second day. Such was the mastery of the bowlers on drying turf that in seven hours and fifty minutes of playing time thirty wickets fell for 369 runs, of which Hutton made nearly one quarter. Although the desperate struggle for runs provided keen interest for spectators, the selectors could have learned little not already known to them. Yardley put in The Rest on winning the toss, and the off-breaks of Laker caused so complete a rout that in 110 minutes they were all out for the lowest total in a match of representative class. The previous smallest score was 30, made by South Africa against England at Port Elizabeth in 1896 and at Edgbaston 1924. On the ground, five miles from his birthplace, on which he had enjoyed many League triumphs for Saltaire, Laker dominated the scene. He took two wickets in his first over and a third before conceding a run; in his fifth over he dismissed four more men before being edged for a second single, and he brilliantly caught and bowled the last man. His full analysis was: 14 overs, 12 maidens, 2 runs, 8 wickets. He spun the ball skilfully, his length was immaculate and his direction perfect. The young batsmen opposed to Laker did not possess the ripe experience needed to cope with his skill under conditions so suited to his bowling. England obtained a lead of 202, chiefly through superlative batting by Hutton, ably assisted by Edrich, against bowling of moderate quality apart from that of Berry, the left-hander, and Jenkins with leg-spin. Berry did not lose accuracy even when Hutton used every possible means to knock him off his length. Hutton, who made 85 out of 155 in two hours, gave a dazzling display of batsmanship on a difficult pitch. Laker again met with early success in The Rest second innings; but Hollies caused chief damage. He turned the ball sharply and varied flight and pace well. Eric Bedser and Spooner made 42 in the only stand. On the sporting Bradford turf the Australians in 1948 and the West Indies earlier in 1950 also were made to look very ordinary.

The Rest

D. J. Kenyon c Evans b Laker	7	– lbw b Hollies	9
D. S. Sheppard lbw b Bailey	4	– b Laker	3
G. H. G. Doggart c Bailey b Laker	2	– st Evans b Hollies	12
P. B. H. May c Hutton b Laker	0	– b Laker	2
D. B. Carr c Bailey b Laker	0	– st Evans b Hollies	2
E. A. Bedser lbw b Laker	3	– c Evans b Hollies	30
R. T. Spooner b Laker	0	– c Yardley b Bedser	22
R. O. Jenkins not out	0	– c Bedser b Hollies	3
R. Berry b Laker	0	– c Yardley b Bedser	16
F. S. Trueman st Evans b Bedser	1	– not out	0
L. Jackson c and b Laker	5	– st Evans b Hollies	1
B 3, l-b 1, w 1	5	B 4, l-b 6, n-b 3	13
	—		—
	27		113

Bowling: *First Innings*—Bailey 6–4–3–1; Bedser 9–3–12–1; Laker 14–12–2–8; Hollies 7–5–5–0. *Second Innings*—Bailey 5–2–6–0; Bedser 9–2–22–2; Laker 18–4–44–2; Hollies 22.4–13–28–6.

England

L. Hutton b Trueman	85	T. G. Evans run out		1
R. T. Simpson st Spooner b Berry	26	J. C. Laker not out		6
W. J. Edrich lbw b Jenkins	46	A. V. Bedser c Jackson b Jenkins		5
J. D. Robertson c Sheppard b Berry	0	W. E. Hollies st Spooner b Berry		4
J. G. Dewes c Doggart b Berry	34	L-b 1, n-b 1		2
N. W. D. Yardley c Trueman b Jenkins	13			—
T. E. Bailey c Spooner b Berry	7			229

Bowling: Jackson 12–3–38–0; Bedser 13–0–60–0; Jenkins 10–0–38–3; Berry 32–10–73–5; Trueman 9–3–18–1.

Umpires: W. H. Ashdown and H. Elliott.

page 99

The new editor, Norman Preston, concluded his first set of Notes by remembering cricket's most distinguished hat-trick.

Death of King George VI

The sudden death in February of King George VI left its gap in cricket as in most other spheres. He was Patron of the Marylebone, Surrey and Lancashire clubs and always received a great welcome at cricket grounds. In his younger days, when Prince Albert, he was a left-handed batsman and bowler of no small ability. There is a ball mounted in the messroom of the Royal Naval College, Dartmouth, commemorating his feat of performing the hat-trick on the private ground at Windsor Castle, where he once bowled King Edward VII, King George V and the present Duke of Windsor with consecutive balls.

pages 829–831

Twenty-one years after West Indies' first Test tour of Australia, they returned to play only the second series between the two countries. In Wisden's review of the tour (1953 edition, page 813) it was noted that "Advance speculation described the visit of West Indies to Australia in 1951-52 as a tour designed to decide the unofficial 'cricket championship of the world'."

Australia v West Indies

Fourth Test Match

At Melbourne, December 31, 1951, January 1, 2, 3, 4, 1952. Australia won by one wicket. No more exciting finish could be imagined than that in which Australia made sure of winning the series and West Indies lost the chance of drawing level at two games each, with the rubber depending upon the final game. Hard though they had fought, the Australians seemed doomed to defeat when their ninth wicket fell in the final innings with 38 runs still needed for victory. Then the two bowlers, Ring and Johnston, defied all the efforts of the West Indies to dislodge them and hit off the runs amid mounting tension. Johnston played a comparatively passive role while Ring hit vigorously, gaining a series of boundaries by lofty drives which may have resulted in catches had the field been set deep enough for this known hitter. Although Ring earned most of the credit, Johnston also played a gallant part and it was fitting that he made the winning hit, a stroke to leg.

A courageous century by Worrell retrieved a bad start by West Indies on the first day when, on a pitch which showed early life, the touring team lost three wickets for 30 runs. During this dangerous period Worrell received a severe blow on the right hand from a ball by Miller, and he batted for the rest of his innings in considerable pain, accentuated by further blows from the ball. Despite this handicap, Worrell showed admirable concentration and in making 108 in three and threequarter hours he hit six fours. During the later stages of his innings he played almost one-handed.

Apart from Worrell, the West Indies batsmen showed lack of judgment, and Christiani and Trim both made the mistake of taking risks in running with such a brilliant fieldsman as Harvey in possession of the ball. Miller took full advantage of a pitch which always gave some help to the pace bowlers, and when Australia batted Trim, too, found conditions to his liking. Three men were out for 49, but once more Miller proved a stumbling-block. Content to play the passive role as partner to the aggressive left-hander Harvey, Miller took part in a fourth-wicket stand of 124, before Trim with the new ball rounded off the innings. Using his feet splendidly, especially to Ramadhin, Harvey hit fifteen fours in a most attractive innings.

Leading by 56, West Indies lost most of their advantage as soon as they began their second innings. Goddard sent in Guillen to open the innings

West Indies

K. Rickards b Miller	15	– lbw b Johnston	22
J. B. Stollmeyer c Langley b Miller	7	– lbw b Miller	54
F. M. Worrell b Lindwall	108	– b Johnston	30
E. D. Weekes c Johnson b Johnston	1	– lbw b Johnson	2
G. E. Gomez c Langley b Miller	37	– b Johnston	52
R. J. Christiani run out	37	– b Miller	33
J. D. Goddard b Miller	21	– lbw b Lindwall	0
S. Guillen not out	22	– c Johnston b Lindwall	0
J. Trim run out	0	– run out	0
S. Ramadhin c Langley b Johnston	1	– run out	0
A. L. Valentine c Lindwall b Miller	14	– not out	1
B 2, l-b 6, w 1	9	B 4, l-b 5	9

1/16 2/29 3/30 4/102 5/194   272   1/0 2/0 3/53 4/60 5/97   203
6/221 7/237 8/242 9/248   6/128 7/190 8/194 9/194

Bowling: *First Innings*—Lindwall 18–2–72–1; Miller 19.3–1–60–5; Johnston 20–1–59–2; Ring 9–0–43–0; Johnson 7–0–23–0; Hole 2–0–6–0. *Second Innings*—Lindwall 17–2–59–2; Miller 16–1–49–2; Johnston 14–2–51–3; Ring 7–1–17–0; Johnson 5–1–18–1.

Australia

J. Moroney lbw b Ramadhin	26	– lbw b Ramadhin	5
A. R. Morris b Trim	6	– lbw b Valentine	12
A. L. Hassett run out	15	– lbw b Valentine	102
R. N. Harvey c and b Ramadhin	83	– b Valentine	33
K. R. Miller b Trim	47	– hit wkt b Valentine	2
G. Hole b Valentine	2	– c Gomez b Worrell	13
R. R. Lindwall lbw b Trim	13	– c Guillen b Ramadhin	29
I. W. Johnson c Guillen b Trim	1	– c Guillen b Ramadhin	6
D. Ring b Trim	6	– not out	32
G. Langley not out	0	– lbw b Valentine	1
W. A. Johnston b Gomez	1	– not out	7
B 12, l-b 4	16	B 14, l-b 4	18

1/17 2/48 3/49 4/173 5/176   216   1/27 2/93 3/106 4/109   (9 wkts) 260
6/208 7/209 8/210 9/215   5/147 6/192 7/218 8/218 9/222

Bowling: *First Innings*—Trim 12–2–34–5; Gomez 13.3–7–25–1; Valentine 23–8–50–1; Ramadhin 17–4–63–2; Goddard 8–0–28–0. *Second Innings*—Trim 10–3–25–0; Gomez 9–1–18–0; Valentine 30–9–88–5; Ramadhin 39–15–93–3; Worrell 9–1–18–1.

with Stollmeyer and followed himself, but Lindwall claimed both Guillen and Goddard in the first over without a run made. On the third day West Indies batted gallantly. Stollmeyer displayed his customary grace, Gomez defended doggedly, and Worrell, well down the order, gave another display of one-handed courage of great value to his side. The final day produced a tense struggle of ever-mounting excitement. Valentine and Ramadhin found the pitch responsive to spin, but Hassett, the Australian captain, batted magnificently. Defending with the greatest determination and patience for over five hours, he was always ready to punish the loose ball. Hassett received good assistance from Harvey and Lindwall, but when he was out the game seemed to be safely in West Indies' hands until the gallant last-wicket stand.

pages 541–542

Surrey v Warwickshire

At The Oval, May 16, 1953. Surrey won by an innings and 49 runs. Members rose as one when the triumphant Surrey team walked from the field having begun their Championship programme with victory in a day. The last and only time that a first-class match had been completed in one day at The Oval was in 1857. Special applause was accorded to A. Bedser who took twelve wickets for 35 runs, and Laker, who performed the hat-trick. Bedser bowled magnificently when play commenced at noon. Unable to obtain a proper foothold on the wet turf, he attacked the leg stump at below normal pace, and, helped by fine catches, he equalled his previous best analysis of eight for 18. Surrey also found the pitch treacherous, but, chiefly through a sound innings by Constable, they took the lead with only two wickets down. The score then went from 50 for two to 81 for seven, and only the aggressiveness of Surridge, who hit three sixes in four balls from Hollies, Laker and Lock enabled them to gain a substantial lead. Lock became the second highest scorer before a blow above the right eye led to a visit to hospital and his retirement from the game. Laker was called into the attack for the first time when Warwickshire batted again and he began the final rout by achieving the first hat-trick of the season. Warwickshire, batting for ten minutes of the extra half hour, were all out in seventy minutes, five minutes less than in their first innings. No Warwickshire batsman was bowled during a day in which 29 wickets fell for 243 runs – a fact that emphasised Surrey's excellent fielding.

Warwickshire

F. C. Gardner c Laker b A. Bedser	7	– c Laker b A. Bedser	7
T. W. Cartwright lbw b A. Bedser	0	– lbw b Laker	9
Don Taylor c Fletcher b A. Bedser	0	– lbw b A. Bedser	20
R. T. Spooner c Whittaker b A. Bedser	16	– c and b Laker	0
H. E. Dollery c Lock b A. Bedser	8	– c Surridge b Laker	0
R. E. Hitchcock c Whittaker b Lock	3	– c A. Bedser b Laker	0
A. Townsend c McIntyre b Lock	7	– run out	0
R. Weeks not out	0	– c Surridge b A. Bedser	0
C. W. Grove c Fletcher b A. Bedser	3	– c Constable b Laker	10
K. R. Dollery c Brazier b A. Bedser	0	– not out	0
W. E. Hollies c Laker b A. Bedser	0	– c sub b A. Bedser	0
L-b 1	1	B 2, l-b 3, n-b 1	6

1/3 2/3 3/8 4/27 5/30   45   1/20 2/22 3/26 4/26 5/26   52
6/36 7/42 8/45 9/45   6/32 7/32 8/49 9/52

Bowling: *First Innings*—A. Bedser 13.5–4–18–8; Surridge 6–1–17–0; Lock 7–2–9–2. *Second Innings*—A. Bedser 13.4–7–17–4; Laker 13–6–29–5..

Surrey

E. A. Bedser b K. Dollery	5	W. S. Surridge b Grove	19
D. G. W. Fletcher c Townsend b Weeks	13	A. V. Bedser not out	5
B. Constable c Grove b K. Dollery	37	G. A. R. Lock retired hurt	27
T. H. Clark c K. Dollery b Hollies	2		
A. F. Brazier c Townsend b Hollies	6	L-b 4, n-b 1	5
G. J. Whittaker b K. Dollery	0		
A. J. McIntyre c and b K. Dollery	9	1/5 2/27 3/50 4/61 5/65	146
J. C. Laker c H. Dollery b Hollies	18	6/77 7/81 8/108 9/119	

Bowling: Grove 10.1–3–29–1; K. Dollery 11–4–40–4; Weeks 8–1–24–1; Hollies 10–4–48–3.

Umpires: E. Cooke and L. Gray.

pages 215–217

Pakistan in England, 1954

In the cricket history of Pakistan the date, Tuesday, August 17, [1954] will live long. On that day at Kennington Oval, Pakistan became the only side to win a Test match on a first visit to England. This victory also enabled them to share the rubber, for each side won one game with the other two left drawn.

Before the tour started no one could have imagined such an outcome to the Test series. Pakistan arrived in England virtually an unknown team and the strength of their extremely young side was estimated to be no better than average county standard. Following the strenuous and closely-fought games with Australia the previous summer, England were not expected to be seriously extended. In actual fact, until the final Test, they were not. In at least two of the first three games England were vastly superior, but except at Nottingham, where they won by an innings and 129 runs, the weather prevented them gaining the success their cricket deserved.

The Pakistan players were the first to admit that they were fortunate to share the rubber, but few people would deny that they won The Oval Test on merit. For England, humiliating though it was at the time, defeat really meant little, but for Pakistan the win had far-reaching effects. It was estimated that interest in the game in that country would be doubled and that thousands of youngsters, inspired by the unexpected result, would become active cricketers. The outcome of this may well be seen when Pakistan next tour England in 1962.

The players were also splendid ambassadors. Rarely has a more popular set of cricketers toured anywhere, and wherever they went they made a host of friends by their modest charm and obvious eagerness to learn. It would be wrong to suggest that they were a particularly talented team, but for all their limitations they lost only three matches, one to England, another to Yorkshire, and the third against a powerful combined side in the final match at Scarborough. Nine victories in first-class matches included that in the fourth Test match, one against Canada and five against counties. The other eighteen games were drawn.

To achieve such a record in a season entirely unsuited to their style of cricket reflected great credit on the side. In match after match they were forced to play on soft, slow turf, generally in cold, depressing weather. The majority of the players were used to matting pitches and warm sunshine, but in most cases batsmen and bowlers adapted themselves well to the changes. One or two of the team, notably Fazal Mahmood and Hanif Mohammad, showed themselves to be in world class and several others displayed plenty of ability. Unfortunately there were not enough top-grade cricketers on whom to call and a few of the party, hard as they tried, scarcely came up to county standard. Thus A. H. Kardar, the captain, and his fellow selectors on the tour found it hard to give everyone an equal share of matches. The need to maintain a well-balanced side meant that the leading players were called upon for practically every game. In a party comprising seventeen besides Khan Mohammad, the Lancashire League cricketer who appeared occasionally, this meant that others spent long spells of inactivity, but it says much for their team spirit that at no time did they show the slightest resentment …

The side proved consistent in batting and steady in bowling, but with plenty of scope for improvement in the field. The catching and groundwork were often weak, though on some occasions appearing quite respectable …

Fazal, the vice-captain, even apart from his magnificent twelve wickets for 99 which played such a vital part in the victory over England, revealed the attributes of a great bowler. Noted for stamina, Fazal was called upon for a tremendous amount of work in the early part of the tour and it was not surprising that he broke down. Following the match with Nottinghamshire on June 19, 21, 22 in which he took eleven wickets, Fazal bowled only in two Test matches during the next month. Neither did he bowl in the last four games. For all that he took most wickets on the tour and he headed the averages with 77 for 17.53. Fazal, undoubtedly one of the big personalities of the season, became the first Pakistan player to find inclusion among *Wisden's* Five Cricketers of the Year …

The brothers Wazir and Hanif Mohammad finished first and second in the batting averages, but Hanif was by far the best batsman in the party. At first almost purely defensive, he later blossomed into a most attractive opening batsman, bringing off delightful all-round strokes with a power his slight build belied. He made nearly 300 more runs than anyone else on the tour. Wazir broke a finger in his second innings, but recovered splendidly and became a valuable middle-of-the-order batsman, with determination and strong defence which proved very necessary when too many batsmen threw away their wickets by recklessness …

Kardar's knowledge of English players and conditions, learned while at Oxford and with Warwickshire, served him well as captain. He made few mistakes and led the side in a quiet, orthodox manner. Fida Hussain, the manager, and Salah-ud-Din, his assistant, also played important roles in the success of the tour. Despite the bad weather, the Pakistanis took back a fair profit and they left behind them happy memories.

pages 858–860

Having retained the Ashes with a 3–1 Test series win in Australia, England concluded their highly successful 1954-55 tour with two Tests in New Zealand.

New Zealand v England

Second Test Match

At Auckland, March 25, 26, 28, 1955. England won by an innings and 20 runs with two days to spare. Hutton's team finished their triumphant tour by setting up a world record. They dismissed New Zealand in the second innings for 26, the lowest total in the history of Test cricket. The previous lowest score was 30, made twice by South Africa against England. The first was at Port Elizabeth in 1895-96 when George Lohmann took eight wickets for seven runs including the hat-trick. The second was at Edgbaston in 1924 when Tate and Gilligan routed South Africa, and Arthur Gilligan was in Auckland on this occasion when Appleyard for the second time in the match took two wickets with successive balls only to be denied the hat-trick.

After winning the toss, New Zealand were soon in trouble against Tyson, losing Leggat and Poore for 13, but Sutcliffe and Reid batted well in a stand of 63 before Sutcliffe, hooking a bouncer, was caught at mid-on. As at Dunedin, Rabone offered a dead bat for two and a half hours and his partnership of 78 in two and a quarter hours with Reid was the best of the match. Dismissing MacGibbon and Colquhoun with the last two balls of the day, Appleyard failed to trap Moir the next morning, but four balls from Statham sufficed to dispose of Moir and Hayes.

Instead of the ideal conditions of the first day, England were confronted with the task of batting on a pitch affected by heavy rain and in light that was dull for most of the day. In addition, more rain which caused two breaks of half an hour left the outfield so heavy that rarely did the batsmen gain full value for their strokes. This was specially true in the case of May whose 48 in two hours included seven threes.

England owed much to Hutton who, going in at number five, saw the total reach 148 for four at the end of the second day. Bailey stayed over two hours with his captain who proceeded to make the highest score of the match before being ninth out soon after lunch when MacGibbon took the new ball. Hutton batted three and a quarter hours. In a final stand Tyson and Statham added 28, two more than New Zealand were about to total.

Actually the issue appeared to be evenly balanced, but in one hour and forty-four minutes the game and the tour were completed. As in Australia, Tyson and Statham were mainly responsible for the collapse by getting rid of the early batsmen. In the seven Tests during the tour, Tyson took 39 wickets and Statham 30.

It was exactly three o'clock on a glorious summer's day when New Zealand began their task. The pitch was dry and not particularly fast, but the ball went through at varying heights and took spin. In forty minutes before tea New Zealand lost Leggat, Poore and Reid for 13 runs.

By clever strategy Hutton brought on Wardle, left-arm slow, to tackle Sutcliffe, New Zealand's talented left-handed batsman. That move made the record lowest score possible as Wardle tempted Sutcliffe into a big hit against his "chinaman" and he was completely deceived and bowled.

With four men out for 14, Appleyard entered the attack, relieving Tyson, and he removed McGregor, Cave, MacGibbon and Colquhoun, who went first ball in each innings. In fact Appleyard claimed three wickets in

New Zealand

B. Sutcliffe c Bailey b Statham	49	– b Wardle	11
J. G. Leggat lbw b Tyson	4	– c Hutton b Tyson	1
M. B. Poore c Evans b Tyson	0	– b Tyson	0
J. R. Reid c Statham b Wardle	73	– b Statham	1
G. O. Rabone c Evans b Statham	29	– lbw b Statham	7
S. N. McGregor not out	15	– c May b Appleyard	1
H. B. Cave c Bailey b Appleyard	6	– c Graveney b Appleyard	5
A. R. MacGibbon b Appleyard	9	– lbw b Appleyard	0
A. R. Colquhoun c sub b Appleyard	0	– c Graveney b Appleyard	0
A. N. Moir lbw b Statham	0	– not out	0
J. A. Hayes b Statham	0	– b Statham	0
B 3, l-b 6, w 4, n-b 2	15		

1/13 2/13 3/76 4/154 5/171	**200**	1/6 2/8 3/9 4/14 5/14	**26**
6/189 7/199 8/199 9/200		6/22 7/22 8/22 9/26	

Bowling: *First Innings*—Tyson 11–2–41–2; Statham 17.4–7–28–4; Bailey 13–2–34–0; Appleyard 16–4–38–3; Wardle 31–19–44–1. *Second Innings*—Tyson 7–2–10–2; Statham 9–2–9–3; Appleyard 6–3–7–4; Wardle 5–5–0–1.

England

R. T. Simpson c and b Moir	23	F. H. Tyson not out	27
T. W. Graveney c Rabone b Hayes	13	R. Appleyard c Colquhoun b Hayes	6
P. B. H. May b Hayes	48	J. B. Statham c Reid b Moir	13
M. C. Cowdrey b Moir	22		
L. Hutton b MacGibbon	53	B 12, l-b 3, n-b 8	23
T. E. Bailey c Colquhoun b Cave	18		
T. G. Evans c Reid b Moir	0	1/21 2/56 3/112 4/112 5/163	**246**
J. H. Wardle c Reid b Moir	0	6/164 7/164 8/201 9/218	

Bowling: Hayes 23–7–71–3; MacGibbon 20–7–33–1; Reid 25–10–28–0; Cave 24–10–25–1; Moir 25.1–3–62–5; Rabone 2–0–4–0.

Umpires: J. C. Harris and J. McLennan.

four balls but Moir again prevented a hat-trick, the ball falling only just short of Graveney who was in great form in the leg trap.

Hutton decided to give Statham and Tyson the chance of making the kill, but one over from Statham sufficed. First he got Rabone leg before with his fourth delivery and finally established the new world record by sending Hayes' middle stump flying. New Zealand's previous lowest scores were 42 and 54 against Australia at Wellington in March 1946.

So MCC won all four matches in New Zealand and finished with the best record of any visiting team to the Antipodes. Large crowds flocked to the New Zealand grounds, the receipts amounting to £26,000, leaving approximately a profit of £16,000 for the benefit of cricket in the two islands.

pages 91–92

Laker's Wonderful Year

By Neville Cardus

Against the Australians in 1956, J. C. Laker bowled himself to a prominence which might seem legendary if there were no statistics to prove that his skill did indeed perform results and deeds hitherto not considered within the range of any cricketer, living or dead.

No writer of boys' fiction would so strain romantic credulity as to make his hero, playing for England against Australia, capture nine first-innings wickets; then help himself to all ten in the second innings. Altogether, 19 for 90 in a Test match. If any author expected us to believe that his hero was not only capable in one chapter of a marvel as fantastic as all this, but also in another chapter, and our earlier chapter, bowled a whole Australian XI out, 10 for 88, the most gullible of his readers would, not without reason, throw the book away and wonder what the said author was taking him for.

Yet as far back as 1950 Laker was hinting that he possessed gifts which on occasion were at any moment likely to be visited by plenary inspiration and accomplish things not only unexpected but wondrous. At Bradford, five miles from his birthplace, Laker, playing for England v The Rest, took 8 wickets for 2 runs in 14 overs – a feat which probably the great S. F. Barnes himself never imagined within mortal bowler's scope – or even desirable.

Against Nottinghamshire at The Oval in 1955, Laker took 6 wickets for 5. Between 1947 and 1953 he did the hat-trick four times.

Obviously the gods endowed him in his cradle with that indefinable power which from time to time generates talent to abnormal and irresistible achievement. And he has done his conjurations – they have been nothing less – by one of the oldest tricks of the bowlers' trade. Not by the new-fangled "swing" and not by "googlies" or Machiavellian deceit by flight through the air, has Laker hypnotised batsmen into helpless immobility, but by off-breaks of the finger-spin type which would have been recognised by, and approved by, cricketers who played in Laker's own county of Yorkshire more than half a century ago. He really follows the great succession of Yorkshire off-spinners – from Ted Wainwright, Schofield Haigh, not forgetting F. S. Jackson, to George Macaulay, reaching to Illingworth of the present day.

Laker's actual finger spin probably has seldom been surpassed on a "sticky" or dusty wicket, in point of velocity and viciousness after pitching. I can think only of Ted Wainwright, Cecil Parkin and Tom Goddard who shared Laker's ability to "fizz" the ball right-handed from the off side. There was more temper in Macaulay's attack than there is in Laker's, more vehemence of character. But for sheer technical potentiality, often for sheer actual spitefulness, Laker's off-spin must be regarded as entirely out of the ordinary, and very much his own.

Any great performer needs to be born at the right time. If Laker had begun to play for Surrey in the 1930s, when wickets at The Oval and on most large grounds were doped and rolled to insensibility, he might have made one or two appearances for Surrey, then vanished from the scene. Or maybe he would have remained in Yorkshire where pitches were never absolutely divorced from nature and original sin.

Laker was clever, too, to begin playing cricket and bowling off-spin after the alteration to the lbw rule dangerously penalised batsmen who had brought to a fine art the use of the pads to brilliant off-breaks pitching off the stumps and coming back like a knife – as Cecil Parkin's frequently did. Laker has been quick to adapt his arts to the deplorably unresourceful footwork of most batsmen of the present period; moreover he has, with the opportune judgment of those born to exceptional prowess, taken advantage of the modern development of the leg-trap.

On a good wicket, his attack naturally loses sting. His tempting slowish flight enables – or should enable – batsmen to get to the pitch of his bowling. He thrives on success in perhaps larger measure than most bowlers. He likes, more even than most bowlers, to take a quick wicket. There is sometimes an air of indolence in his movements, as he runs his loose lumbering run, swinging his arm slowly, but with the flick of venom at the last split second.

At the end of his imperturbable walk back to his bowling mark he stares at the pavilion as though looking for somebody, but looking in a disinterested way. He is entirely what he is by technique – good professional technique, spin, length and the curve in the air natural to off-spin. He does not, as Macaulay and Parkin did, assert his arts plus passion of character and open relentless lust for spoils and the blood of all batsmen.

He is the Yorkshireman, at bottom, true enough; but Southern air has softened a little the native and rude antagonism. Even when he is "on the kill" on a wicket of glue there is nothing demonstrably spiteful in his demeanour; he can even run through an Australian Xl in a Test match, as at Manchester in his "wonderful year", and seem unconcerned.

His bowling is as unassuming as the man himself and on the face of it as modest. That's where the fun comes in, for it is fun indeed to see the leisurely way Laker "sends" his victims one after another, as though by some influence which has not only put the batsmen under a spell, but himself at the same time. Somebody has written that all genius goes to work partly in a somnambulistic way. Jim Laker is certainly more than a talented spinner.

pages 544–547

Surrey in 1957

By Alex Bannister

For the sixth successive year incomparable Surrey carried all before them. Their high skill, ruthless efficiency, matchless team spirit and appetite for quick runs left no reasonable doubt that their record run of Championship victories would be extended. Once they had taken the lead theirs was a lonely supremacy, and in the final table they were separated from Northamptonshire, the runners-up, by the wide margin of 94 points. On August 16 they clinched the title, a date which equalled Warwickshire's post-war record, set in 1951, of winning by the earliest date.

Surrey's policy of persistent aggression from the first ball to the last never wavered, even in the rare threat of defeat. As many as nine of their 21 Championship victories were gained inside two days. Nor was it a coincidence that they scored faster than any other side – an example of their dynamic approach to the game.

Throughout the season Surrey were the dominant side, attracting large crowds wherever they appeared. They played, acted, thought and looked like the magnificent champions they are. Surrey's achievements undoubtedly entitle them to be considered the greatest county combination of all time.

Though it was yet another glorious record of uninterrupted success the season marked a new chapter in Surrey cricket. After five triumphant years Stuart Surridge retired and the captaincy passed to P. B. H. May, England's captain since 1955. As May was an automatic choice to lead the national side again, there were fears that his dual responsibility, and his absence in many county fixtures – he missed nine – would react unfavourably against Surrey. May's services to England virtually meant his sharing the Surrey captaincy with his newly-appointed deputy, senior professional, Alec Bedser.

Bedser was May's own recommendation to the Surrey Committee, and it proved from every conceivable angle a wise and happy choice. Bedser was a brilliant deputy. His wide experience, deep technical knowledge, shrewdness and willingness to encourage the new members earned him a new stature in English cricket. When they played together May made no secret of his reliance on Bedser's advice. At the end of the season May paid the warmest of tributes to the qualities of his vice-captain. "Alec has been splendid in every direction," he said. "So much has depended on him. He and I run the show including team selection."

For the first time since he suffered from shingles when touring with Hutton's team in Australia in 1954-55, Bedser was also once again a great medium-pace bowler, sharing with Lock and Loader the distinction of taking over 100 wickets for his club.

Captain and vice-captain shared the credit for the maintenance of Surridge's legacy of a great team spirit. It was a spirit born of success, and thrived because, by habit and practice, Surrey played as a side and not as a collection of brilliant individualists.

Once again Surrey's international-standard attack was superb; so was the supporting fielding and catching, especially close to the wicket. The sight of their alert fieldsmen crouched near the bat is a familiar and thrilling feature of English cricket. The side's striking power was reflected in the first-class bowling averages. Lock, at the top, took 200 wickets for the second time in three years, including 153 in the Championship at the remarkably low cost of 11.58 apiece. Laker, Loader and the Bedser twins were also in the first ten bowlers to take 70 or more wickets. Whatever the type of pitch Surrey had the bowlers to use it. Loader and Alec Bedser rarely failed to strike with the new ball, and there was Laker and Lock, the world's most dangerous spinning partnership, to follow, with Eric Bedser's off-breaks as good measure.

Under Surridge, who believed catches were to be had off defensive shots if fieldsmen were prepared to stand close enough, Surrey developed a standard of fielding comparable with the greatest. May and Bedser saw to it that their side did not deviate from Surridge's level. Lock again made many breathless catches and Stewart, as the shortest of short-legs, or in any position near the bat, was one of the most daring and brilliant catchers in the country. He took 77 catches, only one short of W. R. Hammond's record established in 1928. Stewart, however, had the rich compensation of creating a new world record for a fielder other than a wicket-keeper by making seven catches at Northampton in June.

To stand at Stewart's "pocket picking" distance at short leg needs more than a safe pair of hands, quick reflexes and a stout heart; it demands complete faith in his bowlers to maintain an accurate length. They never failed him. Barrington, in his first season as a slip, shared with Stewart and Lock the outstanding performance of exceeding 60 catches. Surrey, by having their youngest players in the positions nearest the wicket, further prove this modern theory is the soundest.

Barrington also made a welcome return to form with the bat. He enjoyed his best season since his premature selection for England in 1955 led to his falling off. Stewart and Clark, who was on the fringe of Test honours, also topped the 1,500 mark in all matches, and Constable fell just short of that target. None could match the consistently high performance of May, who scored in his 19 Championship games 1,391 of his first-class aggregate of 2,347 runs.

Generally Surrey could hope for runs down to number nine. Their batsmen cheerfully took risks in the interests of their side; their true worth lay in their determination to give the team's bowlers time and runs in which to dismiss the opposition twice. Surrey's batting has often been unjustly criticised; almost always under-rated. For long periods five Surrey batsmen and five Surrey bowlers were in the averages. The mammoth totals of pre-war Oval days are happily no longer reached. The wicket has undergone a radical change; the lush, beautifully maintained outfield is no longer fast. Runs are harder to come by, and Surrey strive, not necessarily for large, dreary draw-producing totals, but winning ones.

McIntyre lost none of his wicket-keeping ability. Throughout the Test series he stood by as reserve to Evans and there can be little doubt that he is England's second best 'keeper. Keeping to Surrey's varied attack, especially on a pitch helpful to the bowlers, calls for the highest skill and McIntyre was seldom wanting.

A last but not inconsiderable reason for Surrey's triumph was their fund of adequate reserves to fill the gaps left by England's heavy calls. Without their loyal and excellent service Surrey would be hard pressed to maintain their position.

Surrey Results in 1957

| All First-Class Matches | Played 35, Won 25, Lost 4, Drawn 6 |
| County Championship Matches | Played 28, Won 21, Lost 3, Drawn 3, No Decision 1 |

Surrey went on to win their seventh successive Championship in 1958, since when they have finished champions only twice – in 1971 and 1999.

page 108

The Record Individual Innings

Hanif Mohammad, Pakistan's 24-year-old opening batsman, made 499, the world's highest individual score in first-class cricket,* for Karachi against Bahawalpur in the semi-final of the Quaid-e-Azam Trophy at the Karachi Parsi Institute ground on January 8, 9, 11, 12, 1959. This beat the 452 not out by Sir Donald Bradman for New South Wales against Queensland at Sydney in 1929-30.

On a coir matting pitch, Hanif scored 25 in forty minutes on the first evening, 230 in five hours on the second day and 244 in four hours fifty-five minutes on the third day. He was run out when going for his 500 off the last ball of the day. Altogether he batted ten hours thirty-five minutes and hit sixty-four fours. Hanif played superbly, rarely putting the ball in the air, he did not offer a chance and was beaten only once, and then off the pitch. Hanif shared a stand of 259 with Wallis Mathias for the second wicket.

Hanif is one of four brothers all playing in first-class cricket. Three appeared for Karachi in this match; Wazir was captain and the other was Mushtaq.

Note: In the final, a few days later, Abdul Aziz, the Karachi wicket-keeper, died while batting against Combined Services. He was struck on the heart by a slow off-break from Dildar Awan and fell. He died fifteen minutes later on the way to hospital. Play was postponed for a day.

---

* Hanif's score remained the highest first-class innings for 35 years, until being surpassed by Brian Lara's 501 not out for Warwickshire against Durham in 1994.

Bahawalpur

Ijaz Hussain run out	24	– c Waqar b Mahmood	32
Zulfiqar Ahmed c Aziz b Mahmood	0	– c Aziz b Mahmood	8
Mohammad Iqbal b Ikram	20	– c Aziz b Munaf	0
Mohammad Ramzan c Wallis b Ikram	64	– lbw b Munaf	5
Ghiassuddin b Ikram	4	– c Wazir b Ikram	12
Jamil Khalid run out	12	– b D'Souza	4
Farrukh Salim c Aziz b Mahmood	3	– b Ikram	4
Riaz Mahmood b Mahmood	4	– lbw b Mushtaq	10
Asad Bhatti st Aziz b Mushtaq	21	– b Ikram	4
Tanvir Hussan not out	16	– c Aziz b D'Souza	7
Aziz Ahmed b Ikram	8	– not out	5
Extras	9	Extras	17
	185		108

Bowling: *First Innings*—Mahmood 18-4-38-3; Ikram 17-3-48-4; Munaf 8-1-23-0; D'Souza 11-2-42-0; Mushtaq 4-0-19-1; Hanif 1-0-6-0. *Second Innings*—Mahmood 10-2-27-2; Ikram 8-2-10-3; Munaf 9-1-29-2; D'Souza 11-3-17-2; Mushtaq 3-0-8-1.

Karachi

Hanif Mohammad run out	499	Abdul Munaf b Iqbal	18
Alim-ud-Din c Zulfiqar b Aziz	32	Abdul Aziz not out	9
Waqar Hassan c Tanvir b Iqbal	37		
Wazir Mohammad st Tanvir b Jamil	31	Extras	22
Wallis Mathias run out	103		
Mushtaq Mohammad lbw b Aziz	21	(7 wkts dec.)	772

Ikram Elahi, Mahmood Hussain and Antao D'Souza did not bat.

Bowling: Zulfiqar 34-5-95-0; Ramzan 19-0-83-0; Aziz 50-4-208-2; Riaz 9-0-44-0; Ghias 37-3-139-0; Jamil 23-1-93-1; Iqbal 25-3-81-2; Tanvir 3-0-7-0.

Umpires: Daud Khan and Idris Beg.

page 106

The following extract concludes an article by Tom Smith,
who was the Honorary Secretary, and a founder,
of the Association of Cricket Umpires.

Umpiring

In places where "gamesmanship" is accepted it is considered smart to try to deceive the umpire. Fieldsmen appeal at every opportunity, even if they know perfectly well that they have little or no justification. It stands to reason that the only man in a position to judge lbw is the umpire, but even he has difficulties. Yet we have players at mid-off and mid-on, and frequently in other positions, talking about a man being "plumb out". It is ridiculous and absurd, but it can become fashionable and infectious. The bowler who is standing at an angle of 20–30 degrees to the pitch after delivery, and is constantly throwing his hands up to the heavens with disappointment or anguished appeals, is a menace to the game.

This posturing may be amusing to some but it is not so to umpires, and it is not cricket. Youngsters will always imitate their seniors and this behaviour is detrimental to the game as a whole.

There are matches, too, where batsmen who know full well they are out apply all their acting powers and "gimmicks" to try to confuse the umpire. Again, this can become fashionable and considered "clever" and it will be imitated and carried into junior cricket. Fair-minded people know that the umpire has a very small chance against the odds of bowler and batsman. In some cases his life becomes miserable. He grows bitter and unhappy, and thinks seriously about giving up. It is impossible to recruit the right type of man if he has to face hours of worry and anxiety in the field. He does not stick it for very long if he meets the wrong type of players.

My appeal to players in *all* grades of cricket is to recognise the umpire as a vital part of the game. Treat him with respect. Forget silly play-acting and gallery-appealing antics; control bad temper and incidents. Not only will this be doing something for umpires and umpiring but it will make cricket a happy game. It was always intended to be so.

page 951

Obituary: Alec Skelding

SKELDING, ALEXANDER, who died at Leicester on April 17, aged 73, stood as a first-class umpire from 1931 to 1958. He began his cricket career as a very fast bowler with Leicestershire in 1905, but, because he wore spectacles, was not re-engaged at the end of the season. He then joined Kidderminster in the Birmingham League and achieved such success that in 1912 the county re-signed him and he continued with them till 1929. His best season was that of 1927, when he took 102 wickets, average 20.81. Altogether he dismissed 593 batsmen at a cost of less than 25 runs each.

One of the most popular personalities in the game, he always wore white boots when umpiring and he was celebrated for his sense of humour. It was his custom at the close of play to remove the bails with an exaggerated flourish and announce: "And that concludes the entertainment for the day, gentlemen."

"Alec" was the central figure in many amusing incidents. Once in response to an appeal for run out, he stated: "That was a 'photo-finish' and as there isn't time to develop the plate, I shall say not out." In another match a batsman who had been celebrating a special event the previous evening was rapped on the pad by a ball. At once the bowler asked: "How is he?" Said Alec, shaking his head sadly: "He's not at all well, and he was even worse last night." Occasionally the joke went against Alec. In a game in 1948 he turned down a strong appeal by the Australian touring team. A little later a dog ran on to the field, and one of the Australians captured it, carried it to Skelding and said: "Here you are. All you want now is a white stick!"

Asked in his playing days if he found spectacles a handicap, Alec said: "The specs are for the look of the thing. I can't see without 'em and on hot days I can't see with 'em, because they get steamed up. So I bowl on hearing only and appeal twice an over."

One of his most cherished umpiring memories was the giving of three leg-before decisions which enabled H. Fisher of Yorkshire to perform a unique "hat-trick" against Somerset at Sheffield in 1932. "I was never more sure that I was right in each case," he said afterwards, "and each of the batsmen agreed that he was dead in front."

pages 842–844

Australia v West Indies

First Test Match

At Brisbane, December 9, 10, 12, 13, 14, 1960. A tie. Quite apart from gaining a niche in cricket history as the first Test to end in a tie this match will always be remembered with enthusiasm because of its excellent cricket. It was played in a most sporting spirit, with the climax coming in a tremendously exciting finish as three wickets fell in the final over.

Australia, set to score 233 runs at a rate of 45 an hour for victory, crumbled before the fiery, sustained pace of Hall, and lost five wickets for 57. The sixth fell at 92. Then the drama began to build up as Davidson, the Australian all-rounder who enjoyed a magnificent match, was joined by Benaud, in a stand which added 134. They were still together half an hour before time, with 27 needed when Hall took the new ball – a crucial stage.

In the event, however, the West Indies fieldsmen, often at fault during the match, rose to the occasion so that three of the last four batsmen to fall were run out in the desperate race against time. The first run-out came when Benaud called for a sharp single, but Solomon hit the stumps from mid-wicket to dismiss Davidson. Grout came in and took a single off Sobers, so that when the last momentous over from Hall began, six runs were needed with three wickets left.

The first ball hit Grout on the thigh and a leg-bye resulted, from the second Benaud gave a catch at the wicket as he swung mightily. Meckiff played the third ball back to the bowler, but when the fourth went through to the wicket-keeper, the batsmen scampered a run, Hall missing a chance to run out Meckiff as the wicket-keeper threw the ball to him. Grout hit the fifth ball high in the air, Hall attempted to take the catch himself, but the ball bounced out, and another run had been gained. Meckiff hit the sixth ball hard and high to leg, but Hunte cut it off on the boundary as the batsmen turned for the third run, which would have given Australia victory. Hunte threw in superbly, low and fast, and Grout was run out by a foot. So Kline came in to face the last two balls with the scores level. He played the seventh ball of the over towards square leg and Meckiff, backing up well, raced down the wicket, only to be out when Solomon again threw down the wicket with only the width of a stump as his target. So ended a match in which both sides had striven throughout for victory, with no thought of safety first.

West Indies attacked the bowling from the start of the match only to lose three men for 65 before Sobers, who hit a masterly century in just over two hours including fifteen fours, and Worrell mastered the bowling. Solomon, Alexander and Hall added valuable contributions to an innings which yielded 4.5 runs an over despite much excellent pace bowling by Davidson. Australia succeeded in establishing a lead of 52, largely through the determination of Simpson and O'Neill, who made his highest Test score without reaching his very best form.

Indeed, West Indies missed several chances at vital times. More fine bowling by Davidson caused West Indies to battle hard for runs in their second innings and they owed much to some high-class batting from Worrell for their respectable total, swelled usefully on the final morning by a last-wicket stand of 31 between Hall and Valentine.

124

West Indies

C. C. Hunte c Benaud b Davidson	24	– c Simpson b Mackay	39
C. Smith c Grout b Davidson	7	– c O'Neill b Davidson	6
R. Kanhai c Grout b Davidson	15	– c Grout b Davidson	54
G. Sobers c Kline b Meckiff	132	– b Davidson	14
*F. M. Worrell c Grout b Davidson	65	– c Grout b Davidson	65
J. Solomon hit wkt b Simpson	65	– lbw b Simpson	47
P. Lashley c Grout b Kline	19	– b Davidson	0
†F. C. M. Alexander c Davidson b Kline	60	– b Benaud	5
S. Ramadhin c Harvey b Davidson	12	– c Harvey b Simpson	6
W. Hall st Grout b Kline	50	– b Davidson	18
A. L. Valentine not out	0	– not out	7
Extras	4	Extras	23
	453		**284**

1/23 2/42 3/65 4/239 5/243 6/283 7/347 8/366 9/452

1/13 2/88 3/114 4/127 5/210 6/210 7/241 8/250 9/253

Bowling: *First Innings*—Davidson 30–2–135–5; Meckiff 18–0–129–1; Mackay 3–0–15–0; Benaud 24–3–93–0; Simpson 8–0–25–1; Kline 17.6–6–52–3. *Second Innings*—Davidson 24.6–4–87–6; Meckiff 4–1–19–0; Benaud 31–6–69–1; Mackay 21–7–52–1; Kline 4–0–14–0; Simpson 7–2–18–2; O'Neill 1–0–2–0.

Australia

C. C. McDonald c Hunte b Sobers	57	– b Worrell	16
R. B. Simpson b Ramadhin	92	– c sub b Hall	0
R. N. Harvey b Valentine	15	– c Sobers b Hall	5
N. C. O'Neill c Valentine b Hall	181	– c Alexander b Hall	26
L. Favell run out	45	– c Solomon b Hall	7
K. D. Mackay b Sobers	35	– b Ramadhin	28
A. K. Davidson c Alexander b Hall	44	– run out	80
*R. Benaud lbw b Hall	10	– c Alexander b Hall	52
†A. W. T. Grout lbw b Hall	4	– run out	2
I. Meckiff run out	4	– run out	2
L. F. Kline not out	3	– not out	0
Extras	15	Extras	14
	505		**232**

1/84 2/138 3/194 4/278 5/381 6/469 7/484 8/489 9/496

1/1 2/7 3/49 4/49 5/57 6/92 7/226 8/228 9/232

Bowling: *First Innings*—Hall 29.3–1–140–4; Worrell 30–0–93–0; Sobers 32–0–115–2; Valentine 24–6–82–1; Ramadhin 15–1–60–1. *Second Innings*—Hall 17.7–3–63–5; Worrell 16–3–41–1; Sobers 8–0–30–0; Valentine 10–4–27–0; Ramadhin 17–3–57–1.

Umpires: C. J. Egar and C. Hoy.

A fuller description of this match by E. M. Wellings was given in the 1961 Wisden, pages 105–110.

pages 137–139

Notes by the Editor

(Norman Preston)

Disappearance of the Amateur

To many people the abolition of the amateur status in first-class cricket provided yet another big surprise. Four years earlier MCC had conducted a full inquiry into this matter and arrived at certain conclusions which were accepted by the Advisory County Cricket Committee. Among them were the following:–

> The wish to preserve in first-class cricket the leadership and general approach to the game traditionally associated with the Amateur player.
>
> The Committee rejected any solution to the problem on the lines of abolishing the distinction between Amateur and Professional and regarding them all alike as "cricketers".
>
> They considered that the distinctive status of the amateur cricketer was not obsolete, was of great value to the game and should be preserved.

The members of this Committee were: The Duke of Norfolk (chairman), H. S. Altham, G. O. Allen, M. J. C. Allom, Col. R. J. de C. Barber, F. R. Brown, E. D. R. Eagar, C. A. F. Hastilow, C. G. Howard, D. J. Insole, P. B. H. May, C. H. Palmer, Col. R. S. Rait Kerr, A. B. Sellers, Rev. D. S. Sheppard, R. Aird (secretary).

It seems strange that within four years the opinions of some people appear to have been completely reversed. We live in a changing world. Conditions are vastly different from the days of our grandparents; but is it wise to throw everything overboard?

We have inherited the game of cricket. The story of its development during the last hundred years is appropriately given full treatment in this edition of *Wisden*. Right through these hundred years the amateur has played a very important part. In the time of Dr W. G. Grace there was talk that the amateur received liberal expenses. Whether this was true or not, I do not believe cricket, as we know it today, would be such a popular attraction, or so remunerative to the professional, without the contribution which Dr Grace and his contemporaries made as amateurs.

By doing away with the amateur, cricket is in danger of losing the spirit of freedom and gaiety which the best amateur players brought to the game.

On the other hand there is at present a source of talent which has been untapped because of the gulf between the amateur and the professional. This comprises the band of cricketers who could get away from business or other activities for periods during the summer to assist their counties if they could receive compensation for loss of salary. In other words, their employers would be willing to release them, but not to pay their salaries during their absence from work.

The passing of the amateur could have a detrimental effect in the vital matter of captaincy both at County and Test level. True, it was under a professional, Sir Leonard Hutton, that England last regained the Ashes, in 1953, and men like Tom Dollery (Warwickshire), J. V. Wilson (Yorkshire) and Don Kenyon (Worcestershire) have led their counties with distinction.

Because the amateur possessed independent status, the professionals, generally, preferred to have him as captain. Two of the most popular and most successful captains were A. B. Sellers (Yorkshire) and W. S. Surridge (Surrey). Their gifts of leadership were stronger than their batting or bowling ability. Both were great fielders, but if either had been on equal status as a "cricketer" with the professional he might well have been passed over.

Under the new set-up, one presumes there will still be players with a full-time contract while others receive match fees and a minority may still prefer to play solely for the love of the game. One can visualise smaller full-time staffs, particularly if, as many reformers desire, there is a reduction in the number of days allotted to county cricket.

Sir John Hobbs, commenting on the change, said: "It is sad to see the passing of the amateurs because it signals the end of an era in cricket. They were a great asset to the game, much appreciated by all of us because they were able to come in and play freely, whereas many professionals did not feel they could take chances. Now times are different, and I can understand the position of the amateur who has to make his living. You cannot expect him to refuse good offers outside cricket."

page 87

1963
The Centenary of
Wisden Cricketers' Almanack

Notes by the Editor
(Norman Preston)

Wisden itself made an indelible contribution to the summer by the appearance on April 19, 1963, of the 100th edition of "The Cricketers' Bible". The newspapers, television and sound radio were lavish in their praise and they treated it as a national event. I don't think I am giving away any secrets when I say that even the publisher was surprised by the public demand for the Almanack. It ran into three impressions by the printers before everyone was satisfied. Naturally, *Wisden,* which specialises in cricket facts and records, established its own record of sales.*

The firm of John Wisden & Co Ltd commemorated the event by launching The Wisden Trophy, with the approval of MCC and the West Indies Cricket Board of Control, to be played for perpetually between England and West Indies in the same way as England and Australia contest the Ashes. West Indies have become the first holders of the trophy, which is being kept permanently in the Imperial Cricket Museum at Lord's. All the members of the West Indies touring team received a silver replica.

---

*According to the minutes of a meeting on January 7, 1964, of the John Wisden & Co Board of Directors, sales "of the 1963 centenary edition of the Wisden Cricketers' Almanack totalled £22,000 (approximately) with a remaining stock of 900 copies. 31,000 copies [in total] were printed". The record did not last too long. Wisden Almanacks in the 1990s have consistently sold between 35,000 and 40,000 copies.

pages 993–994

Cricket Books, 1963

By John Arlott

1963 has been marked by the publication of a cricket book so outstanding as to compel any reviewer to check his adjectives several times before he describes it and, since he is likely to be dealing in superlatives, to measure them carefully to avoid over-praise – which this book does not need. It is *Beyond a Boundary,* by C. L. R. James (Hutchinson: 25*s.*) and, in the opinion of this reviewer, it is the finest book written about the game of cricket. Only two others can challenge comparison with it. They are, the immortal "Nyren" – to be precise, the section of Nyren's *Young Cricketer's Tutor* called "The Cricketers of My Time" – and Hugh de Selincourt's *The Cricket Match.* Nyren has been for so long the touchstone of all cricket-writing that it is surprising to hear the most knowledgeable students of cricket literature wondering aloud whether, in fact, Mr James's book is better. The crucial factor in the decision probably lies in the fact that "The Cricketers of My Time" is a fragment – little more than 12,000 words long – whereas *Beyond a Boundary,* without waste or excess, runs to some 120,000. *The Cricket Match* may suffer in the eyes of cricketers by virtue of being cast in the form of a novel: that fact, however, should not weigh against it by literary standards. It is as complete and rounded as Mr James's book; but it has not quite the same scope or profundity. There may be a better book about any sport than *Beyond a Boundary*: if so, the present reviewer has not seen it.

After such enthusiasm, it must be admitted that it is not simple to describe *Beyond a Boundary* within reasonable space. Indeed, to some it may not seem like a cricket book at all.

Mr James was brought up in a room overlooking the cricket ground at Tunapuna, in Trinidad: he was a useful, fairly fast, left-arm bowler: and for several summers he reported cricket for *The Manchester Guardian.* But he has also read deeply in philosophy and history, lectured in the United States on English literature, particularly in relation to Shakespeare: and, with Sir Learie Constantine, he conducted the first effective propaganda drive in England for West Indian self-government. The habitual reader of "popular" cricket books may be startled to find that Bernhard Berenson, Matthew Arnold, Edmund Burke, John Milton, Michelangelo, Karl Marx and Charles Dickens have more index-references than Tony Lock, Wesley Hall, Richie Benaud, Trevor Bailey, G. O. Allen or "Patsy" Hendren – or to find T. S. Eliot, Leon Trotsky, Jimmy Durante, Toussaint L'Ouverture, Pablo Picasso and Florence Nightingale mentioned at all. This is not, like most cricket books, a book about cricket in isolation, but a book about cricket and life – the life being that of a man who has studied and thought so widely that he can take as his text "What do they know of cricket who only cricket know?" To answer that question, the author says, "involves ideas as well as facts".

Much of the book deals closely with cricket, though never with cricket divorced from the ideas of the outer world which must, ultimately, condition it. Mr James's savage propaganda drive, as editor of *The Nation*, to replace Gerry Alexander as captain of the West Indies with Frank Worrell is dealt with coldly, but no less dramatically for that. The essay on Wilton St Hill must be the finest portrait of a cricketer ever created in prose – or, for that matter in verse or paint either – and those of Sir Learie Constantine, George Headley, W. G. Grace, "Piggy" Piggott (who may pass unnoticed in the major records, but lives in this book) and George John are also memorable.

The story of the rise of West Indian cricket is interwoven with the West Indian rise to self-government, and with Thomas Arnold, W. G. Grace and the English public school system. The book has fire and contemplation, facts and imagination, breadth and depth. Every cricketer should read this book: if he does not enjoy it, then Richard Tyldesley's words to Neville Cardus about Lancashire cricket, "'t' Pooblic needs eddicäating oop to it", must apply.

page 973

Obituary: Peter the Cat

CAT, PETER, whose ninth life ended on November 5, 1964, was a well-known cricket-watcher at Lord's, where he spent 12 of his 14 years. He preferred a close-up view of the proceedings and his sleek, black form could often be seen prowling on the field of play when the crowds were biggest. He frequently appeared on the television screen. Mr S. C. Griffith, Secretary of MCC, said of him: "He was a cat of great character and loved publicity."

pages 158–160

From 1941 to 1989, a regular feature in Wisden *was
"Dates in Cricket History". In 1966 this section
included a brief history of cricket dress.*

Cricket Dress

Eighteenth Century

Three-cornered or jockey hats, often with silver or gold lace; shirts, generally frilled; nankeen breeches, silk stockings, buckled shoes. The Hambledon Club has sky-blue coats with buttons engraved "C.C." The first uniform of the MCC was in azure blue.

1800–1850

From about 1810–15 trousers begin to replace breeches, though Eton and Harrow still wore the latter in 1830. Tall "beaver" hats, in black or white, became the rule. Shirts no longer frilled, but now worn with rather high collars and spreading bow ties; singlets instead of shirts not uncommon. Wide braces often seen, especially on professionals. Black "Oxford" shoes universal. Belts with metal clasps, for the waist.

Towards the end of this period the tall hat began to give place to a soft and full flannel cap, generally white, or, less commonly, to a straw hat, often rather of a haymaker's shape. Short, white flannel jackets, mentioned as early as 1812, began to appear as forerunners of "the blazer"; T. Lockyer, the Surrey cricketer, is thought to have been the first to wear "a cricket coat".

1850–1880

Under the lead of I Zingari (established 1845) Club cricket colours begin to appear, often as ribbons round the white bowler hats now replacing the tall and straw hats of the previous two decades. Club caps date from about 1850, but Eton may have sported their light blue caps as early as 1831 and the Rugby XI were "habited alike" in 1843. The Winchester XI first wore their blue caps in 1951 and Harrow their striped caps in 1852. The Cambridge "blue" seems to date from 1861, the Oxford "blue" certainly from 1863. Coloured shirts became common as uniform, e.g. a pattern of coloured spots, stripes or checks on a white ground: the All-England XI wore white shirts with pink spots.

The Oxford and Cambridge's XIs for many years wore dark and light blue shirts. The Harlequins, founded 1852, originally wore blue trousers. Rugby School now present sole survival of the coloured shirt.

The term "blazer" is said to have been first applied to the scarlet coats adopted by the Lady Margaret Boat Club (St John's College, Cambridge) as early as 1862, or possibly from the coats worn by the crew at the "Captain's Gig" of HMS *Blazer, c.* 1850. The coloured cricket blazer seems to have appeared at about the same time: the Oxford XI of 1863 wore blue blazers. Shaw and Shrewsbury's team to Australia in 1884-85 wore blazers and caps to match.

Shoes progressively gave place to boots, either brown or white with brown straps.

1880–1895

Coloured shirts disappear. White shirts, with starched or semi-starched fronts, the rule. Ties not so common, but small bow ties in low turned-down starched collars common enough. White buckskin boots were first worn about 1882, but they only gradually superseded the old brown and brown-and-white type. The modern "sweater", probably an evolution from the old "singlet", came in during this period.

1895 to date

Very little change. About the end of the century came soft white hats, in felt or linen, possibly on an Australian model, and in the last twenty years appeared rubber-soled boots, even now worn by some bowlers in dry weather; also sleeveless sweaters.

Umpires' white coats seem first to have been worn in 1861, but as late as 1882 the old uniform of the tall hat or "billycock" and black coat was by no means uncommon.

MCC touring cap and blazer was first worn by the team that visited Australia 1903-04, under the captaincy of Sir Pelham Warner. The cap awarded to England players in Test matches at home was introduced with the approval of King Edward VII in 1908; the award was retrospective for players who had previously represented England in England.

A touring cap bearing the arms of Australia was first worn by the team that visited England in 1890.

Since this history was written, helmets and coloured clothing (the latter in one-day cricket) have been the most conspicuous developments in cricket dress during the last quarter of the twentieth century.

pages 126–132

*Although the 1964 edition had already featured Garry Sobers as one of
the Five Cricketers of the Year, the 1967 edition included the following
portrait by Sir Neville Cardus.*

Sobers – The Lion of Cricket

Cricketer of the Century: Garry Sobers

Garfield St Aubrun Sobers, thirty years old in July 1966 –
the most renowned name of any cricketer since Bradman's
high noon. He is, in fact, even more famous than Bradman
ever was; for he is accomplished in every department of the
game, and has exhibited his genius in all climes and
conditions. Test matches everywhere, West Indies, India,
Pakistan, Australia, New Zealand, England; in Lancashire League and
Sheffield Shield cricket. We can safely agree that no player has proven
versatility of skill as convincingly as Sobers has done, effortlessly, and after
the manner born.

He is a stylish, prolific batsman; two bowlers in one, fastish left-arm,
seaming the new ball, and slow to medium back-of-the-hand spinner with
the old ball; a swift, accurate, slip fieldsman in the class of Hammond
and Simpson, and generally an astute captain. Statistics concerning him
speak volumes.

Sobers holds a unique Test double, over 5,500 runs, and close on 150
wickets. Four years ago he set up an Australian record when playing for
South Australia by scoring 1,000 runs and taking 50 wickets in the same
season. To emphasize this remarkable feat he repeated it the following
summer out there …

Is Sobers the greatest all-round cricketer in history? … It is, of course,
vain to measure ability in one age with ability in another. Material
circumstances, the environment which moulds technique, are different.
Only providence, timeless and all-seeing, is qualified to weigh in the
balance the arts and personality of a Hammond and a Sobers. It is enough
that the deeds of Sobers are appreciated in our own time, as we have
witnessed them. He has, as I have pointed out, boxed the compass of the

world of present-day cricket, revealing his gifts easefully, abundantly. And here we touch on his secret: power of relaxation and the gift of holding himself in reserve. Nobody has seen Sobers obviously in labour. He makes a stroke with moments to spare. His fastest ball – and it can be very fast – is bowled as though he could, with physical pressure, have bowled it a shade faster. He can, in the slips, catch the lightning snick with the grace and nonchalance of Hammond himself. The sure sign of mastery, of genius of any order, is absence of strain, natural freedom of rhythm.

In the Test matches in England last summer, 1966, his prowess exceeded all precedents: 722 runs, average 103.14, twenty wickets, average 27.25, and ten catches … I am not sure that his most impressive assertion of his quality was not seen in the Lord's Test. Assertion is too strenuous a word to apply to the 163 not out scored then; for it was done entirely free of apparent exertion, even though at one stage of the proceedings the West Indies seemed beaten beyond salvage. When the fifth second-innings wicket fell, the West Indies were leading by nine runs only. Nothing reliable to come in the way of batsmanship, nobody likely to stay with Sobers, excepting Holford. As everybody concerned with cricket knows, Sobers and his cousin added, undefeated, 274. It is easy to argue that Cowdrey, England's captain, did not surround Sobers with a close field. Sobers hinted of no technical flaw, no mental or temperamental anxiety. If he slashed a ball when 93, to Cowdrey's hands, Cowdrey merely let us know that he was mortal when he missed a blistering chance. Bradman has expressed his opinion that few batsmen of his acquaintance hit with the velocity and strength of Sobers. And a sliced shot can travel at murderous pace.

At his best, Sobers scores as easily as any left-handed batsman I have seen since Frank Woolley. He is not classical in his grammar of batsmanship as, say, Martin Donnelly was. To describe Sobers' method I would use the term lyrical. His immense power is concealed, or lightened, to the spectator's eye, by a rhythm which has in it as little obvious propulsion as a movement of music by Mozart (who could be as dramatically strong as Wagner!). A drive through the covers by Sobers sometimes appears to be quite lazy, until we see an offside fieldsman nursing bruised palms, or hear the impact of ball striking the fence. His hook is almost as majestic as MacLaren's, though he hasn't MacLaren's serenity of poise as he makes it. I have actually seen Sobers carried round, off foot balance, while making a hook; it is his only visibly violent stroke – an assault. MacLaren, as I have written many times before, dismissed the ball from his presence. The only flaw in Sobers' technique of batsmanship, as far as I and better judges have been able so far to discern, is a tendency to play at a dangerously swinging away off-side ball "with his arms" – that is to say, with his bat a shade (and more) too far from his body. I fancy

Sydney F. Barnes would have concentrated on this chink in the generally shining armour.

He is a natural product of the West Indies' physical and climatic environment, and of the condition of the game in the West Indies, historical and material, in which he was nurtured. He grew up at a time when the first impulses of West Indies' cricket were becoming rationalised; experience was being added to the original instinctive creative urge, which established the general style and pattern – a creative urge inspired largely by Constantine, after George Challenor had laid a second organised basis of batting technique. Sobers, indeed, flowered as West Indies' cricket was "coming of age". As a youth he could look at Worrell, at Weekes, at Walcott, at Ramadhin, at Valentine. The amazing thing is that he learned from all these superb and definitely formative, constructive West Indies cricketers, for each of them made vintage of the sowings of Challenor, George Headley, Constantine, Austin, Nunes, Roach, and Browne – to name but a few pioneers. Sobers began at the age of ten to bowl orthodox slow left-arm; he had no systematic coaching. (Much the same could safely be said of most truly gifted and individual cricketers.) Practising in the spare time given to him from his first job as a clerk in a shipping house, he developed his spin far enough to win a place, 16 years old now, in a Barbados team against an Indian touring side; moreover, he contrived to get seven wickets in the match for 142.

In the West Indies season of 1953-54, Sobers, now 17, received his Test match baptism at Sabina Park, Kingston. Valentine dropped out of the West Indies XI because of physical disability and Sobers was given his chance – as a bowler, in the fifth game of the rubber. His order in the batting was ninth but he bowled 28 overs, 5 balls for 75 runs, 4 wickets, when England piled-up 414, Hutton 215. In two innings he made 14 not out, and 26. Henceforward he advanced as a predestined master, opening up fresh aspects of his rich endowment of gifts. He began to concentrate on batsmanship, so much so that in 1955, against Australia in the West Indies, he actually shared the opening of an innings with J. K. Holt, in the fourth Test. Facing Lindwall and Miller after Australia had scored 668, he assaulted the greatest fast bowlers of the period to the tune of 43 in a quarter of an hour. Then he suffered the temporary set-back which the fates, in their wisdom, inflict on every budding talent, to prove strength of character. On a tour to New Zealand, the young man, now rising twenty, was one of a West Indies contingent. His Test match record there was modest enough – 81 runs in five innings and two wickets for 49.

He first played for the West Indies in England in 1957, and his form could scarcely have given compensation to his disappointed compatriots when the rubber was lost by three victories to none. His all-round record then was 10 innings, 320 runs, with five wickets costing 70.10 each. Next he became a professional for Radcliffe in the Central Lancashire League, where, as a bowler, he relied on speed and swing. In 1958-59 he was one of the West Indies team in India and Pakistan; and now talent burgeoned prodigiously. On the hard wickets he cultivated his left-arm "googlies", and this new study did not in the least hinder the maturing of his batsmanship. Against India he scored 557, average 92.83, and took ten for 292. Against Pakistan he scored 160, average 32.0 and failed to get anybody out for 78.

The course of his primrose procession since then has been constantly spectacular, rising to a climax of personal glory in Australia in 1960-61. He had staggered cricketers everywhere by his 365 not out v Pakistan in 1958; as a batsman he has gone on and on, threatening to debase the Bradman currency, all the time swinging round a crucial match the West Indies' way by removing an important opposing batsman, or by taking a catch of wondrous rapidity. He has betrodden hemispheres of cricket, become a national symbol of his own islands, the representative image on a postage stamp. Best of all, he has generally maintained the *art* of cricket at a time which day by day – especially in England – threatens to change the game into (a) real industry or (b) a sort of out-of-door "Bingo" cup jousting. He has demonstrated, probably unaware of what he has been doing, the worth of trust in natural-born ability, a lesson wasted on most players here. If he has once or twice lost concentration at the pinch – as he did at Kennington Oval in the fifth Test last year – well, it is human to err, occasionally, even if the gods have lavished on you a share of grace and skill not given to ordinary mortals. The greatest ever? – certainly the greatest all-rounder today, and for decades. And all the more precious is he now, considering the general nakedness of the land.

pages 116 and 121–122

The 1968 edition recorded the deaths of several great cricketers,
including S. F. Barnes, M. Leyland and A. A. Mailey. But
the saddest passing was that of Sir Frank Worrell who had died aged 42.
The following tribute is edited from his obituary, written by another
great West Indian cricketing knight, Sir Learie Constantine.

Sir Frank Worrell

Born in Barbados, August 1, 1924
Died in Jamaica, March 13, 1967
Knighted for his services to cricket, 1964

Sir Frank Worrell once wrote that the island of Barbados, his birthplace, lacked a hero. As usual, he was under-playing himself. Frank Maglinne Worrell was the first hero of the new nation of Barbados and anyone who doubted that had only to be on the island when his body was brought home in mid-March of 1967.

Or in Westminster Abbey when West Indians of all backgrounds and shades of opinion paid their last respects to a man who had done more than any other of their countrymen to bind together the new nations of the Caribbean and establish a reputation for fair play throughout the world. Never before had a cricketer been honoured with a memorial service in Westminster Abbey.

Sir Frank was a man of strong convictions, a brave man and, it goes without saying, a great cricketer. Though he made his name as a player, his greatest contribution was to destroy for ever the myth that a coloured cricketer was not fit to lead a team. Once appointed, he ended the cliques and rivalries between the players of various islands to weld together a team which in the space of five years became the champions of the world.

He was a man of true political sense and feeling, a federalist who surely would have made even greater contributions to the history of the West Indies had he not died so tragically in hospital of leukaemia at the early age of 42, a month after returning from India …

Throughout his life, Sir Frank never lost his sense of humour or his sense of dignity … Sir Frank was ever the diplomat … He would always come up with a smile and a loud laugh. West Indians really laugh their laughs. And Sir Frank laughed louder than most of us.

He was a happy man, a good man and a great man. The really tragic thing about his death was that it cut him off from life when he still had plenty to offer the islands he loved. He was only at the beginning. Or was it that the opportunity came to him a bit too late?

Other Tributes

S. C. Griffith (Secretary, MCC): Ever since I first saw him play during the MCC tour of the West Indies, I have thought of Frank Worrell as a great and impressive batsman and a very useful bowler. Even more than that, I have been impressed by his ever growing stature as a leader of cricketers, by his tolerance and understanding, and by the contribution he was making to the game. He was a great friend of mine and like countless other cricketers I shall miss him more than I can say.

P. B. H. May: The game has lost a personality we all admired. He was one of the greatest of the long line of Barbadian cricketers. One associated him with his two colleagues, Weekes and Walcott; but I regard him as the most accomplished of the trio.

Sir Donald Bradman: His name is for ever shrined on the Frank Worrell Trophy which Australia is proud to have created for permanent competition between our two countries. Players of his calibre are rare. Not only was he a truly great and stylish batsman, he was also a fine thinker with a broad outlook.

Richie Benaud: He was a great leader of men and one of the finest cricketers on and off the field in the history of the game. It is difficult to realise that the indolent drawl, the feline grace known all over the world are no more. Few men have had a better influence on cricket.

Ian Johnson: He was easily the greatest captain of modern times. He brought West Indies cricket to the top and set a wonderful example to world cricket.

Alan Barnes (Secretary, Australian Board of Control): His name is indelibly linked with the finest traditions of cricket throughout the world and particularly in the hearts of all Australian cricket lovers.

E. R. Dexter: His reputation as a cricketer is beyond dispute. I found him one of the best captains I have seen or played against.

F. S. Trueman: He was one of the nicest people I ever played against.

J. M. Kilburn: Cricket was always distinguished in the presence of Worrell – Sir Frank. His knighthood was a personal honour to a cricketer of rare quality and an acknowledgement that West Indian cricket had reached the highest level in the world. In his captaincy he won esteem and affection by the calm demeanour in which he cloaked firmness and shrewd tactics. His serenity smoothed ruffled feathers and diminished crises.

pages 402–403

Glamorgan
v
Nottinghamshire

At Swansea, August 31, September 1, 2, 1968. Nottinghamshire won by 166 runs. Nottinghamshire 18 pts, Glamorgan 5 pts. This was the history-making match in which the incredible Garfield Sobers created a new world record by hitting six sixes in a six-ball over. Somehow one sensed that something extraordinary was going to happen when Sobers sauntered to the wicket. With over 300 runs on the board for the loss of only five wickets, he had the right sort of platform from which to launch a spectacular assault, and the manner in which he immediately settled down to score at a fast rate was ominous.

Then came the history-making over by the 23-year-old Malcolm Nash. First crouched like a black panther eager to pounce, Sobers with lightning footwork got into position for a vicious straight drive or pull. As Tony Lewis, Glamorgan's captain, said afterwards, "It was not sheer slogging through strength, but scientific hitting with every movement working in harmony." Twice the ball was slashed out of the ground, and when the last six landed in the street outside it was not recovered until the next day. Then it was presented to Sobers and will have a permanent place in the Trent Bridge Cricket Museum.

All other events were overshadowed by Sobers's achievement, but the rest of the cricket was not without distinction. In the Nottinghamshire first innings Bolus hit a magnificent century in three hours, fifty minutes, including six sixes and fifteen fours. Glamorgan could not match such boldness although Walker batted steadily for his second century of the season in two hours, forty minutes.

With a first-innings lead of 140 Nottinghamshire then lost half their wickets for 70, but again Sobers accomplished the inevitable, scoring 72 out of 94 in nine minutes under two hours. Eventually Glamorgan had to get 280 to win in four hours, but good bowling by Taylor, who made the most of a damp patch caused by overnight rain, resulted in them being dismissed for 113.

Nottinghamshire

J. B. Bolus c sub b Nash	140	– run out		3
R. A. White c Wheatley b B. Lewis	73	– b Cordle		1
G. Frost c A. R. Lewis b Nash	50	– b Nash		2
M. J. Smedley c A. R. Lewis b Nash	27	– c Majid b Cordle		24
†D. L. Murray b Nash	0	– c Cordle b Shepherd		13
J. M. Parkin not out	15	– not out		9
*G. S. Sobers not out	76	– b Shepherd		72
S. R. Bielby (did not bat)		– not out		13
B 4, l-b 7, n-b 2	13	B 1, n-b 1		2

1/126 2/258 3/289   (5 wkts dec.) 394   1/2 2/7 3/7   (6 wkts dec.) 139
4/289 5/308   4/30 5/70 6/124

M. N. Taylor, D. J. Halfyard and B. Stead did not bat.

Bonus points – Nottinghamshire 5, Glamorgan 2.

Bowling: *First Innings*—Wheatley 5–0–22–0; Nash 21–3–100–4; Cordle 3–1–24–0; Walker 32–4–109–0; Shepherd 25–5–82–0; B. Lewis 13–1–44–1. *Second Innings*—Nash 17–4–53–1; Cordle 16–4–41–2; Shepherd 25–10–43–2.

Glamorgan

A. Jones c Murray b Taylor	25	– c Parkin b Taylor		1
R. Davis c Taylor b Stead	0	– b Stead		18
Majid Jahangir c Taylor b Halfyard	41	– c Bolus b Taylor		4
*A. R. Lewis c Bielby b Taylor	0	– c Bielby b White		52
P. M. Walker not out	104	– c Sobers b White		16
†E. Jones lbw b Sobers	29	– c Stead b Taylor		3
A. E. Cordle lbw b Halfyard	4	– c Smedley b Taylor		4
M. A. Nash b Sobers	8	– b White		5
B. Lewis run out	38	– b Taylor		4
D. J. Shepherd c Sobers b Halfyard	0	– b White		4
O. S. Wheatley b White	1	– not out		0
L-b 3, w 1	4	L-b 2		2

1/0 2/46 3/56 4/78 5/137   254   1/40 2/45 3/49 4/85 5/96   113
6/142 7/179 8/252 9/253   6/100 7/100 8/105 9/113

Bonus points – Glamorgan 3, Nottinghamshire 3.

Bowling: *First Innings*—Sobers 20–6–63–2; Stead 9–3–27–1; Taylor 9–2–23–2; Halfyard 31–8–71–3; White 23.2–5–66–1. *Second Innings*—Stead 9–1–26–1; Taylor 16–6–47–5; Halfyard 7–1–29–0; White 8–5–9–4.

Umpires: J. G. Langridge and W. E. Phillipson.

pages 310–311 and 870

Ireland v West Indies

At Sion Mills, Londonderry, July 2, 1969. Ireland won by nine wickets. In some ways this one-day match provided the sensation of the 1969 season.

The West Indies, with six of the team who had escaped on the previous day from defeat in the Lord's Test, were skittled for 25 in this tiny Ulster town on a damp and definitely emerald green pitch. The conditions were all in favour of the bowlers, but the West Indies batsmen fell in the main to careless strokes and smart catching. Goodwin, the Irish captain, took five wickets for 6 runs and O'Riordan four for 18. Both bowled medium pace at a reasonable length and the pitch did the rest. It was not a first-class match, but Ireland's performance deserves a permanent record and therefore we give the full score.

West Indies

G. S. Camacho c Dineen b Goodwin	1	– c Dineen b Goodwin	1
M. C. Carew c Hughes b O'Riordan	0	– c Pigot b Duffy	25
M. L. C. Foster run out	2	– c Pigot b Goodwin	0
*B. F. Butcher c Duffy b O'Riordan	2	– c Waters b Duffy	50
C. H. Lloyd c Waters b Goodwin	1	– not out	0
C. L. Walcott c Anderson b O'Riordan	6	– not out	0
J. N. Shepherd c Duffy b Goodwin	0		
†T. M. Findlay c Waters b Goodwin	0		
G. C. Shillingford not out	9		
P. Roberts c Colhoun b O'Riordan	0		
P. D. Blair b Goodwin	3		
B 1	1	L-b 2	2

1/1 2/1 3/3 4/6 5/6   25   1/1 2/2 3/73 4/78   (4 wkts) 78
6/8 7/12 8/12 9/12

Bowling: *First Innings*—O'Riordan 13–8–18–4; Goodwin 12.3–8–6–5. *Second Innings*—O'Riordan 6–1–21–0; Goodwin 2–1–1–2; Hughes 7–4–10–0; Duffy 12–8–12–2; Anderson 7–1–32–0.

Ireland

R. H. C. Waters c Findlay b Blair	2	G. A. Duffy not out	15
D. M. Pigot c Camacho b Shillingford	37	L. F. Hughes c sub b Carew	13
M. Reith lbw b Shepherd	10	L-b 2, n-b 4	6
J. Harrison lbw b Shepherd	0		
I. Anderson c Shepherd b Roberts	7	1/19 2/30 3/34	(8 wkts dec.) 125
P. J. Dineen b Shepherd	0	4/51 5/55 6/69	
A. J. O'Riordan c and b Carew	35	7/103 8/125	

*D. E. Goodwin and †O. D. Colhoun did not bat.

Bowling: Blair 8–4–14–1; Shillingford 7–2–19–1; Shepherd 13–4–20–3; Roberts 16–3–43–1; Carew 3.2–0–23–2.

Umpires: M. Stott and A. Trickett.

In the same edition, Wisden *reprinted Richard Streeton's report of this match from* The Times *(July 3). The following explanation is quoted from that report.*

When Ireland batted they established a lead of 100 runs and then declared with two wickets in hand – an imperious gesture but an opportunity not to be missed. It had the added advantage of letting the crowd see the touring team bat again.

The official result under the laws of cricket goes down to posterity as a win for Ireland by nine wickets on first innings. The full mathematical details will be pasted in many a scrap-book in Sion Mills, described by a helpful assistant in the local library as having one street, 1,569 souls at the 1966 census and with linen mills providing the main source of employment. In the Caribbean the same details will be regarded with awe for a long time.

page 101–105

Peter May – the Complete Master

By John Woodcock

When Peter May announced his retirement from first-class cricket in 1962, at the young age of thirty-two, it was hoped that he might one day play again. That he has never done so is the reason for an appreciation such as this having been delayed for so long.

Cricket followers bestowed the same peculiar favour upon May as they had upon Denis Charles Scott Compton and John Berry Hobbs. They knew him by his full name. Ask those who played with or against him between 1955 and 1960, or who watched him play, and they will tell you that Peter Barker Howard May was England's finest post-war batsman.

Heredity had nothing to do with it. There was no cricketing thread running through the family. He lacked the instant look of a games player or the natural movements of an athlete. Between the wickets he had a stiff, rather ungainly run. Yet as soon as he appeared in the nets at Charterhouse he was seen to have a most uncommon talent. In his first summer term, when he was still only thirteen, there was a move to play him in the first eleven. Robert Birley, the headmaster, was consulted, and May, for his own good, was made to wait. In the following year, at the age of fourteen and a half, he took a hundred off the Harrow bowling in less than an hour and a half. R. L. Arrowsmith, through whose hands passed a multitude of Carthusian cricketers, writes that "even the things you can teach every boy, to have his boots and pads clean, not to run on the pitch, etc., Peter seemed to know by instinct".

May was fortunate, of course, in the pitches on which he learnt to bat. On the hill at Charterhouse they were fast and true, and at Fenner's they were even truer. In 1950, his first year at Cambridge, four of the University side – John Dewes, Hubert Doggart, David Sheppard and May – were chosen for the Test Trial at Bradford, and by the end of 1951 they had all played for England. May did so for the first time against South Africa at Headingley in 1951, and in his first Test innings he made 138.

By the winter of 1953-54 he was in the West Indies under Len Hutton; by 1954-55 he was Hutton's vice-captain in Australia and New Zealand; and when Len gave up the captaincy it was handed on to May. Still only 26, he wasn't really ready for it; but Trevor Bailey had been passed over, and Sheppard had embarked on the road to Woolwich, and May's place in the England side was assured for years to come. Although he had held the captaincy of Cambridge at soccer he had never done so at cricket, and as Writer P. B. H. May during his National Service in the Royal Navy he had had no experience of leadership. Nor had he yet taken over at The Oval from Stuart Surridge. Yet here he was, handling the England side at a younger age than anyone except A. P. F. Chapman. All things considered he did it well, although I am not sure that we gave him credit for that at the time.

His chief qualities as a captain were his courtesy and his intensity of purpose. He was also unwaveringly straight. His players knew exactly where they were with him, and if at times he was too lenient for their own good that was a fault they enjoyed. He was indulgent with them in Australia in 1958-59, when we lost the Ashes without a good enough fight, and it had been the same in South Africa two years before. The last of his tours, to the West Indies in 1959-60, was also the least happy. He and his manager, Walter Robins, viewed the responsibilities of an MCC side in hopelessly differing ways. May thought they were there primarily to win, Robins primarily to entertain. To make matters worse, Peter became so unwell that the doctors ordered him home before the tour was over. That, in the event, was the end of his captaincy, and he surrendered it, I think, without regret. In only five years he had led England 41 times … Under him England had won 20 Test Matches, drawn 11 and lost 10.

I am writing this on my way to Australia, and we have just flown over India and Pakistan where May never played. Soon we shall be in Melbourne where I can see him now, hitting Ray Lindwall off the back foot with a cold and calculated fury. One after the other Lindwall took his slips away, to reinforce the covers, and they in their turn were left wringing their hands. That was in 1954, when May was one of the four young men who did so much to help Hutton retain the Ashes. The others were Colin Cowdrey, Brian Statham and Frank Tyson.

Back in England, in the summer of 1955, May and Denis Compton carried the English batting. In his seven Test innings, against a South African attack which included such fine bowlers as Heine, Adcock and Tayfield, May failed only twice. In 1956, when Australia were in England, he had another wonderfully successful season, averaging 90 on some far from perfect pitches. In these two home series, against South Africa and Australia, May made 1,035 runs, and in only four out of sixteen innings was he out for fewer than 40.

In the winter of 1956-57, on his first tour as captain, he had his one bad series – against the same South African bowling as he had scattered to the winds in 1955. He began the tour with hundreds in each of his first four innings – against Western Province, Eastern Province, and in successive weeks against Rhodesia. Wherever we went the crowds poured in to see May at the wicket. His mastery seemed complete – until the Tests began. Then the strain of having supported the English batting through two hard series took its toll.

In 1957 and 1958 he was back in form and the outstanding batsman of the English season. His 285 not out, in the first Test match against the West Indies at Edgbaston in 1957, was one of the landmarks of his career. When he went in his side was facing an overwhelming defeat, and he remembers feeling unexpectedly composed. With Cowdrey he shared a fourth-wicket partnership of 411 which gave England a hold on the series and broke the spell that Ramadhin had cast upon England's batsmen since 1950. In Australia in 1958-59 May would have made more runs, I thought, but for the cares of captaincy, and in his nineteen Test innings after that he scored only two more hundreds. His illness in the West Indies in 1959-60 caused him to miss the English season of 1960. In 1961 he made a last and unsuccessful attempt to regain the Ashes which he had lost in 1958-59, and after one more year with Surrey, when he asked not to be considered for England, he retired. Despite frequent petitions from friends and selectors he refused to come back.

On the few occasions that May can still be persuaded to take a bat in his hand, either for charity or a friend, he plays in a different dimension from anyone else in the game. To see him is to be reminded of his class. The on-drive was his particular glory. Though one of the hardest of all strokes to play, he scored many runs with it even as a boy. From wide mid-on to cover point, off front foot and back, his shots had great power, the result of timing rather than strength. The most remarkable stroke I ever saw him play was at Lord's, when from the middle of the ground he hit a medium-pacer high into the Mound Stand, over extra cover and off the *back* foot.

He had a delicate touch with both the late cut and the leg glance; but the hook, and more especially the sweep, were not among his favourite strokes. He was too good a straight hitter to need to sweep, and the hook carried an element of risk which he hardly cared for. Brilliant player though he was, he took few risks, partly because he didn't need to. As for statistics, he paid them more attention than some might suppose. A milestone he would have liked to reach was 100 hundreds. In another two or three years he would have become the first amateur since "W. G." to have made so many, and that would have appealed to him.

At the same time he was a conspicuously unselfish cricketer, always ready to shield a lesser player or to give himself up if he thought it was someone else's turn to bat. He was above pettiness and completely uninterested in gossip, and on tour he was unfailingly loyal to his players. "A good day for the boys" he used to say, even when he knew it wasn't. To the public he was polite but unforthcoming. He gave them his time but not his attention. It was as though he had modelled himself on Hutton. He had the same distant and yet disarming manner, the same flair for the enigmatic reply. Like Len he was quietly scathing about batsmen who played recklessly in a crisis, and bowlers who had a job to make up their minds what field they wanted. Like Hutton, too, he was a masterly player on bad wickets. During the fifties, when Surrey were having their great run in the Championship, the wickets were all in the bowlers' favour. If not specifically prepared to suit Bedser, Lock and Laker, they certainly did so. Yet May batted superbly on them, seldom compromising his wish to attack.

He took over the captaincy of Surrey in 1957, by which time they had been champion county for five successive years, and in 1957 and 1958 they won again. May's predecessor at The Oval was Stuart Surridge, a strong character whose style might have been expected to influence May more than it did. While Surridge was forthright, May was unyielding. He listened to Alec Bedser and one or two of the older Surrey professionals, but generally speaking he had his own way of doing things and he rarely changed it.

It was this spirit of independence which decided him to retire when he did, and to remain in retirement. Although for ten years and more cricket was his whole life, it was never his profession. He enjoyed the pleasure and the success it brought him, and the opportunities it provided of seeing the world. He was quietly delighted with a standing ovation at the Guildhall in Cape Town for having spoken a few sentences in Afrikaans which he had learnt on the ship going out.

He must have enjoyed waving modestly from The Oval balcony whenever Surrey won the Championship or England won a series. As a perfectionist he could take pride in many of his innings. But having reached the age of thirty-two he turned happily enough to the City and the life of a family man. With four daughters he is surrounded now by women and by his wife's horses which he resolutely refuses to ride. He was an England selector from 1965 to 1968* and he serves on numerous committees at Lord's and The Oval, to which no doubt he brings the same gentle determination of his playing career.

---

* Peter May returned to the England selection panel, as chairman, from 1982 to 1988. He died on December 27, 1994, four days short of his 65th birthday.

page 645

*As a half-page filler, the 1972 edition reprinted the following
extract taken from "How's That", the official publication of the
Association of Cricket Umpires.*

Ye Olde Game of Cricket

Here are some extracts from a Code of Laws of Cricket, first published in 1755.

1. Laws for the Bowler

If he delivers ye ball with his hinder foot over ye bowling crease ye Umpire shall call No Ball though she be struck or ye player is bowled out, which he shall do without being asked and no person shall have any right to ask him.

2. Laws for the Umpires

To allow 2 minutes for each man to come in when one is out and 10 minutes between each hand. To mark ye ball that it may not be changed. They are sole judges of all outs and ins, of all Fair and Unfair play or frivolous delays, of all hurts whether real or pretended, and are discretionally to allow what time they think proper before ye game goes on again. In case of a real hurt to a Striker they are to allow another to come in & ye persons hurt to come in again. But are not to allow a fresh man to play on either side on any account. They are sole judges of all hindrances, crossing ye players in running & standing unfair to strike & in case of hindrance may order a notch to be scored. They are not to order any man out unless appealed to by any one of ye players. These Laws are to ye Umpires jointly. Each Umpire is ye sole judge of all nips and catches, ins and outs, good or bad runs at his own wicket & his determination shall be absolute & he shall not be changed for another Umpire without ye consent of both sides. When ye 4 balls are bowled he is to call Over. These Laws are separately. When both Umpires shall call Play 3 times 'tis at ye peril of giving ye game from them that refuse to play.

and

3. When ye ball has been in hand by one of ye keepers or stoppers and ye player has been at home he may go where he pleases till ye next ball is bowled. If either of ye strikers is cross'd in his running ground designedly, which design must be determined by ye Umpires, ye Umpires may order that notch to be scored.

pages 226 and 352

Throwing the Cricket Ball

140 yards 2 feet   Richard Percival, on the Durham Sands, Co. Durham
                    Racecourse, 1884
140 yards 9 inches Ross Mackenzie, at Toronto, 1872

W. F. Forbes, on March 16, 1876, threw 132 yards at the Eton College Sports.
He was then 18 years of age.

William Yardley, while a boy at Rugby, threw 100 yards with his right
hand and 78 yards with his left.

Charles Arnold, of Cambridge, once threw 112 yards with the wind and
108 against. W. H. Game, at The Oval, in 1875, threw the ball 111 yards and
then back the same distance. W. G. Grace threw 109 yards one way and
back 105, and George Millyard 108 with the wind and 103 against. At The
Oval in 1868, W. G. Grace made three successive throws of 116, 117 and
118 yards, and then threw back over 100 yards. D. G. Foster (Warwickshire)
has thrown 133 yards, and in 1930 he made a Danish record with 120.1
metres – about 130 yards.

The above extract appeared in the Cricket Records section,
where it can still be found in the 2000 edition of Wisden.
The 1973 edition also included the following report.

An attempt by the villages of Britain to uncover a man to challenge the record
set up in 1884 when R. Percival threw a cricket ball 140 yards 2 feet at Durham
Sands Racecourse proved abortive. After a nation-wide search for a strong
arm, the best that could be produced for the final at Lord's on September 9, as
a subsidiary to the Village Cricket Championship match, was 106 yards. The
throw was by Michael Richardson, a 17-year-old from Northumberland.

In later editions, Wisden *added "King Billy" the Aborigine as having*
thrown 140 yards at Clermont, Queensland, in 1872, and the following
footnote also appeared in the 1999 edition.

Extensive research by David Rayvern Allen has shown that these traditional records are probably authentic, if not necessarily wholly accurate. Modern competitions have failed to produce similar distances although Ian Pont, the Essex all-rounder who also played baseball, was reported to have thrown 138 yards in Cape Town in 1981. There have been speculative reports attributing throws of 150 yards or more to figures as diverse as the South African Test player Colin Bland, the Latvian javelin thrower Janis Lusis, who won a gold medal for the Soviet Union in the 1968 Olympics, and the British sprinter Charley Ransome. The definitive record is still awaited.

pages 1027–1029 and 1114

The Women's World Cup Competition, 1973

By Netta Rheinberg

In 1777 The Third Duke of Dorset watched the Countess of Derby's XI play a Ladies' Invitation team at The Oaks in Surrey. He wrote afterwards: "What is human life but a game of cricket? And if so, why should not the ladies play it as well as we?" Ever since those days the ladies have been proving his point and certainly, nearly 200 years later, the staging by women cricketers in 1973 of the first ever World Cup Competition has shown beyond a doubt that, thin on the ground as we women cricketers are, we are still not afraid of trying out something new and not lacking in enterprise.*

The whole ambitious project of the World Cup Competition would not have been possible without the financial generosity and support of our patron, Jack Hayward. The two West Indian teams were Government helped, members of the Australian and New Zealand teams paid their own way to and from this country and the Women's Cricket Association also footed the bill for a great deal.

After a two week period of gathering together and settling down in London, Dr Roger Bannister, Chairman of the Sports Council, declared the Competition open at the Civil Service Sports Ground, Chiswick on June 16, at a colourful opening ceremony attended by seven teams from five nations. There should have been a sixth nation, India, who requested inclusion in the Competition, but too late for acceptance; and had difficulties not arisen, there would have been a seventh nationality, South Africa, but the Jamaican and Trinidad & Tobago governments would not permit their teams to play with or against the five South African players who had been invited to join the International team.

One of the most memorable Receptions was that given to all the teams by the Prime Minister at No. 10 Downing Street. Mr Heath, in a short informal speech of welcome, referred to Lady Baldwin, wife of the former Prime Minister and a cricketer of some repute. She was a member of the White Heather Women's Cricket club and she called a committee meeting of the club at No. 10 during the General Strike of 1926.

The competition proper began on June 20 with 21 international matches spread over six weeks and played on different grounds in widely scattered parts of the country, from Bletchley to Bradford, Sittingbourne to Swansea, and Eastbourne to Edgbaston ...

The final "needle" match at Edgbaston between England and Australia proved to be of the highest standard and quality producing some of the best cricket within living memory. England, having won the toss, batted with no sign at all of any tension. Enid Bakewell (118) scored fluently and looked as relaxed as if she had been on the beach. Admittedly she was served a rather tasty diet of all sorts of bowling, which she digested with relish. Her example inspired the team and she received excellent support from Lynne Thomas (40), Rachael Flint (64) and Chris Watmough (32 not out). Those who watched the morning's performance will not easily forget the sparkle of the game in the excellent setting of Edgbaston and under a cloudless sky. During the afternoon, when the Australians' turn came to bat, Princess Anne arrived to watch and stayed to present the cup at the end. After England's batting, Australia's performance came as something of an anticlimax and they never succeeded in mastering the situation. The fielding of both teams was a joy to watch and especially, for England, Jill Cruwys' throwing in from the deep which would put many county players to shame.

At Edgbaston, July 28, 1973: England 273 for 3 (E. Bakewell 118, R. Flint 64, L. Thomas 40, C. Watmough 32 not out) beat Australia 187 for 9 (J. Potter 57, B. Wilson 41, E. Bray 40) by 92 runs.

FINAL TABLE

	Played	Won	Lost	No Decision	Points
England	6	5	1	0	20
Australia	6	4	1	1	17
International XI	6	3	2	1	13
New Zealand	6	3	2	1	13
Trinidad and Tobago	6	2	4	0	8
Jamaica	6	1	4	1	5
Young England	6	1	5	0	4

* The 1974 edition also included the following report, which confirmed that the men's game would follow the women's lead by staging a World Cup tournament in 1975.

The International [Cricket] Conference at their annual meeting at Lord's on July 25, 26, 1973, approved a plan put forward by the Test and County Cricket Board for a tournament in England in 1975 involving all the current Test playing countries. The games would be 60 overs a side, with the competition organised in two groups of four countries, each playing one another on a League basis, and the leading two sides in each group proceeding to the semi-finals. The final would be at Lord's on the normal Saturday of the Lord's Test. The countries to be invited to complete an entry of eight teams would be East Africa and Sri Lanka.

A sponsor was to be sought to defray the costs. Ten per cent of the profits would go to the United Kingdom as the promoters, with 7½ per cent to each of the seven other countries. The remaining 37½ per cent would be divided between non-competing members of the ICC and an International Coaching Fund.

pages 67–68

The Pleasures of Cricket

By HRH The Duke of Edinburgh, KG, KT, President of the MCC 1949 and 1974-75

Watching cricket without *Wisden* is almost as unthinkable as batting without pads. There is a widely held and quite erroneous belief that cricket is just another game. It is true that games are played and cricket is played, but there is very much more to it than that. It can be as brutal as rugby and as delicate as chess; it requires all the grace and fitness of athletics, but at the same time it requires the psychological insight and judgement of master politicians. Any similarity between a Test team on tour and a bunch of cricketers having a jolly time only exists in the romantic imaginations. Not that I have ever had first-hand experience of a touring team, but I have played cricket and I have been to most of the cricketing countries of the world. Occasionally, there is a match which might be described as a game, but otherwise the whole thing bears a closer resemblance to Wellington's campaign in the Peninsular War than to so many "flannelled fools" amusing themselves in the sun. Then there are the statistics, courtesy of *Wisden,* which add their particular dimension.

I enjoy everything about cricket. I suppose I must have played the game off and on from the age of eight until about forty-eight, and I am sure I shall go on watching it as long as I can. Exactly how I came to be President of the MCC in 1949 escapes me at the moment, but I do not mind admitting that I remember how inordinately proud I was. I suppose I must have been one of the very few village, with a dash of club, cricketers to step into this legendary position. Now, 25 years later, I am, if anything, prouder still to be so closely associated once again with this most English of games and to preside over the destinies of that most English of institutions, the Marylebone Cricket Club at Lord's.

A lot has changed, of course, although the game itself is much the same. 1962 saw the end of the distinction between Gentlemen and Players, and it was during my term of office that twenty-six distinguished retired Players were invited to become Hon. Members of the MCC. In those days it was assumed that sports and games would be self-supporting and commercial sponsorship was hardly known. There was a bit of League cricket, more generally appreciated in the north than in the south, but I do not think anyone ever dreamed that one-day league and knock-out games would ever develop the way they have. However, even then it was appreciated that the first-class game would become almost entirely professional and therefore it would be necessary to have rather more cricket to keep the players fully occupied and to cover costs.

For the moment, cricket looks pretty healthy. The recent Test series in Australia has stirred up some splendid arguments and these are just as much a part of the game as everything else. I shall only start to worry if cricket ever ceases to be a topic of heated discussion over drinks in pubs and clubs.

At one time it looked as if it might become a purely spectator sport, but there are signs that people are re-discovering the pleasures of actually playing the game and, who knows, perhaps even schools and universities may notice that they are missing something.

To attempt to see into the future at this time of financial and social confusion would be folly, but there is no harm in making a few suggestions. It seems to me unwise to place too great a reliance on a growing or even on a steady contribution of commercial sponsorship to the first-class game. First-class cricket, including international competition, is essential to the game as a whole but it would not be in the best interests of cricket if the first-class game became too widely separated from club and other levels of the game. There are hopeful signs that the administrators are aware of the need to improve the structure.

If the game is to flourish in the future, there are two absolutely vital requirements. In the first place, clubs must be allowed to be viable organisations. Secondly, the younger generations need the encouragement of sympathetic teachers and the expert instruction of competent coaches.

In the meantime, we have the first World Cup type of competition to look forward to this summer, as well as an intriguing series against the Australians.

For the active players in schools, villages and clubs, the fixture lists have been more or less completed; the pavilions dusted out; hats, pads, flannels and other essential equipment pulled out from behind the golf clubs and walking sticks; and the pitches are being prepared for another and, I hope, successful attempt to improve the statistics of last year.

pages 318–319

The First World Cup Final

Australia v West Indies

At Lord's, June 21, 1975. West Indies won by 17 runs and Prince Philip presented the Cup amidst hilarious scenes to their talented captain, the Man of the Match, Clive Lloyd, just before nine o'clock on a glorious summer's evening. From 11 a.m. till 8.43 p.m. the cricketers from the Caribbean had been locked in a succession of thrills with the cricketers from the Southern Cross. It might not be termed first-class cricket, but the game has never produced better entertainment in one day.

The deciding factor was the wonderful hundred by Clive Lloyd after Ian Chappell had won the toss and invited the West Indies to bat. Until Lloyd arrived at 50 for three, Chappell had set a fairly tight field and his battery of quick seam bowlers had kept the West Indies under subjection. Australia gained the initiative when Fredericks hooked a bouncer high over fine leg for six only to lose his balance and tread on his wicket. Greenidge spent eighty minutes crawling to 13 and a rash cut by Kallicharran ended in a flick to the wicket-keeper.

Then came Lloyd and at once he showed himself master of the situation.

He hooked Lillee in majestic style, square for six, and then put Walker off the back foot past cover with disdainful ease. At the other end Lloyd had the dependable Kanhai as a willing anchor man – he did not score for 11 overs – and so the pair put on 149 together in 36 overs. Lloyd hit two sixes and twelve fours and was at the crease only one hour and forty-eight minutes while making his scintillating hundred off 82 balls. More powerful hitting came from Boyce and Julien so that Australia required 292 to lift the Cup.

Although they challenged to the very end and might have won had they shown some discretion when trying to steal precious runs, they contributed to their own destruction, for as many as five men were run out by the brilliant West Indies fielders. Kallicharran began their troubles with a dazzling slip catch which removed McCosker, while the amazing Richards threw down the stumps twice from backward square leg and also enabled Lloyd to break the wicket at the bowler's end when Ian Chappell hesitated and then set off for the third impossible run.

Nevertheless, Turner and particularly Ian Chappell played extremely well before their mishaps, but West Indies always had the edge until near the end when Thomson and Lillee threw their bats, adding 41 in their attempt to win a lost cause. It was the longest day of the year; the longest day in cricket history and one that those who were there and the millions who watched it on television will never forget. The full attendance was 26,000 and the paying crowd produced gross receipts of £66,950, a record for a one-day match in England.

West Indies

R. C. Fredericks hit wkt b Lillee		7
C. G. Greenidge c Marsh b Thomson		13
A. I. Kallicharran c Marsh b Gilmour		12
R. B. Kanhai b Gilmour		55
*C. H. Lloyd c Marsh b Gilmour		102
I. V. A. Richards b Gilmour		5
K. D. Boyce c G. S. Chappell b Thomson		34
B. D. Julien not out		26
†D. L. Murray c and b Gilmour		14
V. A. Holder not out		6
L-b 6, n-b 11		17

A. M. E. Roberts did not bat.

1/12 2/27 3/50 4/199 5/206 6/209 7/261 8/285   (8 wkts, 60 overs) 291

Bowling: Lillee 12–1–55–1; Gilmour 12–2–48–5; Thomson 12–1–44–2; Walker 12–1–71–0; G. S. Chappell 7–0–33–0; Walters 5–0–23–0.

Australia

A. Turner run out		40
R. B. McCosker c Kallicharran b Boyce		7
*I. M. Chappell run out		62
G. S. Chappell run out		15
K. D. Walters b Lloyd		35
†R. W. Marsh b Boyce		11
R. Edwards c Fredericks b Boyce		28
G. J. Gilmour c Kanhai b Boyce		14
M. H. N. Walker run out		7
J. R. Thomson run out		21
D. K. Lillee not out		16
B 2, l-b 9, n-b 7		18

1/25 2/81 3/115 4/162 5/170 6/195 7/221 8/231 9/233   (58.4 overs) 274

Bowling: Julien 12–0–58–0; Roberts 11–1–45–0; Boyce 12–0–50–4; Holder 11.4–1–65–0; Lloyd 12–1–38–1.

Umpires: H. D. Bird and T. W. Spencer.

pages 95–97

Five Cricketers of the Year

Cricketer of the Century: Vivian Richards

By Tony Cozier

The modern generation of cricket followers were provided with an ample illustration of what the legendary Don Bradman's domination of the game must have been like in the 1930s by the exploits of Isaac Vivian Alexander Richards, the West Indian batsman, during the first eight months of 1976.

In the eleven Tests he managed to cram into that period, Richards accumulated 1,710 runs with the style and consistency of a great player. No other batsman in the history of the game had scored nearly so many in a calendar year although, it must be admitted, Bradman and others before the recent expansion of Test cricket never had the opportunity to bat as frequently.

Even so, the fact that Richards maintained his phenomenal form in three separate series in three different parts of the world enhanced the excellence of his feat. His sequence started with scores of 44, 2, 30, 101, 50 and 98 against the "lethal" Australian fast bowling in the final three Tests of a series which, otherwise, proved disastrous for the West Indies. It continued in the Caribbean, in the four-Test series against India, with scores of 142, 130, 20 run out, 177, 23 and 64 against the best spinners in the game. It culminated in the English summer when, in the sunshine against bowling of no outstanding merit, he helped himself to 829 runs in seven innings – including scores of 291, 232 and 135.

His aggregate in the Tests in England was the highest by any West Indian in a single series and, yet, he was forced to miss the second Test through illness.

If he fails to make another run in Test cricket, Richards' performances in 1976 will always be a source of conversation for the enthusiasts – and inspiration to young batsmen. Indications are, however, that Richards has only just started on what should be a prolific career.

He was born on March 7, 1952 on the island of Antigua … His advance to the heights which he has already achieved reflects the changing structure of West Indian – and, indeed, world – cricket in the past decade or so. It has only been in that period that teams from the Windward and Leeward Islands have been included in the mainstream of first-class cricket in the West Indies, joining the four more developed territories of Barbados, Guyana, Jamaica and Trinidad which, for years, exclusively provided players for the Test team.

Nevertheless, cricket has always been played and followed with no less fervour in the smaller islands of the English-speaking Caribbean than it has been in the larger ones and opportunity was all their players lacked. That has now been provided with the Windwards and Leewards competing in the annual Shell Shield (senior) and Benson and Hedges Trophy (junior) championships as well as playing against touring teams.

Richards and others of his generation had no obstacles as those before them did. One such had been Richards' father, Malcolm, Antigua's leading fast bowler for many years, to whom first-class cricket could only be a dream. At least he has had the satisfaction of seeing three of his sons reach that level. In addition to Vivian, Donald, a fast-medium bowler, and Mervyn, a batsman, have represented the Leeward Islands.

It was clear from his school days that Vivian possessed something special as a natural ball player. He was chosen for Antigua in cricket and soccer when still in his teens and was the idol of the crowds. It was this which probably delayed his entry into first-class cricket for an incident, involving his home crowd during an inter-island match, brought him a two-year suspension in 1969.

Given out caught, Richards had indicated to the umpire and his adoring spectators that he had not hit the ball and stamped off in obvious annoyance. The result was a chain reaction among the crowd, which stopped play and chanted "No Vivi, No Match". Shockingly, the officials bowed to the mob, overruled the decision and allowed Richards to continue. Even though he allowed himself to be stumped immediately on resumption, Richards had to shoulder the blame and was banned.

It was not until the 1972 season, at the age of 20, that he could be chosen for the Leeward and Combined Islands teams in the domestic West Indian competitions and he quickly attracted attention with an innings of 82 against the touring New Zealanders. His natural ability was unmistakable, both with the bat and in the field. Yet he lacked application and he regularly got himself out when seemingly well set.

Two developments early in 1973 had a beneficial effect on his future. The first was a spell at Alf Gover's Cricket School in London, financed by public subscription which sent him and another promising young Antiguan, Andy Roberts by name, for the summer. In that time, Richards played club cricket in Taunton, Roberts in Southampton and, by the following year, both were making their presence felt in county cricket for Somerset and Hampshire respectively.

Richards' association with Somerset began when he was spotted playing for Antigua against a touring English club team, the Acorns, which included several Somerset members. His stint in the day-to-day atmosphere of county cricket has unquestionably benefited Richards and he pays glowing tribute to the advice and guidance offered him by his county captain, Brian Close.

In fact, before he had played a first-class match for Somerset, Richards had not been able to discipline himself sufficiently to score his maiden first-class century in the Caribbean. It was, therefore, an inspired choice by the West Indian selectors when they picked him, with no convincing statistical background, for the tour of India, Sri Lanka and Pakistan in 1974-75. That Rohan Kanhai might have been given the place that eventually went to Richards represented a courageous selection.

Since then, Richards has gone from strength to strength. He gained a place in the Test team in the first instance only because Lawrence Rowe was unavailable with eyesight problems but, since making his debut at Bangalore 1974, he has missed only one Test – and that through illness.

After two failures against Chandrasekhar in that first Test, Richards revealed ideal temperament with an undefeated 191 in his next innings at New Delhi. Even when he has failed to score many, his value in the field, in any position, is inestimable. His run-out of three batsmen in the 1975 Prudential Cup Final at Lord's was as decisive as Clive Lloyd's memorable century.

In Australia, during the 1975-76 series, Richards always appeared the most comfortable of the West Indian batsmen, but he seemed to be slipping back into his old habit of needlessly giving his wicket away when set. The decision was taken for him to open the batting mainly because the position was a selectorial problem, partly because it was felt that the responsibility would encourage Richards to concentrate more.

It proved an astute move, for it started Richards on his succession of big scores. Ideally, however, he is a number three and, after the experiment in Australia, it is in that position that he has batted since.

Self-confidence, without arrogance, is one of Richards' hallmarks. Another is the unconfined enjoyment he gets out of the game. Both will be tested when he is forced to endure the barren periods which are the lot of all cricketers, great and humble alike. For the year 1976, however, Vivian Richards stood on top of the cricketing world and enjoyed it.

The other four Cricketers of the Year in 1977 were J. M. Brearley, C. G. Greenidge, M. A. Holding and R. W. Taylor.

pages 130–132

The Centenary Test Match

Australia Victorious Again by 45 Runs

By Reg Hayter

At Melbourne, March 12, 13, 14, 16, 17, 1977. An occasion of warmest reunion and nostalgia, the cricket continuously compelling, a result straining credulity. Hans Ebeling, former Australian Test bowler and the inspiration of it all, should have been christened Hans Andersen Ebeling.

From Ebeling, a vice-president of the Melbourne Cricket Club, originated the suggestion to signalise 100 years of Test Cricket by a match between England and Australia on the same ground – in 1877 the Richmond Police Paddock – on which David Gregory's team beat James Lillywhite's all-round professional England side.

The Victorian Cricket Association and the Melbourne Cricket Club co-operated to bring this about and, with sponsorship from Qantas, TAA, Benson and Hedges and the Melbourne Hilton Hotel, a masterpiece of organisation resulted in an event which none fortunate enough to be present could forget. Unlucky were those who missed it.

Arrangements were made for the England team visiting India to extend their tour to play an official Test in the same month as the 1877 Test, and invitations to attend as guests were sent to the 244 living cricketers who had played for Australia or England in the series. All but 26 of these were able to accept for an event unique in history.

The oldest Australian Test player present was the 87-year-old Jack Ryder. Even though suffering from near blindness, the 84-year-old Percy Fender made the enervating air journey from Britain as the oldest English representative. He was accompanied by his grandson, Jeremy, who became his cricketing eyes. Poor health alone prevented E. J. ("Tiger") Smith and Herbert Sutcliffe to travel and, for the same reason, Frank Woolley could not leave Canada.

Of those who went to Melbourne many told unusual stories. Colin McCool was marooned in his Queensland home by floods and had to be hauled up from his front lawn by helicopter for the airport. Jack

Rutherford's train broke down and he finished the journey to the airport by taxi. Denis Compton – who else? – left his passport in a Cardiff hotel and, but for the early start to the pre-flight champagne party at London Airport which enabled a good friend to test the speed limits on the M4, would have missed the plane.

Some ex-England players – Harold Larwood, Peter Loader, Tony Lock, Barry Knight, Frank Tyson – already lived in Australia and the Australian Neil Hawke flew home from England. The gradual gathering of all at the Hilton Hotel, 200 yards across the Jolimont Park from the Melbourne Oval, brought meetings and greetings of unabated happiness. Not a hitch, not one.

Fittingly, this was also Melbourne's Mardi Gras, a week called "Moomba", the aboriginal word for "let's get together and have fun". After a champagne (much was drunk between London and Melbourne and back) breakfast and an opening ceremony on which ex-Test captains accompanied the teams on to the field, the crowd were also given the opportunity of a special welcome to all the former Test players.

Greig called correctly to Greg Chappell's spin of the specially-minted gold coin and chose for England to field first. Probably he felt apprehension about his batsmen facing Lillee while moisture remained in the pitch. The resolute fast-medium bowling of Willis, Old and Lever, helped by Underwood's customary left-handed accuracy and breathtakingly supported in the field, appeared to justify Greig's decision in Australia's dismissal for 138 in front of a crowd of over 61,000.

Australia, handicapped by the early departure of McCosker, who fractured his jaw when a ball from Willis flew off his hand into his face, were always on the defensive. England's batting buckled even more swiftly against Lillee, at the zenith of his form and speed, and Walker – Australia's fielding being no whit inferior to that of England.

That was the last of the bowling mastery. On the second, third and fourth days Australia increased their first innings lead of 43 so much that their declaration left England 463 to win at 40 an hour.

Marsh, who had already beaten Grout's record of 187 Test victims, added to his triumph by his first Test century against England, and Walters joyfully rode his fortune in the manner that has charmed so many cricket admirers of the cavalier approach to batsmanship. Yet the spotlight centred on the 21-year-old David Hookes who won his place on the forthcoming tour to England with an innings straight from the fount of youth. This six feet, two inches powerful left-handed batsman, who had scored five centuries in 1976-77 Sheffield Shield cricket, strode to the crease with a confidence even more apparent when he struck Greig for five fours in an over – off, pull, cover, mid-wicket, cover.

Then it was England's turn. And, in the presence of the Queen and the

Duke of Edinburgh – during an interval they drove round the ground and were hugely acclaimed – royally did they apply themselves. Well as Amiss, Greig, Knott and Brearley batted, however, the innings to remember was played by Randall, a jaunty, restless, bubbling character, whose 174 took England to the doorstep of victory. The Australian spectators enjoyed his approach as much as Indian crowds had done on the tour just finished.

Once, when Lillee tested him with a bouncer, he tennis-batted it to the mid-wicket fence with a speed and power that made many a rheumy eye turn to the master of the stroke, the watching Sir Donald Bradman. Words cannot recapture the joy of that moment.

Another time, when Lillee bowled short, Randall ducked, rose, drew himself to his full five feet eight, doffed his cap and bowed politely. Then,

Australia

I. C. Davis lbw b Lever	5	– c Knott b Greig	68
R. B. McCosker b Willis	4	– c Greig b Old	25
G. J. Cosier c Fletcher b Lever	10	– c Knott b Lever	4
*G. S. Chappell b Underwood	40	– b Old	2
D. W. Hookes c Greig b Old	17	– c Fletcher b Underwood	56
K. D. Walters c Greig b Willis	4	– c Knott b Greig	66
†R. W. Marsh c Knott b Old	28	– not out	110
G. J. Gilmour c Greig b Old	4	– b Lever	16
K. J. O'Keeffe c Brearley b Underwood	0	– c Willis b Old	14
D. K. Lillee not out	10	– c Amiss b Old	25
M. H. N. Walker b Underwood	2	– not out	8
B 4, l-b 2, n-b 8	14	L-b 10, n-b 15	25

138   1/33 2/40 3/53   (9 wkts dec.) 419
1/11 2/13 3/23 4/45 5/51   4/132 5/187 6/244
6/102 7/114 8/117 9/136   7/277 8/353 9/407

Bowling: *First Innings*—Lever 12–1–36–2; Willis 8–0–33–2; Old 12.4–39–3; Underwood 11.6–2–16–3. *Second Innings*—Lever 21–1–95–2; Willis 22–0–91–0; Old 27.6–2–104–4; Greig 14–3–66–2; Underwood 12–2–38–1.

England

R. A. Woolmer c Chappell b Lillee	9	– lbw b Walker	12
J. M. Brearley c Hookes b Lillee	12	– lbw b Lillee	43
D. L. Underwood c Chappell b Walker	7	– b Lillee	7
D. W. Randall c Marsh b Lillee	4	– c Cosier b O'Keeffe	174
D. L. Amiss c O'Keeffe b Walker	4	– b Chappell	64
K. W. R. Fletcher c Marsh b Walker	4	– c Marsh b Lillee	1
*A. W. Greig b Walker	18	– c Cosier b O'Keeffe	41
†A. P. E. Knott lbw b Lillee	15	– lbw b Lillee	42
C. M. Old c Marsh b Lillee	3	– c Chappell b Lillee	2
J. K. Lever c Marsh b Lillee	11	– lbw b O'Keeffe	4
R. G. D. Willis not out	1	– not out	5
B 2, l-b 2, w 1, n-b 2	7	B 8, l-b 4, w 3, n-b 7	22

95   1/28 2/113 3/279 4/290 5/346   417
1/19 2/30 3/34 4/40 5/40   6/369 7/380 8/385 9/410
6/61 7/65 8/78 9/86

Bowling: *First Innings*—Lillee 13.3–2–26–6; Walker 15–3–54–4; O'Keeffe 1–0–4–0; Gilmour 5–3–4–0. *Second Innings*—Lillee 34.4–7–139–5; Walker 22–4–83–1; Gilmour 4–0–29–0; Chappell 16–7–29–1; O'Keeffe 33–6–108–3; Walters 3–2–7–0.

Umpires: T. F. Brooks and M. G. O'Connell.

felled by another bouncer, he gaily performed a reverse roll. This helped to maintain a friendly atmosphere in what, at all times, was a serious and fully competitive match.

The Australians responded. When Randall was 161, umpire Brooks gave him out, caught at the wicket. Immediately Marsh intimated that he had not completed the catch before dropping the ball. After consultation, the umpire called Randall back. Would that this spirit was always so! At the end of the game Randall was awarded the first prize of 1,600 dollars as the Man of the Match. To be chosen ahead of the superb Lillee, whose colleagues chaired him from the field when he finished the match with an analysis of eleven for 165, was a feat indeed.

Some time after it was over someone discovered that the result of the 226th Test between the two countries – victory by 45 runs – was identical, to the same side and to the very run, with that of the 1877 Test on the same ground. Hans "Andersen" Ebeling had even scripted the final curtain.

page 694

John Player Sunday League, 1978

Hampshire Snatch Title on Run-Rate

Hampshire became the John Player League champions for the second time, their previous success being in 1975. On the final day of the season, Somerset, who have never won any county competition, led by four points from Hampshire and Leicestershire, and a tie would have sufficed to give them first place. However, having gone down to Sussex in the Gillette Cup final the previous day, they were beaten by two runs at Taunton by Essex*. Meanwhile, Leicestershire gained an easy win over Derbyshire at Leicester and Hampshire mastered Middlesex at Bournemouth by 26 runs.

So three sides, Hampshire, Somerset and Leicestershire, each finished with 48 points, and the honour went to Hampshire who had much the best "higher run-rate" per over throughout the season. In deciding the final positions, "most

---

* *Somerset needed 11 runs from the last over, and 5 from the final two balls, to tie the match and so win the League.*

wins" will carry the day, and if these are equal, as was the case in this instance, "most away wins" count. Again, though, the sides were equal, and consequently the third consideration, "higher run-rate", came into operation.

FINAL TABLE

		Played	Won	Lost	No Result	Points	6s	4 wkts
1 – Hampshire (4)		16	11	3	2	48	39	5
2 – Somerset (9)		16	11	3	2	48	24	2
3 – Leicestershire (1)		16	11	3	2	48	17	3
4 – Worcestershire (13)		16	10	5	1	42	21	6
5 – Lancashire (16)		16	9	6	1	38	27	4
6 – Essex (2)		16	7	6	3	34	16	3
7 – Yorkshire (13)		16	7	7	2	32	18	2
8	Derbyshire (9)	16	6	7	3	30	20	3
	Sussex (4)	16	6	7	3	30	12	1
10	Glamorgan (8)	16	6	8	2	28	16	4
	Kent (6)	16	6	8	2	28	13	3
	Surrey (13)	16	6	8	2	28	19	3
13	Nottinghamshire (12)	16	4	7	5	26	19	1
	Northamptonshire (17)	16	5	8	3	26	25	1
15 – Middlesex (3)		16	5	9	2	24	13	6
16 – Warwickshire (9)		16	4	11	1	18	15	1
17 – Gloucestershire (6)		16	3	11	2	16	23	1

Run-rate for first three places: Hampshire 5.355, Somerset 4.580, Leicestershire 4.265.

1977 positions in brackets.

pages 83 and 87

Norman Preston died on March 6, 1980, aged 76, just after the 1980 edition went to press. He had been editor of Wisden *since 1952 when he succeeded his father, Hubert Preston. The following extracts are from his final Editor's Notes.*

Notes by the Editor

(Norman Preston)

The 1979 season produced some of the most exciting cricket in the long history of the game. To my mind, foremost were the feats of Essex and Somerset in carrying off the four major titles. Neither county had previously won any major competition, although in recent years both had become serious challengers.

Then there was the wonderful effort by India who, when facing a target of 438 in the last of their four Tests, came within 9 runs with two wickets in hand of achieving a sensational victory at The Oval. Although India did not succeed, there was a personal honour for Sunil Gavaskar. For more than eight hours he batted faultlessly for his 221 and left no doubt in my mind that he is now the No. 1 opening batsman in the world.

Earlier in the season, West Indies again proved supreme in the Prudential World Cup, from which India were eliminated in the preliminary rounds. Last year the World Cup grossed £359,700, of which just over half – £180,000 – came from the two matches at Lord's. No wonder the International Cricket Conference have agreed to stage another World Cup in England in 1983 and have planned to make the competition a four-yearly event.

However …

The old saying "It is not cricket" used to be universal when something shady was done in any walk of life, but in modern times cricket has so often blotted its copybook that one rarely hears the term these days. It certainly applied when Somerset, to ensure their passage to the Benson and Hedges Cup quarter-finals, cut short their match against Worcestershire at Worcester to exactly seventeen balls, including one no-ball. It was all over in eighteen minutes, and the Somerset players left the ground fourteen minutes later.

Somerset entered the match with nine points from previous contests, and they had the faster rate of taking wickets than either of their challengers in Group A, Worcestershire and Glamorgan, both with six points. Somerset risked nothing by declaring after one over and allowing Worcestershire no chance to improve their wicket-taking rate. Somerset were within the law governing the competition – it has since been changed – but they showed no consideration to their sponsors or the spectators. Brian Rose, the Somerset captain, was condemned in the cricket world for his action, although I understand it was planned by some members of his team.

Donald Carr, secretary of the TCCB said: "Somerset's action is totally contrary to the spirit of the competition." Colin Atkinson, the Somerset president and a former captain of the county, tried unsuccessfully to have the match replayed. Within eight days, the TCCB, at an emergency meeting, banned Somerset for their "indefensible" Cup declaration, and their place was given to Glamorgan, who played and lost to Derbyshire at Cardiff.

pages 90–93

John Woodcock, cricket correspondent of The Times *since 1954,
succeeded Norman Preston as editor.
He began his first set of Notes with the following observations.*

Notes by the Editor
(John Woodcock)

*"This leads us to the much greater question of the desirability of further
altering the Law of leg before wicket." (1934)*

   *"As to the events of the past year, the happiest man in the country must
have been the born pessimist. In the course of 16 months our cricketers have
lost a rubber in Australia, West Indies and South Africa in turn." (1936)*

   "Of great leg-break bowlers there was none." (1939)

   *"The fast natural pitch, made as level as a billiard table by mowing,
rolling and watering, would increase greatly the likelihood of a definite
result in county matches." (1944)*

   *"In short … English cricket needs an injection of culture and
enterprise." (1952)*

These extracts are taken from this corresponding article on the last five
occasions that a new editor of *Wisden* has taken over, and they all, to some
degree, apply today. The Law of leg before is still under discussion;
England are still losing successive rubbers to Australia and West Indies;
there are now no English leg-break bowlers, let alone any great ones; "fast
natural pitches" remain as elusive as ever; and English batsmanship is in
need once again of "an injection of culture".

   So when I sound a cautionary note, or a sombre one, it will be in the
established tradition of these notes. *Déjà vu* you may think. There is one
aspect, even so, of the year under review which is new and of great concern.
This is the manner and frequency with which famous players have flouted
the authority of the umpires. In all the years that *Wisden* has been published,
there can have been no more shocking photograph than that, to be found in
the illustration section [of the 1981 edition], of Michael Holding, the
distinguished and richly talented West Indian fast bowler, kicking the

stumps out of the ground in a Test match in New Zealand – for no other reason than that he disagreed with an umpire's decision.

Unbridled dissent

Nor was this an isolated example of such unbridled dissent. In the same Test series Colin Croft, another of the West Indian fast bowlers, having lost his temper, sent an umpire flying as he ran in to bowl. In India, at much the same time, the umpires were being denounced by the touring Pakistanis; in Perth, Dennis Lillee, the great Australian, held up play for ten minutes in a Test match between England and Australia while he argued with the umpires and his own captain over the use of an aluminium bat in which he had a proprietorial interest. Technically Lillee had a point, there being nothing in the Laws at that time, though there is now, to say that a bat must be made of wood; morally, as he must have known, he should have done as the umpires asked him.

As disconcerting as these individual cases of defiance was the way in which they were glossed over by those whose responsibility it was to make an example of the players concerned. In New Zealand, the West Indian manager, himself a former Test player, blamed the umpires for what was happening. No wonder that when the West Indians left for home the New Zealand cricketing public, to quote R. T. Brittenden in his summary of the tour, "was glad to see the back of them". In Australia, the Chairman of the Australian Cricket Board said that he could not understand what all the fuss was about over Lillee's insubordination. Ian Chappell, an outstanding batsman and conspicuously successful captain of Australia, was suspended once, and subsequently given a second suspended sentence, for tilting at the precept that the umpire's decision is final; but in Australia, as elsewhere, the standards of cricketing discipline have in recent years been regularly compromised.

Towards the end of 1980, however, it began to seem as though those who administer the game were themselves seeing the red light. In West Indies Gerry Gomez, a member of the West Indian Board of Control, advocated a series of fines aimed at calling the players to order. There was a move among members of the International Cricket Conference to appoint independent "observers" to Test series. From Pakistan came a suggestion that Test umpires should be empowered to send players off the field. Even in Australia the senior players, or most of them, were looking for ways of keeping the hoodlums at bay.

The Centenary Test Fracas

This great jamboree, arranged to celebrate 100 years of Test cricket between England and Australia in England, had been eagerly awaited. Its counterpart, at Melbourne in 1977, had been a wonderful success ... Last summer's match was ill-fated from the start. Some would say that the hours from eleven o'clock until six o'clock on the Saturday were like a nightmare. So incensed were certain members of MCC by the middle of the afternoon that play was not in progress, owing, as they thought, to the obstinacy of the umpires, that a scuffle took place on the steps of the pavilion, in which the umpires, one or two members, and the captains were involved. As a result of it, the umpires were shaken, the reputation of MCC was damaged and the occasion impaired.

Two and a half months later, following what MCC described as a "thorough inquiry" – which included taking the evidence of the umpires, the captains and a number of members, and studying a BBC film recording of the incident – Peter May, President of MCC, wrote in a letter to all members of the club that "appropriate disciplinary action" had been taken. He made the point, too, that it was no more fitting for members of a club publicly to question the decision of the umpires, let alone abuse them, than for players to do so on the field. If good is to come from a sorry affair, it will be to see that efforts are redoubled to provide the best possible covering on all first-class grounds, especially those where Test matches are staged. As many have said, it seems laughable to be able to land a man on the moon yet to have discovered no adequate way of protecting the square at Lord's.

pages 326–328

England v Australia

Third Cornhill Test

By Alan Lee

At Leeds, July 16, 17, 18, 20, 21, 1981. England won by 18 runs. A match which had initially produced all the wet and tedious traits of recent Leeds Tests finally ended in a way to stretch the bounds of logic and belief. England's victory, achieved under the gaze of a spellbound nation, was the first this century by a team following on, and only the second such result in the history of Test cricket.

The transformation occurred in less than 24 hours, after England had appeared likely to suffer their second four-day defeat of the series.

Wherever one looked, there were personal dramas: Brearley, returning as captain like England's saviour: Botham, who was named Man of the Match, brilliant once more in his first game back in the ranks: Willis, whose career has so often heard the distant drums, producing the most staggering bowling of his life when his place again seemed threatened.

Others, too, had good reason to remember this game. It was the first time in nineteen Tests that Willey had been a member of a victorious side, there were wicket-keeping records for both Taylor (all first-class cricket) and Marsh (Tests), Dyson made his maiden century for Australia, and Lillee moved further up the list of bowling immortals. But if the statisticians revelled in such facts, they were, for most of us, submerged in the tension of a climax as near to miraculous as a Test ever can have been.

None of this had seemed remotely likely on the opening day when the familiar slate-grey clouds engulfed the chimneys which stretch away from the Kirkstall Lane End. Australia, one up in the series, were unchanged: England made two changes, Woolmer standing down for Brearley and Old returning on his home ground at the expense of Emburey. England thus went in with four seamers and only Willey to provide a measure of spin. It was a selectorial policy which caused considerable discussion. Brearley later confessed he lost sleep on the first night for fear that it had been a mistake. As things transpired, however, it was largely irrelevant.

Australia, having chosen to bat, ended the first day in fine health at 203 for three, the extra hour having reduced lost time to only fifty minutes. Dyson batted diligently for his century, playing chiefly off the back foot, and survived one chance, to Botham in the gully, when 57. Chappell, who supported Dyson staunchly in a stand of 94 for the second wicket, was twice reprieved – by Gower and Botham again – so England, not for the first time this summer, suffered for their ineptitude in the field. The other talking-point of the day concerned Headingley's new electronic scoreboard, which had a mixed reception, being difficult to see from most parts of the ground when the sun began to sink.

It will come as a surprise when, in future years, people look back on a Test of such apparently outrageous drama, to know that the second day was pedestrian in the extreme. Botham, to some degree, salvaged English pride by taking five more wickets, all of them in an after-tea spell costing 35 runs, and finishing with six for 95. Naturally, the assumption was drawn that he is a more effective player without leadership duties. Despite his efforts, Australia extended their score to 401 for nine, thanks to half-centuries from Hughes and Yallop. It was another day of patchy weather and patchy cricket, completed when Gooch and Boycott saw out an over apiece from Lillee and Alderman without mishap.

At this stage, the odds seemed in favour of a draw. An England win was on offer generously though by no means as extravagantly as 24 hours later when Ladbrokes, from their tent on the ground, posted it at 500 to 1. The reason for their estimate was a truncated day on which England were dismissed for 174 and, following on 227 behind, lost Gooch without addition. Australia's seamers had shown what could be done by bowling straighter and to a fuller length than their counterparts. Other than Botham, who opted for all-out aggression and profited by a swift 50, England at no stage commanded and were occasionally undone by deliveries performing contortions at speed. Botham fell victim to just such a ball from Lillee and the catch by Marsh was his 264th in Tests, beating Knott's record.

The third day ended with unhappy scenes similar to those seen at Lord's, when spectators hurled cushions and abuse at the umpires. On this occasion, Messrs Meyer and Evans had walked to the middle, wearing blazers, at five to six, after a lengthy stoppage for poor light. They consulted their meters and summoned the covers, abandoning play just before the hour. With cruel irony, the light improved instantly, the sun was soon breaking through and the large crowd was incited to wrathful demands for explanations as to why they were not watching the prescribed extra hour. Once more, it seems, confusion in interpretation of the playing regulations was the cause of the ill feeling: they stated only that conditions must be fit for play at the scheduled time of finish and not, as the umpires thought, that play must actually be in motion. Whether it was, in fact, fit at six o'clock is open to doubt, but the TCCB soon adjusted the ruling so that play in future Tests in the series could restart at any stage of the extra hour.

This heated diversion seemed likely to achieve nothing more than a stay of sentence for England, a view which appeared amply confirmed by late afternoon on the Monday. England were then 135 for seven, still 92 behind, and the distant objective of avoiding an innings defeat surely their only available prize. Lillee and Alderman had continued where Saturday's disturbances had forced them to leave off, and for all Boycott's skilful resistance, the cause seemed lost. Boycott, who batted three and a half hours, was sixth out to an lbw decision he seemed not to relish, and when Taylor followed quickly, the England players' decision to check out of their hotel seemed a sound move. Three hours later, the registration desks around Leeds were coping with a flood of re-bookings, Botham having destroyed the game's apparently set course with an astonishing, unbeaten 145, ably and forcefully aided by Dilley. Together, they added 117 in 80 minutes for the eighth wicket, only 7 short of an England record against Australia. Both struck the ball so cleanly and vigorously that Hughes's men were temporarily in disarray; when Dilley departed after scoring 56 precious runs, Old arrived to add 67 more with Botham, who still had Willis as a partner at the close, with England 124 ahead.

Botham advanced his unforgettable innings to 149 not out before losing Willis the next morning, but Australia, needing 130, still remained clear favourites. Then, at 56 for one, Willis, having changed ends to bowl with the wind, dismissed Chappell with a rearing delivery and the staggering turnabout was under way. Willis bowled as if inspired. It is not uncommon to see him perform for England as if his very life depended on it, but this was something unique. In all, he took eight wickets for 43, the best of his career, as Australia's last nine wickets tumbled for 55 runs despite a stand of 35 in four overs between Bright and Lillee. Old bowled straight and aggressively and England rose to the need to produce an outstanding show in the field. Yet this was Willis's hour, watched or listened to by a vast invisible audience. At the end, the crowd gathered to wave their Union Jacks and chant patriotically, eight days in advance of the Royal Wedding.

Takings were £206,500 and the attendance 52,566.

Australia

J. Dyson b Dilley	102	– (2) c Taylor b Willis 34
G. M. Wood lbw b Botham	34	– (1) c Taylor b Botham 10
T. M. Chappell c Taylor b Willey	27	– c Taylor b Willis 8
*K. J. Hughes c and b Botham	89	– c Botham b Willis 0
R. J. Bright b Dilley	7	– (8) b Willis 19
G. N. Yallop c Taylor b Botham	58	– (5) c Gatting b Willis 0
A. R. Border lbw b Botham	8	– (6) b Old 0
†R. W. Marsh b Botham	28	– (7) c Dilley b Willis 4
G. F. Lawson c Taylor b Botham	13	– c Taylor b Willis 1
D. K. Lillee not out	3	– c Gatting b Willis 17
T. M. Alderman not out	0	– not out 0
B 4, l-b 13, w 3, n-b 12	32	L-b 3, w 1, n-b 14 18

1/55 2/149 3/196 4/220 5/332   (9 wkts. dec.) 401   1/13 2/56 3/58 4/58 5/65   111
6/354 7/357 8/396 9/401   6/68 7/74 8/75 9/110

Bowling: *First Innings*—Willis 30–8–72–0; Old 43–14–91–0; Dilley 27–4–78–2; Botham 39.2–11–95–6; Willey 13–2–31–1; Boycott 3–2–2–0. *Second Innings*—Botham 7–3–14–1; Dilley 2–0–11–0; Willis 15.1–3–43–8; Old 9–1–21–1; Willey 3–1–4–0.

England

G. A. Gooch lbw b Alderman	2	– c Alderman b Lillee 0
G. Boycott b Lawson	12	– lbw b Alderman 46
*J. M. Brearley c Marsh b Alderman	10	– c Alderman b Lillee 14
D. I. Gower c Marsh b Lawson	24	– c Border b Alderman 9
M. W. Gatting lbw b Lillee	15	– lbw b Alderman 1
P. Willey b Lawson	8	– c Dyson b Lillee 33
I. T. Botham c Marsh b Lillee	50	– not out 149
†R. W. Taylor c Marsh b Lillee	5	– c Bright b Alderman 1
G. R. Dilley c and b Lillee	13	– b Alderman 56
C. M. Old c Border b Alderman	0	– b Lawson 29
R. G. D. Willis not out	1	– c Border b Alderman 2
B 6, l-b 11, w 6, n-b 11	34	B 5, l-b 3, w 3, n-b 5 16

1/12 2/40 3/42 4/84 5/87   174   1/0 2/18 3/37 4/41 5/105   356
6/112 7/148 8/166 9/167   6/133 7/135 8/252 9/319

Bowling: *First Innings*—Lillee 18.5–7–49–4; Alderman 19–4–59–3; Lawson 13–3–32–3. *Second Innings*—Lillee 25–6–94–3; Alderman 35.3–6–135–6; Lawson 23–4–96–1; Bright 4–0–15–0.

Umpires: D. G. L. Evans and B. J. Meyer.

pages 1141–1142

Cricket in India, 1981-82

By P. N. Sundaresan

Normally peak interest in cricket in India is reached during a Test series, but the countless fans who flocked to see the Tests against England in the 1981-82 season felt disappointed. Fortunately for them the knockout matches of the Ranji Trophy championship, taken up after the Englishmen had departed, proved lively and keen, with the final between Delhi and Karnataka providing a fitting climax.

Delhi were declared winners on their first-innings lead, but what a match of high drama it turned out to be! Under the rules of the championship the final is a five-day affair, but in the event of the first innings of the two teams not being completed on the fifth day, the match may be prolonged until a result on first innings is obtained. It was on the afternoon of the sixth day when Delhi succeeded in their exciting bid to overtake Karnataka's first-innings score of 705. This was the first occasion on which such an extension of play had had to be made.

Unfortunately, it was not just the exciting nature of the cricket that drew attention to the later stages of the Ranji Trophy. Some matches were marred by the disorderly behaviour of unruly elements. Umpire Reporter's decision to uphold a close-in catch against T. E. Srinivasan, who was batting in his best style in Tamilnadu's first innings against Delhi, led to a vociferous demonstration at the end of the day's play. A section of the crowd threatened to disrupt play if the umpire failed to change his decision. Next day, the simmering discontent of the spectators exploded into a minor riot when a similar decision was given against Vasudevan, to which the batsman, as in the other earlier case, showed his displeasure. The spectators marched on to the ground, and one of the umpires was assaulted. Play had to be called off shortly before lunch and was resumed only after the Tamilnadu captain, Venkataraghavan, and others had pacified the crowd.

A decision by umpire Rajan Mehra against Viswanath, the local favourite, sparked off trouble at Bangalore in Karnataka's semi-final against Bombay. Viswanath, reputed to be a "walker", stayed a while before leaving after being given out caught. Later he explained that it was a gesture of disappointment at getting out when he was in good form, but the incident provoked the spectators to rush on to the ground, mob the two umpires, and set fire to one of the sightscreens. This riot forced the abandonment of play fifteen minutes before the end of the second day, and only after strong appeals from officials of the Karnataka Cricket Association was it resumed on the following morning. Another unacceptable incident in the same match concerned Gavaskar, Viswanath's brother-in-law. Entering at No. 7 in Bombay's second innings, he batted alternately left- and right-handed. Although this did not offend the Laws of Cricket, it was in poor taste, and Gavaskar was later censured for his conduct by the Working Committee of the Indian Board. The Umpires Advisory Panel, in a report to the Board, said that Gavaskar's gesture was not in keeping with a cricketer of distinction and should be termed as a bad example for the young cricketers of India.

At the end of the season the umpires sub-committee of the Indian Cricket Board met to discuss the incidents, and held the players responsible. It felt that the mob was infuriated by their gesticulations against the umpires. The committee was also of the view that mob violence sometimes resulted from adverse comments by commentators on the decisions of umpires, and wrote to the Ministry of Information and Broadcasting to frame guidelines for the commentators so that they should confine themselves to the factual description of matches.

Gavaskar had the highest aggregate of 632 runs in the Ranji Trophy, but perhaps the credit for outstanding batsmanship should go to [Delhi's] Mohinder Amarnath. After his two efforts in the quarter-final against Tamilnadu on a turning pitch, and his great innings of 185 runs in 487 minutes in the final, there was keen disappointment when he was not included in the Indian team to England.

While the season confirmed the form of established players, it also threw up a number of future Test prospects. Of these, Gursharan Singh and Maninder Singh of Delhi and L. Sivaramakrishnan of Tamilnadu stood out. Gursharan Singh, a stocky, turbaned Sikh, hit the headlines with a century against the touring England team at the start of the season and ended it with another in the Ranji Trophy final against Karnataka. His bold approach and his range of strokes created a fine impression. Maninder Singh, a tall young bowler on the lines of Bedi, showed much promise and perseverance. In his first season in the championship he collected 40 wickets, including a return of fourteen for 122 against Punjab in the North Zone league. Sivaramakrishnan, in the only match he played for Tamilnadu, revealed great promise as an orthodox leg-spinner. These three youngsters are all ripe to be blooded in Test cricket.

Both Ashok Ghosh of Bihar and Zulfiqar Parkar of Bombay established new wicket-keeping records of ten dismissals in a match. Ghosh's feat was against Assam and Parkar's against Maharashtra. In each case, nine of the dismissals were catches.

page 1201

Obituary: George Headley

HEADLEY, GEORGE ALPHONSO, MBE, who died in Jamaica on November 30, 1983, aged 74, was the first of the great black batsmen to emerge from the West Indies. Between the wars, when the West Indies batting was often vulnerable and impulsive, Headley's scoring feats led to his being dubbed "the black Bradman". His devoted admirers responded by calling Bradman "the white Headley" – a pardonable exaggeration. In 22 Tests, when the innings could stand or fall on his performance, Headley scored 2,190 runs, including ten centuries – eight against England – with an average of 60.83. He was the first to score a century in each innings of a Test at Lord's, in 1939, and it was a measure of his ability that from 1929 to 1939 he did not have a single bad Test series. By the start of the Second World War he had totalled 9,532 runs in first-class cricket with an average of 72.21. Afterwards, though not the power that he had been, he extended his aggregate to 9,921 runs, with 33 centuries and an average of 69.86.

Born in Panama, where his father had helped to build the Canal, Headley was taken to Jamaica at the age of ten to perfect his English – Spanish had been his first tongue – and to prepare to study dentistry in America. At school he fell in love with cricket, but he might still have been lost to the game had there not been a delay in getting his passport for the United States. While he was waiting, Headley was chosen to play against a visiting English team captained by the Hon. L. H. Tennyson.

Though not yet nineteen, he had innings of 78 in the first match and 211 in the second, and dentistry lost a student. Surprisingly he was not chosen for the 1928 tour of England immediately afterwards, but in the home series against England in 1929-30 he scored 703 runs in eight Test innings, averaging 87.80. His scores included 21 and 176 in his first Test, 114 and 112 in the third and 223 in the fourth. In 1930-31 in Australia he scored two more Test centuries and ended the tour with 1,066 runs. Clarrie

Grimmett described him as the strongest on-side player he had ever bowled against. In 1932, in a single month, he hit 344 not out (his highest-ever score), 84, 155 not out and 140 against another English side to visit Jamaica. Against sterner opposition and in more difficult conditions in England in the following year, he averaged 66 for the tour, scoring a century on his first appearance at Lord's and taking 224 not out off Somerset. In the second Test at Manchester he made 169 not out, a score he improved upon with 270 not out at Kingston in the 1934-35 series.

Headley was of medium build, compact, balanced and light on his feet. Like most great batsmen he was a superb back-foot player and seldom made a hurried shot. Sir Leonard Hutton, who saw him at his best in 1939, declares he has never seen a batsman play the ball later. It was hard to set a field for him, such was his genius for collecting runs with his precise placement of the ball. In League cricket in England Headley also excelled. At every level of the game, in fact, he scored an avalanche of runs with a style and brilliance few of any age have matched. His contribution to the strength and power of modern West Indies teams cannot be exaggerated.

George Headley's son, Ron, also played Test cricket for West Indies, and Ron Headley's son, Dean, has played Test cricket for England. The Headleys are the only family to have three generations of Test cricketers.

pages 279–281

The West Indians in England, 1984

By Christopher Martin-Jenkins

As far as the records are concerned, the 1984 West Indians, under the captaincy of Clive Lloyd, were unique. No country had hitherto achieved a 100 per cent record in a full Test series in England. Apart from one limited-overs international, at Trent Bridge early in their tour, not a game was lost.

Only four other rubbers of five games or more in the history of Test cricket have finished with a similar whitewash for one of the competing teams, and Lloyd's West Indians must rank as the equals at least of the others on this very short list: Australia against England in 1920-21 and

South Africa in 1931-32, England against India in 1959, and West Indies, under another of their elder statesmen, Frank Worrell, against India in 1961-62.*

Blessed by a dry summer, maturely led, strong and adaptable in batting, possessing in Roger Harper the best West Indian off-spinner since Lance Gibbs, and basing their attack on a formidably fit and hostile hand of fast bowlers, Lloyd's was a team of almost all the talents. Whatever may have appeared to be the case on paper, they relied on no special individuals. There was a man for every moment.

The most gifted batsman in contemporary world cricket, Vivian Richards, began the tour in the kind of form, and mood, which had enabled him to score 829 runs in seven Test innings in England in 1976. In the two one-day Texaco Trophy matches which West Indies won he totally dominated the England bowling, producing at Old Trafford perhaps the most powerful innings ever seen in one-day cricket at this level. Then, in the first Test at Edgbaston, he made a century almost as a matter of course, playing as if a hundred was the least that he, and everyone else, expected. If this suggests over-confidence, it is no more than the truth. Thereafter he played like a millionaire and in doing so enjoyed no luck, so that it was not Richards but Greenidge and Gomes who took the main batting honours in the Tests. Both hit four first-class centuries on the tour and two against England. Greenidge, in fact, reached a thousand runs in only sixteen first-class innings at an average of 82.23. Gomes made 841 from seventeen innings at 70.08.

Gomes let his figures talk for him. Phlegmatic and undemonstrative, he stroked the ball with a light touch and relished a tough challenge … Greenidge batted with the air of a man in control of every situation. Seldom can he have played on such a high plane of inspired brilliance as when seizing the second Test from England on the last day at Lord's. His second double-hundred of the series, at Old Trafford in the fourth Test, was less attractive and fluent, yet his defence was seemingly unpierceable and his judgement in attack quite flawless as he set about locking England out of the game …

In the field the West Indians were as impressive as at any time during the Lloyd era. The close-catching and out-fielding were slick and sure. One of the most memorable moments of the tour occurred at Lord's when England's Geoff Miller, blithely sauntering along on a second run after the ball had been played wide of Eldine Baptiste on the long-leg boundary, was

---

* Since 1984 there have been two more 5–0 series in Test cricket, both involving West Indies: in the Caribbean in 1985-86 they repeated their demolition of England, but in 1998-99, on their first tour of South Africa, they suffered their first 5–0 series defeat.

amazed to see a missile fizzing past him to break the stumps at the bowler's end from some 80 yards away. If this stands out ahead of the many brilliant slip catches, taken by a variety of fielders, it is perhaps because the latter were two-a-penny.

But the invincibility of the West Indians was based again upon their relentless fast bowling. Joel Garner, towering above the batsmen, was the most consistently dangerous; Malcolm Marshall, wiry as a whippet, was the fastest. Michael Holding, graceful but intelligently menacing, bowled mainly off a shorter run than of old but was still capable of taking vital wickets with near-unplayable balls; and Baptiste bowled with admirable stamina and accuracy, if not with quite as much ferocity as the others …

There were no passengers in the party. Whenever it was threatened, someone came to the rescue, as when Desmond Haynes, after a lean series, played the match-winning innings in the final victory at The Oval which took West Indies' run of Test successes to eight out of eight, following a one-sided series against Australia in the Caribbean.

Such praise, however, must be tempered by two reservations. Before the tour began, the West Indies Cricket Board refused to agree to the Test and County Cricket Board's idea of insisting on a reasonable minimum number of overs in a day, an expedient which had worked well in England in 1982 and 1983. As a result both sides bowled their overs in the Test matches at a rate which was unacceptably low. Over the series, England averaged 13.4 overs an hour, West Indies 13.5. Only at Old Trafford, when Pocock, Cook and Harper bowled long spells, did either side maintain a rate of more than 15 overs an hour.

Equally typical of contemporary cricket, for which West Indies, being the best team in the world, have set the trend, the bouncer was used by their fast bowlers to such an extent that batting against them became as much an exercise in self-defence as in defence of the wicket. Andy Lloyd and Paul Terry both sustained serious injury while playing for England. Several others were hit on the helmet. Uneven pitches and poor batting techniques partially explained this, but so, too, did the West Indian strategy (aped by other teams but most effectively carried out by themselves) of digging the ball in short and watching the hapless batsmen dance to their tune.

West Indian Tour Results

Test matches	Played 5: Won 5.
First-class matches	Played 14: Won 8, Drawn 6.
Non first-class matches	Played 9: Won 4, Lost 1, Drawn 4.

174

pages 328–329

National Village Championship Final, 1985

At Lord's, September 1, 1985. Freuchie beat Rowledge by virtue of having lost fewer wickets with the scores level, so becoming, in the bicentenary year of Scottish cricket, the first Scottish village to win the final. Rowledge had won the toss and batted first, but against tigerish Scottish fielding the runs came slowly. Dunbar, whose 33 was top score of the match, and Offord were both run out by Andrew Crichton. Freuchie's captain and president, David Christie, saw the score to 134 for seven, when he was run out off the last ball of the 39th over, whereupon in great excitement in the gloaming of St John's Wood, the ninth-wicket pair played out a maiden 40th over to ensure victory. Freuchie, with kilts swirling and their piper skirling at their head, had marched into Lord's, where the national dress, including tie and jacket, was permitted wear in the Pavilion. Freuchie won £500 and Rowledge £250.

Rowledge

R. E. C. Simpson c A. N. Crichton b Cowan .	6
A. P. Hook b McNaughton	28
N. S. Dunbar run out	33
C. Yates b D. Y. F. Christie	10
†P. Offord run out	0
R. J. Dunbar c Irvine b Trewartha	12
*A. J. Prior b Trewartha	6
P. R. Cooper b Cowan	12
B. A. Silver c Wilkie b Trewartha	0
A. B. Field not out	10
J. Reffold lbw b Trewartha	0
L-b 9, w 7, n-b 1	17
	—
1/15 2/56 3/73 4/74 5/94 (39.3 overs)	134
6/108 7/117 8/117 9/133	

Bowling: Cowan 9–1–25–2; McNaughton 9–0–31–1; B. Christie 9–0–28–0; D. Y. F. Christie 5–0–17–1; Trewartha 7.3–0–24–4.

Freuchie

M. Wilkie b Field	10
†A. S. Duncan c Yates b Silver	16
A. N. Crichton lbw b Field	0
G. Wilson c Offord b Yates	14
D. Cowan b Silver	16
S. Irvine c and b Prior	24
G. Crichton not out	24
T. Trewartha b Reffold	1
*D. Y. F. Christie run out	11
B. Christie not out	0
B 6, l-b 8, w 2, n-b 2	18
1/23 2/25 3/42 (8 wkts, 40 overs)	134
4/52 5/85 6/91	
7/101 8/134	

N. McNaughton did not bat.

Bowling: Field 9–1–15–2; Reffold 6–1–25–1; Prior 9–0–31–1; Yates 9–0–31–1; Silver 7–0–18–2.

Umpires: R. Axworthy and R. H. Duckett.

pages 1026 and 1029

Austral-Asia Cup, 1985-86

By Qamar Ahmed

The first Austral-Asia Cup tournament, played in Sharjah in April as part of the Cricketers' Benefit Fund Series, was won by Pakistan off the last ball of the final against India. With 4 runs needed to win, Javed Miandad struck Chetan Sharma's final delivery for his third six.

India, put in to bat, were given an excellent start by Gavaskar, Srikkanth and Vengsarkar, who put on 200 for the loss of only one wicket. However, they slumped from 216 for two to 245 for seven when Imran

FINAL

INDIA v PAKISTAN

At Sharjah, April 18, 1986. Pakistan won by one wicket. Toss: Pakistan.
Man of the Match: Javed Miandad. *Man of the Tournament:* S. M. Gavaskar.

India

K. Srikkanth c Wasim b Qadir	75	†C. S. Pandit not out		0
S. M. Gavaskar b Imran	92			
D. B. Vengsarkar b Wasim	50	L-b 6, w 2, n-b 1		9
K. Azad b Wasim	0			
*Kapil Dev b Imran	8	1/117 2/216 3/216	(7 wkts, 50 overs)	245
Chetan Sharma run out	10	4/229 5/242		
R. J. Shastri b Wasim	1	6/245 7/245		

M. Azharuddin, Madan Lal and Maninder Singh did not bat.

Bowling: Imran 10-2-40-2; Wasim 10-1-42-3; Manzoor 5-0-33-0; Mudassar 5-0-32-0; Qadir 10-2-49-1; Tauseef 10-1-43-0.

Pakistan

Mudassar Nazar lbw b Chetan	5	Wasim Akram run out		3
Mohsin Khan b Madan Lal	36	†Zulqarnain b Chetan		0
Ramiz Raja b Maninder	10	Tauseef Ahmed not out		1
Javed Miandad not out	116			
Salim Malik run out	21	L-b 11		11
Abdul Qadir c sub (R. Lamba) b Kapil Dev	34	1/9 2/39 3/61	(9 wkts, 50 overs)	248
*Imran Khan b Madan Lal	7	4/110 5/181 6/209		
Manzoor Elahi c Shastri b Chetan	4	7/215 8/235 9/241		

Bowling: Kapil Dev 10-1-45-1; Chetan 9-0-51-3; Madan Lal 10-0-53-2; Maninder 10-0-36-1; Shastri 9-0-38-0; Azharuddin 2-0-14-0.

Umpires: D. M. Archer and A. Gaynor.

Khan and Wasim Akram returned to the attack. Pakistan's requirement of just under 5 an over drifted to 9 with ten overs remaining, but Miandad and Abdul Qadir picked up the rate in their fifth-wicket stand of 71 and Miandad kept the impetus going with exciting running between the wickets. His 110, as he faced the final ball from Chetan Sharma, contained only two sixes and two fours, but with India's field set to prevent a third four, he won the match in the most dramatic manner. It was Pakistan's first major success in a limited-overs tournament and they won $40,000 in prize money.

Five countries participated in the tournament: Australia, New Zealand and Sri Lanka, in addition to India and Pakistan. Sri Lanka, as winners of the Asia Cup, qualified automatically for the semi-finals, where they were joined by the winners of the first-round matches, India and Pakistan, plus New Zealand, who went through as the first-round loser with the lesser margin of defeat. Following a practice established in previous competitions in Sharjah, neutral umpires were employed, D. M. Archer and A. Gaynor, from West Indies, standing in all five matches.

pages 44–46

Notes by the Editor

(Graeme Wright)

The refusal of Chris Broad, England's opening batsman, to leave the wicket when given out in the First Test in Pakistan [1987-88] cannot be condoned. He received a reprimand but was subject to no other disciplinary measure. On a rainy day at Nottingham, he would do well to read Sections One and Two of the Professional Golfers' Association code of ethics and thank his lucky stars he is a professional cricketer and not a golfer. Cited in mitigation were the frustrations of the England players which had been allowed to build up during the tour as a result of some bad umpiring. Sympathy was the prevailing sentiment. In the next Test match, at Faisalabad, Gatting lost his temper and indulged in an unedifying confrontation with Shakoor Rana. The nation was then held spellbound by the spectacle of two grown men standing on their dignity without a square inch of moral ground to support them. At the time of writing, no action had been taken against Gatting.

Whether or not it should have been, time will provide an answer. A glance at what has happened in two other sports, however, suggests it should have been. Rugby union and tennis have suffered at lower levels from the example of ill discipline at the highest level. When the British Lions rugby team toured South Africa in 1974, and won a series there for the first time, part and parcel of their game plan was the now infamous "99 call". In the event of provocation or aggression against a Lions forward, his fellow forwards would immediately pitch into the opposition. The purpose was two-fold. It showed the opposing side that the Lions could not be intimidated, and it made it impossible for the referee to send off any one player for retaliation. The consequences of this policy are still being felt today in club rugby, especially in Wales where a lack of discipline leads to outbursts of violence throughout the season. In tennis, the boorish behaviour of some leading players has permeated through to junior ranks so that coaches in England now complain that their young charges could win Wimbledon on the strength of their tantrums, but lack the tennis skills to match them.

I doubt if there is a cricketer anywhere who has not been upset by an umpire's decision especially when – as can happen in club and village matches – that umpire has affiliations with "the other side". But without the unchallenged acceptance of the principle that the umpire's word is final, what chance does the game have? Professional sportsmen set the standards of behaviour for those who play the game at all levels, just as those in authority have a responsibility to ensure that they do. A cricket master, reporting on his school's season for *Wisden,* informed us that he had lost three senior players for disciplinary reasons. "All I can say after nineteen years with the XI", he wrote, "is that a schoolmaster must uphold behaviour standards, even at the cost of losing his best players."

Like it or not, the England captain has a responsibility to English cricket … For Gatting, after the flush of success in Australia, 1987 was not the happiest of years. At Edgbaston, there was an incident when the umpires stood in the middle, waiting to restart the Test match there after an interruption for bad light, only for the England team to remain closeted in their dressing-room, oblivious of the umpires' reappearance. Of the four Test series played fully under his captaincy to the end of 1987, three had been lost. And it might even be argued that, had he not been so concerned with standing up for his "rights" at Faisalabad, that series might have been drawn and not lost. England, by dint of some good cricket, had fought their way into a favourable position. At times, it was almost as if the prince had placed the crown on Falstaff's head and walked away.

Never has cricket been more in need of firm leadership. The events in Pakistan showed that the management, in which I include the captain, instead of retaining a position from which they could provide leadership, allowed themselves to be drawn into the coterie of the players to the extent that sympathy for them was allowed to outweigh the most important issues.

Leadership is not simply issuing commands. As in business, it is a matter of understanding employees, conditions, resources and competition. History is something to be drawn upon; not put behind and forgotten. One wonders if in the offices of the TCCB there is a desk with a drawer filled with past managers' and captains' reports which have never been read again. This past tour was not the first to Pakistan by a cricket team, and nor will it be the last. Gatting had toured there twice before with England teams. He knew what the conditions were like and, as captain, should have helped his side rise above them. He could not; nor, it appears, could the Tour Manager or the Cricket Manager. Even the Chairman of the Cricket Council and TCCB, Raman Subba Row, was so moved by the players' pity for themselves that, without the sanction of the Board, he gave the players a bonus of £1,000 each. My first thought was to wonder how a soldier serving in Northern Ireland felt about that.

Gatting's outburst, of course, drew public support from those who suppose that Britain should stand up to the indignities perpetrated upon it by other countries, especially those of the third world. They ignore that what gives a nation its civilisation is its ability to accept these provocations without feeling a need to retaliate. It is an ability to judge when an issue is so morally wrong that action must be taken which makes a country great. A spat with an umpire in a cricket match is not one of these occasions.

page 1103

World Record Partnership

A world record partnership of 664 runs unbroken for the third wicket was compiled by two schoolboys during the Harris Shield tournament for Bombay schools. Vinod Kambli, a sixteen-year-old left-hander, and fourteen-year-old Sachin Tendulkar were playing for Sharadashram Vidyamandir (English) against St Xavier's High School at the Sassanian Ground (Azad Maidan) in Bombay on February 23, 24, 25, 1988. Kambli hit three sixes and 49 fours in his innings of 349 not out and followed it by taking six wickets for 37, bowling off-breaks, as St Xavier's were dismissed for 145, leaving Sharadashram Vidyamandir (English) the winners by 603 runs. Tendulkar's 326 not out contained one six and 48 fours. Details of the innings are as follows.

Sharadashram Vidyamandir (English)

A. Ranade c N. Dias b Sanghani	42	A. Muzumdar, P. Bhiwandkar, M. Phadke, S.
†R. Mulye c Bahutule b Sanghani	18	Sinha, S. Jadhav, R. Bashte and S. Ambapkar did
V. Kambli not out	349	not bat.
*S. Tendulkar not out	326	
B 5, l-b 3, w 5	13	

1/29 2/84   (2 wkts dec.) 748

Bowling: A. Sanghani 22–1–98–2; S. Sasnur 14–0–79–0; M. Walawalkar 22–0–161–0; J. Kothari 7–0–38–0; S. Bahutule 27–0–182–0; S. Saherwala 2–0–31–0; K. Apte 26–0–149–0.

pages 1189–1192

Obituary: Gubby Allen

ALLEN, SIR GEORGE OSWALD BROWNING (GUBBY), CBE, TD, who died on November 29, 1989, aged 87, had a stronger influence on the welfare and development of cricket than anyone since Lord Harris over a period of more than 50 years. For his services to the game he was made CBE in 1974 and knighted in 1986. Sir George ("Gubby", as he was universally known) was born in Sydney on July 31, 1902. His father, believing firmly in the value of an English education, brought the family to England when he was six. A mere 27 years later he was elected to the committee of MCC. By impressing his seniors with his strong views and a general interest in the game, he had quickly been recognised as good committee material, and by 1933 he was treading the corridors of power, familiarising himself with the inner workings of Lord's. He was ten years younger than the next youngest member of the committee. He had been elected to the Middlesex committee in 1931.

After service in the Second World War, early on in an anti-aircraft battery and later as an intelligence officer, rising to the rank of lieutenant-colonel, Allen returned to Lord's fully aware that cricket needed revitalising and determined to bring this about …

He was President of MCC in 1963-64, and in 1964 he became Treasurer, holding this influential post for twelve years. As Treasurer he had much to do with the setting up of the Cricket Council with its subordinate executive bodies, the Test and County Cricket Board and the National Cricket Association. During all this time he was England's representative on ICC. His deep knowledge and unique ability to advise on any aspect of cricket was based on his playing experience at the highest level.

Allen remained a true amateur and played first-class cricket only when his work in the City permitted. He took trouble to keep himself fit by playing squash regularly and playing good-quality club cricket at weekends. That he was able to step up a gear and invariably make his mark was a tribute to his natural ability and dedication. He had a superb action with a rhythmical run-up and full follow-through, and it needed only a little fine tuning to be running smoothly …

In all he played in 265 matches, making 9,232 runs for an average of 28.67, capturing 788 wickets at 22.23, and taking 131 catches; he was a splendid close fielder. He took ten wickets in a match on nine occasions. His Test record was 750 runs at 24.19 and 81 wickets for 29.37. With his death cricket lost one of its most devoted and dedicated servants. Active almost to the end, he returned to his home from hospital to die only a pitch's length from the Pavilion at Lord's and the stand next door now named after him.

Sir Donald Bradman, AC, writes: Despite the knowledge that the prognosis was bad, it was with great sadness that I learned of the death of Sir George (Gubby) Allen. I had known him for 69 years and he was the sole English survivor of the team which played against us in that memorable Lord's Test of 1930. Over that long period of almost seven decades I made many wonderful and cherished English friends. Sadly the great majority have passed away, and at the time of his death Gubby was probably closer to my heart than anyone else in England. From our very first acquaintance we found ourselves on the same wavelength and this affinity never changed.

Gubby achieved fame as a Test cricketer, but his greatest contribution to the game was when in 1932-33 he refused to be browbeaten by England's captain, Douglas Jardine, and risked being sent home from Australia rather than bowl bodyline, which he believed and said was contrary to the well-being of the game of cricket. His stand displayed courage of the highest order, and the cricket world will for ever be in his debt.

Four years later, in 1936-37, he captained England in Australia. I had the privilege of being Australia's captain, and together we resolved to expunge the memories of 1932-33 and to restore cricket to its rightful place as a sport wherein opponents would strain every nerve and sinew to win but never at the expense of sportsmanship and friendship. I still cherish the letter he wrote me at the end of the tour in which he expressed his personal pride that the slate had been wiped clean and that cricket relationships between Australia and England had been restored to their rightful pinnacle.

Although that series ended our contests on the field of play, Gubby's life and mine continued to follow similar paths in that we both made our livelihoods out of stock and share broking, and that we both dedicated ourselves to cricket administration, an area which presented significant differences of opinion between England and Australia. The culmination of these differences came just before the proposed Australian tour of England in 1961 over the vexed question of what constituted a fair delivery. Enormous publicity had been given to the bowling actions of certain Australians, and the situation of virtually trial by the media became well nigh intolerable – so much so that Bill Dowling and I were despatched to England by air for consultations with our English counterparts.

In essence the problem was thrown into the laps of Harry Altham and Gubby Allen (representing England) and Bill Dowling and myself, representing Australia. There were very frank exchanges of views and much argument, but in the end the measures adopted, which brought an end to the crisis, became possible only because both Gubby and I had implicit faith in the integrity of each other. The final outcome was an agreement for a "throwing truce" during the first five weeks of the 1961 season (of which I was the instigator) and the drafting of a new Law concerning a "fair" delivery, for which Gubby became responsible. History shows that our method of buying time proved of immense value.

Gubby and I wrote to one another frequently exchanging views on matters appertaining to cricket wherein we had reservations or futuristic thoughts. On the off-side lbw Law, Gubby admitted that he supported with enthusiasm the change to the present rule, but he later regretted his decision and thought a mistake had been made. After many years he felt the alteration had made a fundamental change for the worse in the technique of batsmanship, pandering to defensive forward play and militating against the back-foot exponent. In the bowling department he felt that the new rule encouraged in-swing bowling, whereas the health of cricket would have been better served by bowlers being encouraged to make the ball leave the bat. In retrospect he believed it would have been wiser to have left the lbw Law as it was and to have increased the size of the stumps. I wonder if history will ever see eye to eye.

Unfinished business of quite recent origin was his complete agreement with me that the change to the front-foot no-ball Law was a mistake and had set up a quite unsatisfactory rule. Whilst firm in this view, he had not finally come to terms with the issue because he had been unable to devise a wording which would satisfy him for reverting to the back-foot jurisdiction. Tragic that his thinking and wisdom are no longer available to us and the problem remains.

Over the years England has produced a string of wonderful cricket administrators who devoted their lives to cricket, men of the stature of Lord

Hawke, Lord Harris, Harry Altham and others, whose contribution can never be quantified. But I say with sincerity and conviction that nobody in history has left a legacy of dedication and service to the game greater than Gubby Allen. His arguments were always powerful but reasoned, based on his playing skill and knowledge, as well as his understanding of the need for democratic solutions.

I deeply mourn the loss of a staunch friend and colleague, tempered by the gratitude that I had been privileged to share with him a mutual labour of love which deeply enriched our respective lives and which contributed to the well-being of the game we both cherished so much.

pages 1158–1159 and 1161

Cricket in New Zealand, 1989-90

By C. R. Buttery

The 1989-90 Shell Trophy went to Wellington, who won four of their ten matches and were the only team to finish the season undefeated. This was quite a remarkable achievement. At the halfway stage they were in last place, and were given little chance of overtaking Auckland, the competition leaders and clear favourites for the title. However, victories in their next three games took Wellington to the top of the points table, and despite intensive efforts by Auckland and Canterbury to dislodge them, they were able to maintain their lead. Batsmen Andrew Jones and Bruce Edgar were a tower of strength, and Jonathan Millmow, a tall fast bowler, took 33 wickets, which earned him a place in the New Zealand side to tour England later in the year.

Unfortunately for Wellington, the season will be remembered for their farcical tactics at the end of the third day of their return match against Canterbury. In order to narrow the 94-run gap between the two sides, in the hope of then buying the last two wickets to win the game, Wellington captain Erwin McSweeney incurred the wrath of cricket purists by instructing his bowlers to toss up a series of deliberate no-balls. In the penultimate over, comprising 22 balls, Robert Vance conceded a record 77 runs (1444664614116666600401), 69 coming from the bat of the Canterbury wicket-keeper, Lee Germon. In the circumstances the question of whether Germon's feat should go in the record books is debatable. As it turned out, McSweeney's tactics almost cost him the game, which ended in a draw with the scores level after the final over, bowled by Evan Gray, had produced a further 17 runs. The scoreboard attendants could not keep up with the rapid run-rate from the last two overs, and neither side realised how close Canterbury were to victory until the match was over.

Canterbury could feel justifiably pleased at finishing runners-up to Wellington, although they were undoubtedly a little frustrated to be only one run short of winning their final-round match. Victory then would have made the Shell Trophy theirs. Even so, it was an excellent result for a team which had languished in the lower half of the competition for the previous four seasons ...

The defending Shell Trophy champions, Auckland, were expected to do well, and for the first half of the season they alternated between first and second in the table. However, at crucial times they lost up to six players for Test duties, including their opening batsmen, John Wright and Trevor Franklin, wicket-keeper Ian Smith, and the fast bowlers, Danny Morrison and Martin Snedden. Their other fast bowler, Willie Watson, was injured midway through the series and took no further part in the competition. As a result, Auckland failed to win any of their last four games and finished third behind Wellington and Canterbury. Wright had a marvellous season, captaining New Zealand to victory against India and Australia and also heading the national batting averages with 818 runs at 81.80.

Central Districts were probably the unluckiest team in the competition. They lost to Northern Districts by only one run, and two matches later a combination of rain and bad light prevented them from beating Otago. A victory in either of these matches would have won them the Shell Trophy. Nevertheless, their fourth placing was considerably better than the previous year, when they finished last. The batting was very much dependent on Martin Crowe and Mark Greatbatch, both of whom missed games because of international commitments.

Shell Trophy, 1989-90

	Played	Won	Lost	Drawn	Pts 1st Inns	Pts Total
Wellington	10	4	0	6	14*	57
Canterbury	10	3	1	6	16	52
Auckland	10	2	3	5	28	50
Central Districts	10	2	5	3	24	48
Otago	10	2	2	6	22*	42
Northern Districts	10	2	4	4	16	40

Win = 12 pts; lead on first innings = 4pts.
* First-innings points share in one match.
Wellington were penalised 5 points, Otago 4 points, and Auckland 2 points for failing to achieve an average of seventeen overs per hour during the competition.

pages 58–59

The Lancashire League Celebrates Its Centenary

By Chris Aspin

When east Lancashire was full of cotton mills, you could sometimes see 78 tall black chimneys from the old wooden score box in the top corner of Church cricket ground. I counted them once, during the local holiday week. On other days, sharp-eyed spectators could discern about a dozen through the sooty haze, and it would surprise me if as many as that now rise above Accrington, Great Harwood and the distant brickfields of Clayton-le-Moors. The smoking mills, familiar for so long to spectators at Lancashire League matches, have gone. The Pennine air is refreshingly clean this centenary year, though it will probably be too sharp at times for the overseas professionals who have followed in the steps of Learie Constantine, Ray Lindwall, Everton Weekes, Clive Lloyd, Dennis Lillee, Viv Richards and a host of other immortals in order to play in what is widely regarded as the world's foremost league. The fourteen clubs have always insisted on keeping the game for local players – overseas amateurs regularly offer their services in vain – and have been rewarded with the loyal, often passionate, support of a numerous following. The aggregate attendance at the seven games on a Sunday usually exceeds that at Old Trafford.

There have been many times when I have wondered why cricket ever took root in these parts. Snow has more than once prevented play, and the sight and feel of cold Lancashire rain falling from a pewter sky is almost enough to put people off the game for ever. But on a sunny afternoon, with noble hills providing the backcloth to a keenly contested game involving two world-class professionals, there are few better cricketing occasions. Though Lancashire League clubs are often criticised for paying large fees for Test stars, few are likely to abandon a tradition which began with men like McDonald, Headley and Constantine during the inter-war years, and which now provides amateurs with a rare chance to pit their skills against the world's best. Long before the League was formed in 1892, clubs regularly engaged English professionals with first-class and Test experience. And for important matches they occasionally included three or four paid men, causing resentment among opponents who could afford only one or two. The control of professionalism was one of the stated aims of the Lancashire League. Two pros were allowed in the early years, but since 1900 the number has been one.

Many of the older clubs can trace their roots to the enthusiasm for cricket which was fired at public schools attended by the sons of mill owners and professional men. The Blackburn club, East Lancashire, is unusual in having been started by officers of the town's volunteer corps, and its stars included A. N. (Monkey) Hornby, the Lancashire and England player, who was a member of one of the county's oldest cotton families. Most of these players were batsmen. Professionals were engaged to coach and to bowl, with working men occasionally helping out in the nets. Some of the enthusiasts became good enough to be included in the teams, and by the time the League was formed, artisans were well represented both on the field and in the committee rooms.

Mills worked till noon on Saturdays well into this century; and to enable spectators to see a full match, wickets were pitched at two o'clock. Today the starting time is 1.45 p.m., but since limited-overs cricket came in twenty years ago, there has been no fixed finishing time. As many games are now played on Sundays as on Saturdays. Sponsorship has become increasingly important, though bar takings and the renting of rooms provide most of the income.

If I could choose one match from the thousands which have been played during the past 100 years, it would be that between Rawtenstall and Nelson in 1931. It brought into conflict the great Sidney Barnes, aged 59, but still a bowler without equal, and the young Learie Constantine, the cricketing phenomenon, who was the greatest single attraction any league has known. "Connie", as everyone called him, often said that the 96 he scored in front of a vast crowd that afternoon was the best innings he ever played. The duel with Barnes, who took seven for 68, was cricket at the very highest level and was remembered vividly long after the result of the match was forgotten. Nelson won by 72 runs. Constantine was professional for Nelson from 1929 to 1937, and in those nine seasons he gained seven championship medals. Against Accrington in 1934 he took all ten wickets for 10 runs.

Looking over the club records, one sees that bowlers had their best years in the early decades of the competition. One would certainly have liked to watch Sam Moss, the Manchester shoemaker, who burst into league cricket in the 1890s. In his first game as professional for Haslingden in 1896, he took five wickets in eight balls – all bowled – and for Bacup four years later he finished with 143 wickets at 8.2. Publicans throughout the district put up glass cases to display the stumps he broke, and those who saw Moss were in no doubt that they had never come across anyone faster. Nowadays batsmen have the upper hand, and the recent policy of rearranging games hit by the weather has helped them to score more runs than ever before. The Australian, Peter Sleep, professional for Rishton, and the Rawtenstall amateur, Peter Wood, both achieved Lancashire League aggregate records last season.

Over the years, the Lancashire League has provided Lancashire and England with many fine players. Eddie Paynter, who worked in the brick-fields at Clayton-le-Moors and who played for Enfield at both the start and the end of his career, was one of the best known. After his performances for England during the Australian tour of 1932-33, the League presented him with a pair of silver candlesticks. Accrington have the distinction of nurturing David Lloyd and Graeme Fowler, two other left-handers who have played for their country, and many League players have gone to other counties. In 1939, five Bacup-born players were in the first-class game.

Nelson have won the Lancashire League championship eighteen times; East Lancashire and Burnley thirteen times each. During the past decade, Haslingden have gained most of the honours, winning the championship in six of the last nine seasons and being runners-up twice. The knockout competition for the Worsley Cup, started in 1919, has been won thirteen times by East Lancashire.

pages 14–15

After six years as editor, and eight as assistant editor
(to Norman Preston and John Woodcock) before that, Graeme Wright
was succeeded by Matthew Engel. The following extract is from his first
set of Editor's Notes, in the 1993 edition.

Notes by the Editor

(Matthew Engel)

The Gower Affair

The finishing touches are being put to these notes as England go down to defeat in the Calcutta Test, a few days after the members of MCC held a special general meeting and rejected, by 6,135 votes to 4,600, a motion of no confidence in England's Test selectors proposed by 286 dissident members against the strong opposition of the MCC committee. The vote in the hall, as opposed to the postal ballot, was in favour of the motion by 715 to 412, and it would have been clear to a neutral, fair-minded observer, if one was present, that the proponents won the debate as well.

The meeting was called because the selectors had left out Gower and, only slightly less controversially, Jack Russell and Ian Salisbury from the tour of India; Salisbury, who had flown out to act as a net bowler, was later asked to join the tour. Ted Dexter's refusal to give the reasons for Gower's omission was widely seen as arrogant; Keith Fletcher, the new England manager, did offer an explanation – that too many batsman would have been in their mid-30s – which was quite incredible. One expects managers to lie, fib or obfuscate when they have a record to defend; it was a shock for it to happen on Fletcher's first day. Gower's omission created a furore not seen in 25 years since the selectors left out Basil D'Oliveira, with consequences that went far beyond the loss of a Test match or two, from a tour of South Africa.

Since MCC no longer directly controls English cricket it was not a logical forum for public discontent, but it was a very effective one. The club committee made it their business to defend, if not the selection, then at least the selectors' right to do as they wanted without hindrance – so it was sometimes implied – from the ignorant masses. At various times, the committee and their supporters suggested that it was wrong to criticise selectors before the team had played, because that was pre-judgment; it was wrong to criticise during the tour, because that constituted disloyalty to the England team; and of course it was wrong to criticise afterwards, because that meant hindsight, and any fool can have that. The use of the word disloyalty is particularly interesting in this context. We will come back to that in a moment.

There was no sustainable cricketing case for the omission of Gower from a Test series against India. No one seriously made one. Selectors have always had their own secret agenda: prejudices against certain players considered to be unsuitable tourists. In the old days men were sometimes omitted because they did not buy their round at the bar; these days they are more likely to be left out because they do.

Many players throughout history have had their Test careers aborted or curtailed because of these personal defects, real or perceived. It is, however, entirely bizarre that those defects should suddenly be discovered in the cricketer who has played more Test matches for England than anyone in history.

There are many criticisms that can legitimately be made of Gower as a cricketer and, above all, as a captain; Graham Gooch's period of captaincy since 1989 has been marked by a dedication and determination that have often been quite magnificent. But the English cricket public, as I was saying earlier, have remained loyal to their Test team in a manner unmatched elsewhere in the world. The modern player who has most reciprocated that loyalty has been Gower. Between 1978-79 and 1986-87 he went on nine successive winter tours. The following year, understandably, he asked for a break. Since then he has been willing to play for England any time, anywhere, even to the point of something close to public humiliation by Gooch in Antigua in 1990. He did not go on any rebel tour nor is there any evidence (as there is for some other players who subsequently trumpeted their loyalty) that he seriously contemplated it. The contrast with Gooch – his decision to go to South Africa in 1981-82, his refusal, for understandable family reasons, to tour Australia in 1986-87, his need to have Donald Carr fly out to Antigua in 1986 to persuade him to stay because some politician had criticised him, the fact that he planned to skip the (abandoned) India tour of 1988-89 until he was offered the captaincy, even his insistence on not going to Sri Lanka this year – is very stark.

This party for India was chosen last September at a moment when reconciliation was being offered all round, to John Emburey for instance. Now Emburey is a fine cricketer and a nice man. But he is the only person in the whole shabby history of these enterprises who actually signed up for rebel tours to South Africa on two separate occasions. Short of standing on the square at Lord's on the Saturday of a Test match and giving a V-sign to the Long Room, it is hard to imagine how anyone can have shown greater unconcern about whether he plays for England or not. For him, forgiveness was instant. For Gower, there was none. The whole business reflected badly on English cricket; the dissidents were right to make themselves heard.

pages 21–23

Five Cricketers of the Year

Cricketer of the Century: Shane Warne

By Vic Marks

 When Martin Crowe announced just before the 1993 Ashes series that Shane Warne was the best leg-spinner in the world, few alarm bells clanged in England. Such a declaration could be interpreted as an attempt to restore the confidence of Kiwi batsmen, notoriously vulnerable against spin, who had just been undermined by Warne. Moreover, no Australian wrist-spinner had made a significant impact in an English Test series since the days of Grimmett and O'Reilly between the wars. England, it was assumed, had to quell McDermott and Hughes to have a chance of retrieving the Ashes.

Such a complacent misconception was dispelled at Old Trafford by Warne's first delivery in Test cricket in England. It was bowled to Mike Gatting, an acknowledged master of spin. Warne does not indulge in low-risk "looseners" and that first ball was flicked vigorously out of the back of the hand. It set off on the line of Gatting's pads and then dipped in the air further towards the leg side until it was 18 inches adrift of the stumps; by this time Gatting was beginning to lose interest, until the ball bounced, turned and fizzed across his ample frame to clip the off bail. Gatting remained rooted at the crease for several seconds – in disbelief rather than dissent – before trudging off to the pavilion like a man betrayed. Now the Englishmen knew that Crowe's assessment was more than propaganda.

Throughout six Tests they could never master Warne. He bowled 439.5 overs in the series, took 34 wickets – surpassing Grimmett's 29 in the five Tests of 1930 – and also managed to concede under two runs per over, thereby flouting the tradition of profligate wrist-spinners buying their wickets. Some English batsmen were completely mesmerised; Robin Smith, England's "banker" in the middle order, was unable to detect any of his variations and had to be dropped. The admirable Gooch could obviously distinguish the googly from the leg-spinner, yet Warne still disposed of him five times in the series. Once Gooch carelessly clubbed a full toss to mid-on, but otherwise he was dismissed while playing the appropriate defensive stroke, the surest indication that Warne has a special talent.

Ominously for Test batsmen of the 1990s, Warne is not yet the complete wrist-spinner. His googly is not so penetrating or well-disguised as Mushtaq Ahmed's, which is one reason why he employs it so infrequently. His flipper is lethal if it is on target, but it often zooms down the leg side. But he is the most prodigious spinner of the ball of the last three decades, a gift which causes deceptive in-swing as well as excessive turn. He is also remarkably accurate, but if ever his control is threatened, he can regroup by bowling around the wicket to the right-handed batsman, thereby restricting him to just one scoring stroke, a risky sweep. Hence in the Ashes series his captain, Border, was able to use him as both shock and stock bowler.

Warne's success in 1993 was a triumph for the Australian selectors as well as his own resolve. They might easily have discarded him as a liability early in his career. Shane Keith Warne, born in a smart bayside suburb of Melbourne on September 13, 1969, did not display many of the hallmarks of his predecessors – Grimmett, O'Reilly and Benaud – in his youth. Bleached blond hair, a stud in his ear plus a fondness for the good life, which caused his waistline to expand with alarming speed, and an aversion to discipline, which in 1990 led to his departure under a cloud from the Australian Cricket Academy in Adelaide, do not reflect the perfect credentials for the modern Australian Test cricketer. Yet the selectors trusted their judgment.

They pitched him into two Test matches against India in January 1992, after just four Sheffield Shield appearances, in which he had taken eight wickets. He had shown form on tour in Zimbabwe and against the West Indians. None the less, his state captain Simon O'Donnell expressed public reservations. Warne took one for 228 against the Indians and the gamble seemed to have backfired. Warne was then invited by Rod Marsh to return to the Academy, where he was coached by another reformed larrikin, Terry Jenner. Warne was now prepared to make the sort of sacrifices that impress Australians: he gave up beer, trained hard, lost 28 pounds and was rewarded by selection for the tour to Sri Lanka in August 1992.

In Colombo, having yielded 107 runs from 22 wicketless overs in the first innings of the opening Test, Warne took three for 11 from 5.1 overs in the second as Australia conjured a dramatic victory. His victims were only tailenders, but it was a start. That Border entrusted him with the ball at all at such a crucial moment did wonders for his confidence. His seven for 52 against West Indies at Melbourne in December 1992 was an isolated success in that series but confirmed his match-winning potential. But his efforts in New Zealand (17 wickets in three matches) and in last summer's Ashes series have established Warne as an integral cog, perhaps the integral cog, of the Australian team.

On a broader scale he has triggered a mini-renaissance in the art of wrist-spin bowling. In the summer of 1993 young village cricketers could be spied on the outfield, no longer seeking to emulate Curtly Ambrose or Merv Hughes, but attempting to ape the more subtle skills of Warne. For that we should all be grateful.

The other four Cricketers of the Year in 1994 were D. C. Boon, I. A. Healy, M. G. Hughes and S. L. Watkin.

pages 17–18 and 21

Looking at Lara

In 52 days between April 16 and June 6, 1994, Brian Lara became the first batsman in history to score seven centuries in eight first-class innings. Even more remarkable were his first and last innings in this sequence. The first was 375 for West Indies against England in Antigua, the highest individual Test innings. The last was 501 for Warwickshire against Durham, the highest individual first-class innings. The 1995 edition marked these sensational achievements.

The Coach

Bob Woolmer, the Warwickshire coach in 1994, is believed to be the only man to have seen both Hanif Mohammad's old record 499 and Lara's 501.

It was a freak that I saw the Hanif innings. I was at prep school at Tonbridge and my father was working in Karachi. I was flown out on a BOAC Comet 4. That was a story in itself: we were actually forced down by fighters in Baghdad, where there was political trouble. I was 11 and I was very scared. Dad dropped me at the ground at Karachi where Hanif was closing in on the record and then he went to work. I don't remember much about it. There was a big crowd, a matting wicket, a very rough outfield and a bloke getting run out. My father asked me what happened and I said: "Well, someone got 499, Dad." Lara's innings is a bit clearer in my mind. At lunch, Brian said to me, "What score's the first-class record?" I said, "499. You're not going for that?" He said, "Well, are you thinking of declaring?" And Dermot Reeve said, "Well, sort of. We'll see how it goes." So it was agreed he could at least go for the Warwickshire record 305, and I said to Dermot, "Let him go the whole way." He was just so single-minded, it was always inevitable, almost mystical. I don't think I remember any one shot in the innings so much as a Sunday League stroke at Taunton a couple of weeks earlier, against Payne of Somerset, when he flat-batted him into the old stand. I just remember him getting the 501 and his face. He signed a picture for me of his pull with the front foot off the ground. He put: "Try to teach this one, coach." I shall frame that.

Mushtaq Mohammad, who played in the Karachi match, raced to Edgbaston from his office in Birmingham, having been tipped off by a phone call when Lara was past 450, but arrived too late.

The Scorer

Alex Davis, a retired quantity surveyor and Warwickshire scorer since 1990, was also the scorer on the England tour of the West Indies. He is thus believed to be the only man to have watched every ball of both Lara's record-breaking innings.

For me, the two innings are very different, because the first I was doing manually in a scorebook, whereas the second I was doing on the computer and a manual scoresheet, so I was working twice as hard. And the second one was scored at such a rate, we kept having to answer the phone to the press to give the details of each of the fifties. At one time the pressman said: "Shall I stay on for the next 50?" The advantage of the computer is that it does do the adding-up for you, so you don't have to do so much cross-checking. When there's 800 runs on the board that makes a difference. There wasn't a problem of space, because I was doing it on a linear system, down the page. But then I copied it on to the standard scoresheet. Fortunately, with the 375, Simmons and Williams were out for eight and three, so there was loads of space to spread Lara. With the other one it wasn't so easy because of the runs the other players made, so I had to dodge round the spaces. So far as I know, I'm the only person who saw both all the way through. A lot of people didn't bother coming to Edgbaston on the Monday because the game looked completely dead and we had a semi-final at The Oval on the Tuesday. Mike Smith, who was the England manager in Antigua, missed it. My wife Christine normally comes and she never misses a ball: she used to score for Warwickshire Colts and she saw all the 375. But the general feeling was it wouldn't be much of a day. I got a terrible telling off for not ringing up. But she'd have had to come in on public transport from Solihull. And you can't do that with cricket. It used to happen when our son played: she used to ring up and tell me he was doing well and by the time I got there he'd be out.

The Bowler

Anderson Cummins, the Barbadian fast bowler, was 12th man for West Indies during the 375, but was playing for Durham and on the opposing side for the 501.

I had a good idea he was capable of record-breaking innings after seeing his

277 against Australia at Sydney. He's the type of individual who wants to be the best at what he does and that means going for records. He was running into form when he made his 375 against England. It was a very flat wicket and he set his stall out to produce something big. I don't think there was much else England could have done. With that sort of ability and determination, it was going to be very difficult to dislodge him. He started slowly but confidently. He didn't miss much. He has the natural art of picking the gaps and he played better and better. I never thought of the record until he was past 200, but we were all behind him to go for it. We had won the series and we knew it was something he wanted. When he made his 501 against Durham we bowled very well at him early on. We tried to exploit him stepping across his stumps early in his innings and we had our chances. He could have been out first ball. Knowing the type of player he is, I knew he would go for it if I banged one in. It lobbed off the end of his bat just out of my reach. He was on ten when I bowled him with a no-ball. It was a deliberate leg-stump yorker and he stepped inside it. But he started to play really well after about 90 minutes at the crease. I had batted on the pitch and I knew it was as flat as hell, and the way the game went it was set up for Lara to do something like that. Things usually go better for people who really believe in themselves. He was helped by the short boundary, which meant he could clip the ball off his stumps and it would go for six, but I was very impressed by his stamina. I knew he had the ability, but to concentrate for that long and keep going was amazing. I don't think anybody thought we had given it to him. Nobody flagged and we stuck at it right to the end. People forget that the match ended in a draw. We could have set something up to give them a target, but we were a bowler short because David Graveney was injured and at that stage of the Championship we didn't want to give anybody points.

The Man Himself

The 375 in the Antigua Test match was on a marble top of a pitch, ideal for batting. I knew if we won the toss we would make a big score and it did cross my mind it would give me a chance of scoring another double-hundred in Tests. But it was only after the first day's play, when I was on 164, that I thought it might be a big innings, maybe a world record. The next morning I started carefully, playing out two maiden overs from Angus Fraser. I knew it was up to me. If I kept my concentration and didn't do anything rash, I knew I had a chance of making history. I was not too tense. The tension only got to me in the early hours of the next morning when I woke much earlier than usual, and my mind was churning over what it would mean to me if I managed to score 46 more runs. My whole life flashed through my mind. I thought of all the people who had faith in me. I knew I couldn't let them down. The year before in Australia I was given a chance of breaking the record when I passed 200 in the Sydney Test but was run out on 277. That was the best innings of my career and still is. Most players never have a second opportunity. I knew I had to do it this time. The Antiguan innings was chanceless. I played a little sketchily on the third morning but I didn't give a chance. The one that went wide of Jack Russell's glove was a foot or so away from him. The 501 at Edgbaston was different in so many respects. The pitch was not quite so good but the outfield was faster. And obviously Durham's attack wasn't anywhere near as good as England's. On the Friday night I batted so poorly that I was bowled off a no-ball and dropped behind by Chris Scott at 18. "Jeez, I hope he doesn't go on and get a hundred," he said. At tea I went to the nets to try and correct the faults in my batting. It was unbelievable that both records should be broken in such a short space of time. The 375 was more important because it was in a Test match, but I will cherish both records. Test cricket is the highest form of cricket and to have broken the record of Sir Garfield Sobers in a Test in the West Indies meant more to me than anything I had achieved before. If only my father who did so much for me had been there to share the moment with me.

pages 34–35 and 1203–1204

Miracle in Queensland (Somewhat Belated)

By Gideon Haigh

"It behoves the young players of the present day to prove themselves throughout the cricket struggles that are ahead of them, to be worthy in every way of the honour conferred on their association by the conference of the Sheffield Shield States in the year 1926."

> *E. H. Hutcheon, Queensland cricketer and historian.*

It took 68 years and nearly 500 matches before Queensland cricketers proved equal to their behoving: at 3.52 p.m. precisely, Tuesday March 28,

1995, was transformed into VQ Day, when the state beat South Australia by an innings and 101 runs and finally took custody of Australia's symbol of interstate cricket supremacy.

To make himself audible above the celebratory din of his "Banana Army" of supporters, and to adjust to the sensation of victory, captain Stuart Law enunciated his post-match remarks carefully: "We have won the Shield. It does sound strange saying it. It's just a fantastic feeling to finally have that thing in our room, to hold it up above our heads and feel really proud. It's been the longest week ever. We've won it. Now we can get on with enjoying life again" …

The last time Queensland were in possession of the Shield was before their opening match in 1926, when it was borrowed from New South Wales for a shop window display. In the meantime, the nearest they had come was winning the Bougainville Sheffield Shield, contested by Australian soldiers in the South Pacific who were awaiting repatriation after VJ Day. This Shield was actually the casing of a military shell.

In 1995, however, the real Shield arrived. The players took it on a three-day tour in a Government plane round the state's vast hinterland. There was a ticker-tape parade in Brisbane itself, a vintage car cavalcade in Mackay, an escort by Harley-Davidson bikers in Mount Isa, and a quick trip to Kynuna (population: 25). It was all such a novelty that in one town they left it behind.

Fortune toyed with Queensland from their admission to join New South Wales, Victoria and South Australia in the Shield in 1926-27. Set 400 to win in their first match by NSW's Alan Kippax, local captain Leo O'Connor was run out by debutant Gordon Amos for 196, only 19 short of victory, and he saw his side lose by a paltry eight runs …

In that first match, ten of the Queensland team had been born in the state. But an amazing squad could be assembled from Queensland's VIPs (Very Imported Players): extra-colonials Colin McCool, Ray Lindwall, Greg Chappell, Jeff Thomson, Dirk Wellham, Ian Davis, Ray Phillips, Allan Border and Paul Jackson; extra-continentals Kepler Wessels, Majid Khan, Vivian Richards, Tom Graveney, Graeme Hick, Alvin Kallicharran, Rusi Surti, Ian Botham and Wes Hall.

It is a squad to beat the world, but not the rest of Australia. While a few gave their all, others gave only some and at least a handful provided precious little. Queensland seemed in some seasons likelier to win the FA Cup than the Sheffield Shield. And that the most consciously patriotic and occasionally separatist Australian state should acquire such a dependency struck many as eccentric. The Olympic swimming coach Laurie Lawrence wrote, after Queensland crumbled again a couple of years ago: "Imports are not the answer, or at least they are not the answer that will give any

Queenslander any satisfaction." … Law's squad were, if not native, at least long resident in the state: Border's career with NSW and left-arm spinner Jackson's prior duties in Victoria are now some yellow books back.

Blown in from such outposts as Toowoomba, Wondai, Bileola, Kingaroy, Innisfail and Mundubberra, and mingling the born-again Border and the indestructible Carl Rackemann with the supple skills of tyros like Martin Love, Jim Maher, Wade Seccombe and Andrew Symonds, they played with resource and without regret.

The Gabba was being refurbished and the schedule proved too inflexible to allow the Sir Leslie Wilson Stand a few day's grace for the

SHEFFIELD SHIELD FINAL, 1994-95

QUEENSLAND v SOUTH AUSTRALIA

At Brisbane, March 24, 25, 26, 27, 28, 1995. Queensland won by an innings and 101 runs. Toss: South Australia.

Close of play: First day, Queensland 36-0 (T. J. Barsby 11*, M. L. Hayden 14*); Second day, Queensland 409-3 (M. L. Love 114*, A. R. Border 26*); Third day, Queensland 501-4 (A. R. Border 76*, J. P. Maher 6*); Fourth day, South Australia 59-2 (P. C. Nobes 24*, D. S. Lehmann 14*).

South Australia

B. A. Johnson c Hayden b Bichel	4	– c Hayden b Jackson	10
P. C. Nobes c Law b Tazelaar	0	– b Tazelaar	100
*J. D. Siddons c Border b Rackemann	8	– c Seccombe b Rackemann	3
D. S. Lehmann c Seccombe b Tazelaar	12	– c Tazelaar b Bichel	62
J. A. Brayshaw run out	53	– c Seccombe b Rackemann	16
D. S. Webber c Seccombe b Bichel	33	– c and b Law	91
†T. J. Nielsen b Jackson	53	– lbw b Tazelaar	0
J. N. Gillespie c Seccombe b Rackemann	18	– c Rackemann b Jackson	39
P. E. McIntyre c Rackemann b Jackson	9	– c Law b Bichel	2
S. P. George b Rackemann	15	– c Bichel b Jackson	4
M. A. Harrity not out	0	– not out	0
B 1, n-b 8	9	B 4, l-b 8, n-b 10	22

1/4 2/6 3/26 4/30 5/93   214   1/31 2/34 3/142 4/194 5/253   349
6/126 7/179 8/189 9/210   6/253 7/314 8/335 9/347

Bowling: *First Innings*—Bichel 19–4–54–2; Tazelaar 20–3–45–2; Rackemann 18–6–54–3; Law 10–3–26–0; Jackson 14.4–5–34–2. *Second Innings*—Bichel 29–6–90–2; Tazelaar 21–6–65–2; Rackemann 30–10–86–2; Jackson 37.2–9–81–3; Border 1–0–1–0; Law 3–1–14–1.

Queensland

T. J. Barsby c Gillespie b Johnson	151	P. W. Jackson not out	11
M. L. Hayden c Nielsen b Harrity	74	D. Tazelaar b McIntyre	22
M. L. Love c Nielsen b Brayshaw	146	C. G. Rackemann lbw b McIntyre	7
*S. G. Law c Webber b George	11		
A. R. Border b Johnson	98	B 1, l-b 14, w 3, n-b 34	52
J. P. Maher c Nielsen b Gillespie	36		—
†W. A. Seccombe c Harrity b Gillespie	18	1/144 2/336 3/376 4/479 5/553	664
A. J. Bichel c Nielsen b Gillespie	38	6/565 7/618 8/618 9/652	

Bowling: Harrity 46–12–129–1; George 33–8–102–1; Gillespie 35–10–112–3; McIntyre 49.5–10–176–2; Johnson 22–1–96–2; Brayshaw 14–5–34–1.

Umpires: D. B. Hair and P. D. Parker.

final, though spectators enlisted the debris in their visions of victory. The Brisbane bard, "Rupert" McCall – a modern-day Albert Craig – wrote this pre-match doggerel for the Brisbane *Courier-Mail*:

> Let's get out there and win 'cos we're the best team in the land,
> Let's demolish South Australia like the Leslie Wilson Stand.

Which Queensland did. Their 664 was more than enough to overwhelm South Australia and, since a draw was going to be enough anyway, locals were able to savour the prospect of victory for at least three days before its arrival. Grown men – as they do in all the best sports stories – wept. John Maclean, chairman of the Queensland Cricket Association, greeted century-maker and player-of-the-season Trevor Barsby with tears of joy running down his face saying: "You don't know what you've done." He probably didn't. And that may have been why he and his team-mates were able to do it.

pages 31–32 and 1048–1049

A Night to Remember

By David Hopps

Colombo had known much grief in the weeks leading up to the World Cup final. The bomb on January 31 [1996] that killed about 90 people had brought terrorism back to the heart of the capital. And it undermined Sri Lanka's hopes that their co-hosting of the tournament would promote tourism and investment, as well as providing funds for an expansion of cricket facilities throughout the country.

Australia, having just been involved in a bitter series against Sri Lanka, had already voiced some reluctance to fulfil their fixtures in the country, on the grounds that some of their players had received hate mail and feared for their safety, for reasons connected with cricket rather than politics. The atrocity in Colombo justified their quick withdrawal. Even the pleas of the Sri Lankan Government, whose array of security measures included an offer to fly the team in from Madras or The Maldives, failed to change their minds.

West Indies soon followed Australia's example, without bothering to consult their players, leaving only two relatively minor sides, Kenya and Zimbabwe, to play fixtures which passed off without incident. That was only some compensation. In the early stages of the tournament, the mood in this most gracious and easy-going of countries was one of demoralisation and betrayal.

The night of March 17 provided handsome recompense. To be on Galle Face Green, a traditional Colombo meeting point overlooking the Indian Ocean, shortly after Sri Lanka's triumph over Australia in the final in Lahore was to witness a joyful outpouring of national pride. With most Sri Lankans preferring to watch the final in small family groups, the capital was eerily deserted for much of the day but, as night fell, the streets abruptly came alive to the blaring of car horns and the explosion of fireworks.

Some people had privately expressed their reluctance to join the Galle Face parade, fearing that there could be no more crushing time for the Tamil Tigers to launch another attack than at the moment of the country's greatest sporting achievement. But many suppressed their fears as tens of thousands streamed along the sea-front in just about every form of transport known to man.

Even in its most harrowing times, Sri Lanka has rung to the sound of laughter and it was impossible to walk a few yards along Galle Face Green without another invitation to join an impromptu street party. The walk back to the hotel as the sun began to rise was made more unsteadily. Whisky and arrack (the local firewater distilled from coconut) flowed, and Bob Marley music blared from the back of cars and open-top trucks, upon which rapturous youngsters danced precariously. Among the most soulful songs was "This Land Belongs to Us", and such lyrics cannot be sung in Sri Lanka without a sense of underlying weariness caused by years of terrorist warfare.

Cricket had always been a unifying force, offering recreation for Sinhalese, Tamil, Moslem and Christian alike. Now it had given the nation a chance to forget. The schools in Colombo had only just reopened after the Tigers' warning to the Government to "build smaller coffins". Now young children wandered freely and ecstatically through the throng.

According to Sri Lankan folklore, Nadiya – the jackal – is despised as the lowest of all animals, because of its willingness to eat the crow, which is regarded as the dustbin of Sri Lanka. Australia's forfeit of their group match in Colombo had caused their High Commissioner to be greeted with the call of Nadiya – "Hu, Hu, Hu" – at the prize-giving ceremony following Sri Lanka's victory against Kenya in Kandy. As televisions focused on a defeated Australian team, the jackal sounded for a final time. It was the response of a country getting even, and relishing every minute, of it.

WORLD CUP FINAL, 1996

AUSTRALIA v SRI LANKA

At Lahore, March 17, 1996. Sri Lanka won by seven wickets. Toss: Sri Lanka.
Man of the Match: P. A. de Silva. *Most Valued Player of the Tournament:* S. T. Jayasuriya.

Australia

*M. A. Taylor c Jayasuriya b de Silva	74	†I. A. Healy b de Silva	2
M. E. Waugh c Jayasuriya b Vaas	12	P. R. Reiffel not out	13
R. T. Ponting b de Silva	45	L-b 10, w 11, n-b 1	22
S. R. Waugh c de Silva b Dharmasena	13		
S. K. Warne st Kaluwitharana		1/36 (2) 2/137 (1) (7 wkts, 50 overs) 241	
b Muralitharan .	2	3/152 (3) 4/156 (5)	
S. G. Law c de Silva b Jayasuriya	22	5/170 (4) 6/202 (6)	
M G. Bevan not out	36	7/205 (8) Score at 15 overs: 82-1	

D. W. Fleming and G. D. McGrath did not bat.

Bowling: Wickremasinghe 7–0–38–0; Vaas 6–1–30–1; Muralitharan 10–0–31–1; Dharmasena 10–0–47–1; Jayasuriya 8–0–43–1; de Silva 9–0–42–3.

Sri Lanka

S. T. Jayasuriya run out	9
†R. S. Kaluwitharana c Bevan b Fleming .	6
A. P. Gurusinha b Reiffel	65
P. A. de Silva not out	107
*A. Ranatunga not out	47
B 1, l-b 4, w 5, n-b 1	11

1/12 (1) 2/23 (2) (3 wkts, 46.2 overs) 245 .
3/148 (3) Score at 15 overs: 71-2

R. S. Mahanama, H. P. Tillekeratne, H. D. P. K. Dharmasena, W. P. U. J. C. Vaas, G. P. Wickremasinghe and M. Muralitharan did not bat.

Bowling: McGrath 8.2–1–28–0; Fleming 6–0–43–1; Warne 10–0–58–0; Reiffel 10–0–49–1; M. E. Waugh 6–0–35–0; S. R. Waugh 3–0–15–0; Bevan 3–0–12–0.

Umpires: S. A. Bucknor and D. R. Shepherd. Referee: C. H. Lloyd.

Note: Eight of the Australian team went on to win the next World Cup, in 1999.

page 1320

*One of the most popular features of the modern-day
Wisden is the "Cricket Round the World" section.
The 1998 edition included reports from 33 different
non-Test playing countries, some of whom
competed in the European Nations Cup,
which climaxed in an extraordinary final.*

European Nations Cup, 1997

France retained the Nations Cup at Zuoz, Switzerland, in astonishing circumstances. They beat Germany by one run in a pulsating 50-over final. The unwitting hero was France's last man, David Bordes, who was hit on the forehead, and staggered through for a single at the end of the French innings before collapsing with a fractured skull. With two balls left, Germany, chasing 267, were 260 for nine: a top-edge fumbled by third man plopped over the rope for six. The Germans completed the two runs they needed for victory while the last ball was still skying to mid-on, where Valentin Brumant eventually caught it. So the Bordes head-bye proved a match-winner. He had to spend the next two weeks in hospital, and was ill for some time but, happily, was able to resume playing indoor cricket before Christmas. Bordes normally bats with a helmet but did not bother this time because he had only the one ball to face. In a group game against Switzerland, Germany scored 467 for one in their 50 overs including an unbroken stand of 349 between Shamaz Khan, a Pakistani-born naturalised German, and Abdul Bhatti. Shamaz scored 200 not out and Bhatti 179 not out.

*Another popular feature of the modern-day Wisden is the "Chronicle"
section, which includes cricketing items of curiosity reported in the media
during the previous year. The following is a selection from the 1999 edition.*

Chronicle of 1998

- Players at the annual Reedybrook Ashes, in the Queensland outback,
  killed several pythons and one Taipan snake while looking for lost
  balls. (*Australian Cricket*, January 1998.)

- Magistrates in Gampaha, Sri Lanka, were told that Mrs Thushanee
  Priyadarshani was forced to stay under the bed for several hours at a
  stretch because she refused to worship her husband's favourite pictures,
  showing a film star, and Test player Roshan Mahanama. (*The Island*,
  Colombo, January 8, 1998.)

- The disgruntled parents of a teenage boy stopped play at a school
  tournament to protest against his omission from the Tamil Nadu team.
  They held up the start of the inter-state Under-14 tournament in
  Chennai for nearly 40 minutes by sitting on the pitch. "Injustice has
  been done to my son Pramod Doss," said his father Deva Doss. "It
  surprises me how a boy good enough to be in the Under-16 city squad
  cannot find a place in the Under-14 state XI." They were finally
  persuaded to leave by officials. (*The Hindu*, January 31, 1998.)

- The Prince of Wales declared himself "absolutely knackered" after
  facing three balls from a schoolboy at the Sinhalese Sports Club on a
  royal visit to Colombo today. (*Evening Standard*, February 5, 1998.)

- An Under-13 team from the Baranagar Ramakrishna Mission, batting
  one man short, were bowled out for nought by the Bournvita team in a
  match between rival cricket coaching centres in Calcutta. The innings
  lasted just 18 minutes. Sayak Ghosh took six of the wickets, including
  a hat-trick, then hit the winning boundary from the second ball. (*The
  Hindu*, May 11, 1998.)

- A team of Blanks played a match against Staffordshire club Cannock Wood, when Alan Blank, a member of the club, put together an eleven entirely composed of his relatives. It filled in a blank day in the club fixture list. There were eight Blanks and three relations with a different surname. Two of the team, father and son, were both called David Blank. Another Blank umpired, and other clan members provided what the club said was a record attendance. (*Express & Star*, Wolverhampton, June 1, 1998.)

- A magpie stopped play at Ryde on the Isle of Wight. It swooped and stole the keys from the ignition of a motorised roller which was about to roll the pitch. The start was delayed until a tractor could tow the roller away. (*The Times*, June 3, 1998.)

- MCC received a letter addressed to a Mr O. F. Time, who had been selected to be one of the first to receive a brochure "full of beautiful items for home or boardroom". Stephen Green, curator of the Lord's museum, presumed that the letter was intended for Old Father Time, who he regretted was unable to enter into any correspondence. (*The Times*, June 8, 1998.)

- Village cricketers at Over, Cambridgeshire, continued playing in honour of lifelong supporter Sid Wright who died, aged 86, while watching a game. "It's what Sid would have wanted," said a club spokesman. (*Daily Mail*, June 12, 1998.)

- Jennifer Christian drove on to the field in the middle of a match in Dorset, slid to a halt, flung her car keys at the man fielding in the gully and ran off, leaving their two children strapped in the car. Her husband Eric drove off after her and took no further part in the game, between the Dorchester Third Eleven and the Parley Montys from Wimborne. He refused to comment, but team-mates believed he had promised to look after the children that afternoon. (*Daily Mail*, June 19, 1998.)

- The chief executive of South African cricket, Ali Bacher, failed to make a planned speech in the President's Box at the Lord's Test, because he was trapped in the ladies' toilet. He had wandered in there in error to read through his notes. (*The Express*, June 28, 1998.)

- A match between Hoveringham and the Inland Revenue in Nottinghamshire was stopped for more than five minutes when a naked woman drove across the outfield on a quad bike. (*The Times*, July 1, 1998.)

- Play in a Suffolk Premier League match was stopped by two police cars chasing a drunken moped rider across the outfield. Deben Valley were batting against the Ipswich and East Suffolk team at Woodbridge when the rider appeared, waving at the police and taunting them. He eventually fell off and was arrested. (*Daily Mail*, July 7, 1998.)

- Flying ants forced the abandonment of the Worcestershire Borders League game at Alvechurch against Dominies & Guild. Fifteen-year-old Dominies batsman Richard Wilkinson was forced to flee the crease when the ants began to emerge from a nest next to him. Play resumed after a kettle of boiling water was poured on the nest but, ten minutes later, the ants returned and the game was called off. "The whole wicket turned silver," said Dominies captain Glyn Wilks. "Every time anyone went near the wicket they just flew up in a storm." The ants probably saved his team: they were 98 for five chasing 241. (*Worcester Evening News*, August 10, 1998.)

- At a celebration match to open the new pavilion at Buckie in north-east Scotland, Fraser McBean had his car window broken by a six from another player. When McBean batted himself, he hit a six into the hole that was already there. (*The Scottish Cricketer*, September 1998.)

- An impromptu game of cricket in the gents' toilet at the Dutch Open Championships led to English badminton internationals Peter Knowles and Colin Haughton being suspended for ten weeks and six weeks respectively. They played with a cleaners' brush and a bar of soap; Knowles reacted angrily when there were complaints. (*Daily Telegraph*, October 20, 1998.)

- The treasurer of Builth Wells Cricket Club in Wales, sent out to buy a strimmer to keep the ground under control, bought two goats for £20 to do the job instead. (*Daily Telegraph*, December 11, 1998.)

Wisden's Cricketers
of the Year, 1900–2000

1900	*Five Cricketers of the Season:* J. Darling, C. Hill, A. O. Jones, M. A. Noble, Major R. M. Poore.
1901	*Mr R. E. Foster and Four Yorkshiremen:* R. E. Foster, S. Haigh, G. H. Hirst, T. L. Taylor, J. Tunnicliffe.
1902	L. C. Braund, C. P. McGahey, F. Mitchell, W. G. Quaife, J. T. Tyldesley.
1903	W. W. Armstrong, C. J. Burnup, J. Iremonger, J. J. Kelly, V. T. Trumper.
1904	C. Blythe, J. Gunn, A. E. Knight, W. Mead, P. F. Warner.
1905	B. J. T. Bosanquet, E. A. Halliwell, J. Hallows, P. A. Perrin, R. H. Spooner.
1906	D. Denton, W. S. Lees, G. J. Thompson, J. Vine, L. G. Wright.
1907	J. N. Crawford, A. Fielder, E. G. Hayes, K. L. Hutchings, N. A. Knox.
1908	A. W. Hallam, R. O. Schwarz, F. A. Tarrant, A. E. E. Vogler, T. G. Wass.
1909	*Lord Hawke and Four Cricketers of the Year:* W. Brearley, Lord Hawke, J. B. Hobbs, A. Marshal, J. T. Newstead.
1910	W. Bardsley, S. F. Barnes, D. W. Carr, A. P. Day, V. S. Ransford.
1911	H. K. Foster, A. Hartley, C. B. Llewellyn, W. C. Smith, F. E. Woolley.
1912	*Five Members of the MCC's Team in Australia:* F. R. Foster, J. W. Hearne, S. P. Kinneir, C. P. Mead, H. Strudwick.
1913	John Wisden: Personal Recollections.
1914	M. W. Booth, G. Gunn, J. W. Hitch, A. E. Relf, Hon. L. H. Tennyson.
1915	J. W. H. T. Douglas, P. G. H. Fender, H. T. W. Hardinge, D. J. Knight, S. G. Smith.
1916-17	No portraits appeared.
1918	*School Bowlers of the Year:* H. L. Calder, J. E. D'E. Firth, C. H. Gibson, G. A. Rotherham, G. T. S. Stevens.
1919	*Five Public School Cricketers of the Year:* P. W. Adams, A. P. F. Chapman, A. C. Gore, L. P. Hedges, N. E. Partridge.
1920	*Five Batsmen of the Year:* A. Ducat, E. H. Hendren, P. Holmes, H. Sutcliffe, E. Tyldesley.
1921	P. F. Warner.
1922	H. Ashton, J. L. Bryan, J. M. Gregory, C. G. Macartney, E. A. McDonald.
1923	A. W. Carr, A. P. Freeman, C. W. L. Parker, A. C. Russell, A. Sandham.
1924	*Five Bowlers of the Year:* A. E. R. Gilligan, R. Kilner, G. G. Macaulay, C. H. Parkin, M. W. Tate.
1925	R. H. Catterall, J. C. W. MacBryan, H. W. Taylor, R. K. Tyldesley, W. W. Whysall.
1926	J. B. Hobbs.
1927	G. Geary, H. Larwood, J. Mercer, W. A. Oldfield, W. M. Woodfull.
1928	R. C. Blunt, C. Hallows, W. R. Hammond, D. R. Jardine, V. W. C. Jupp.
1929	L. E. G. Ames, G. Duckworth, M. Leyland, S. J. Staples, J. C. White.
1930	E. H. Bowley, K. S. Duleepsinhji, H. G. Owen-Smith, R. W. V. Robins, R. E. S. Wyatt.
1931	D. G. Bradman, C. V. Grimmett, B. H. Lyon, I. A. R. Peebles, M. J. Turnbull.
1932	W. E. Bowes, C. S. Dempster, James Langridge, Nawab of Pataudi sen., H. Verity.
1933	W. E. Astill, F. R. Brown, A. S. Kennedy, C. K. Nayudu, W. Voce.
1934	A. H. Bakewell, G. A. Headley, M. S. Nichols, L. F. Townsend, C. F. Walters.
1935	S. J. McCabe, W. J. O'Reilly, G. A. E. Paine, W. H. Ponsford, C. I. J. Smith.
1936	H. B. Cameron, E. R. T. Holmes, B. Mitchell, D. Smith, A. W. Wellard.
1937	C. J. Barnett, W. H. Copson, A. R. Gover, V. M. Merchant, T. S. Worthington.
1938	T. W. J. Goddard, J. Hardstaff jun., L. Hutton, J. H. Parks, E. Paynter.
1939	H. T. Bartlett, W. A. Brown, D. C. S. Compton, K. Farnes, A. Wood.
1940	L. N. Constantine, W. J. Edrich, W. W. Keeton, A. B. Sellers, D. V. P. Wright.
1941-46	No portraits appeared.
1947	A. V. Bedser, L. B. Fishlock, V. (M. H.) Mankad, T. P. B. Smith, C. Washbrook.

1948	M. P. Donnelly, A. Melville, A. D. Nourse, J. D. Robertson, N. W. D. Yardley.
1949	A. L. Hassett, W. A. Johnston, R. R. Lindwall, A. R. Morris, D. Tallon.
1950	T. E. Bailey, R. O. Jenkins, John Langridge, R. T. Simpson, B. Sutcliffe.
1951	T. G. Evans, S. Ramadhin, A. L. Valentine, E. D. Weekes, F. M. M. Worrell.
1952	R. Appleyard, H. E. Dollery, J. C. Laker, P. B. H. May, E. A. B. Rowan.
1953	H. Gimblett, T. W. Graveney, D. S. Sheppard, W. S. Surridge, F. S. Trueman.
1954	R. N. Harvey, G. A. R. Lock, K. R. Miller, J. H. Wardle, W. Watson.
1955	B. Dooland, Fazal Mahmood, W. E. Hollies, J. B. Statham, G. E. Tribe.
1956	M. C. Cowdrey, D. J. Insole, D. J. McGlew, H. J. Tayfield, F. H. Tyson.
1957	D. Brookes, J. W. Burke, M. J. Hilton, G. R. A. Langley, P. E. Richardson.
1958	P. J. Loader, A. J. McIntyre, O. G. Smith, M. J. Stewart, C. L. Walcott.
1959	H. L. Jackson, R. E. Marshall, C. A. Milton, J. R. Reid, D. Shackleton.
1960	K. F. Barrington, D. B. Carr, R. Illingworth, G. Pullar, M. J. K. Smith.
1961	N. A. T. Adcock, E. R. Dexter, R. A. McLean, R. Subba Row, J. V. Wilson.
1962	W. E. Alley, R. Benaud, A. K. Davidson, W. M. Lawry, N. C. O'Neill.
1963	D. Kenyon, Mushtaq Mohammad, P. H. Parfitt, P. J. Sharpe, F. J. Titmus.
1964	D. B. Close, C. C. Griffith, C. C. Hunte, R. B. Kanhai, G. S. Sobers.
1965	G. Boycott, P. J. Burge, J. A. Flavell, G. D. McKenzie, R. B. Simpson.
1966	K. C. Bland, J. H. Edrich, R. C. Motz, P. M. Pollock, R. G. Pollock.
1967	R. W. Barber, B. L. D'Oliveira, C. Milburn, J. T. Murray, S. M. Nurse.
1968	Asif Iqbal, Hanif Mohammad, K. Higgs, J. M. Parks, Nawab of Pataudi jun.
1969	J. G. Binks, D. M. Green, B. A. Richards, D. L. Underwood, O. S. Wheatley.
1970	B. F. Butcher, A. P. E. Knott, Majid Khan, M. J. Procter, D. J. Shepherd.
1971	J. D. Bond, C. H. Lloyd, B. W. Luckhurst, G. M. Turner, R. T. Virgin.
1972	G. G. Arnold, B. S. Chandrasekhar, L. R. Gibbs, B. Taylor, Zaheer Abbas.
1973	G. S. Chappell, D. K. Lillee, R. A. L. Massie, J. A. Snow, K. R. Stackpole.
1974	K. D. Boyce, B. E. Congdon, R. G. W. Fletcher, R. C. Fredericks, P. J. Sainsbury.
1975	D. L. Amiss, M. H. Denness, N. Gifford, A. W. Greig, A. M. E. Roberts.
1976	I. M. Chappell, P. G. Lee, R. B. McCosker, D. S. Steele, R. A. Woolmer.
1977	J. M. Brearley, C. G. Greenidge, M. A. Holding, I. V. A. Richards, R. W. Taylor.
1978	I. T. Botham, M. Hendrick, A. Jones, K. S. McEwan, R. G. D. Willis.
1979	D. I. Gower, J. K. Lever, C. M. Old, C. T. Radley, J. N. Shepherd.
1980	J. Garner, S. M. Gavaskar, G. A. Gooch, D. W. Randall, B. C. Rose.
1981	K. J. Hughes, R. D. Jackman, A. J. Lamb, C. E. B. Rice, V. A. P. van der Bijl.
1982	T. M. Alderman, A. R. Border, R. J. Hadlee, Javed Miandad, R. W. Marsh.
1983	Imran Khan, T. E. Jesty, A. I. Kallicharran, Kapil Dev, M. D. Marshall.
1984	M. Amarnath, J. V. Coney, J. E. Emburey, M. W. Gatting, C. L. Smith.
1985	M. D. Crowe, H. A. Gomes, G. W. Humpage, J. Simmons, S. Wettimuny.
1986	P. Bainbridge, R. M. Ellison, C. J. McDermott, N. V. Radford, R. T. Robinson.
1987	J. H. Childs, G. A. Hick, D. B. Vengsarkar, C. A. Walsh, J. J. Whitaker.
1988	J. P. Agnew, N. A. Foster, D. P. Hughes, P. M. Roebuck, Salim Malik.
1989	K. J. Barnett, P. J. L. Dujon, P. A. Neale, F. D. Stephenson, S. R. Waugh.
1990	S. J. Cook, D. M. Jones, R. C. Russell, R. A. Smith, M. A. Taylor.
1991	M. A. Atherton, M. Azharuddin, A. R. Butcher, D. L. Haynes, M. E. Waugh.
1992	C. E. L. Ambrose, P. A. J. DeFreitas, A. A. Donald, R. B. Richardson, Waqar Younis.
1993	N. E. Briers, M. D. Moxon, I. D. K. Salisbury, A. J. Stewart, Wasim Akram.
1994	D. C. Boon, I. A. Healy, M. G. Hughes, S. K. Warne, S. L. Watkin.
1995	B. C. Lara, D. E. Malcolm, T. A. Munton, S. J. Rhodes, K. C. Wessels.
1996	D. G. Cork, P. A. de Silva, A. R. C. Fraser, A. Kumble, D. A. Reeve.
1997	S. T. Jayasuriya, Mushtaq Ahmed, Saeed Anwar, P. V. Simmons, S. R. Tendulkar.
1998	M. T. G. Elliott, S. G. Law, G. D. McGrath, M. P. Maynard, G. P. Thorpe.
1999	I. D. Austin, D. Gough, M. Muralitharan, A. Ranatunga, J. N. Rhodes.
2000	C. L. Cairns, R. Dravid, L. Klusener, T. M. Moody, Saqlain Mushtaq.

The Wisden Trophy

[*Patrick Eagar*

The wording on the plaque reads: "This Trophy, to be competed for between England and West Indies in 1963 and succeeding Test series, was presented by Wisden's to commemorate the publication of the 100th edition of *Wisden's Cricketers' Almanack.*"

In 1963 and 1966, the Wisden Trophy was won by West Indies. England then won it in 1967-68 and 1969, before it was regained by West Indies in 1973. They began the 2000 series having retained it ever since.